Conceptual Issues In Psychology

London: Routledge, 1992 0415039258

Conceptual issues in psychology

This new edition of *Conceptual Issues in Psychology* provides the most comprehensive textbook available for students of the philosophy and theory of psychology. In a direct and lucid style, it provides a broad treatment of the main conceptual issues in psychology, explaining what they are, outlining the main approaches to them, and showing their relative merits and demerits.

In the first part of the book, the author covers the more substantive philosophical questions such as free will and determinism, consciousness, and the relation between body and mind. Empirical work in psychology which is relevant to these problems is considered, and the methodological problems of introspection and sources of artefact in experimentation are discussed. In the second section of the book Dr Valentine deals with different theoretical approaches and types of explanation within psychology such as behaviourism, reductionism, computer modelling and purposive explanation.

Conceptual Issues in Psychology will give students a thorough understanding of the philosophical and theoretical aspects of psychology and a balanced view of the controversies surrounding the nature of psychology.

Elizabeth R. Valentine is Lecturer in Psychology at the Royal Holloway and Bedford New College, University of London.

Conceptual issues in psychology

Second edition

Elizabeth R. Valentine

LONDON AND NEW YORK

First published 1982
by George Allen and Unwin

Second edition published in 1992 by
Routledge, 11 New Fetter Lane, London EC4P 4EE

Reprinted 1993, 1995 and 1997

Simultaneously published in the USA and Canada
by Routledge
29 West 35th Street, New York, NY 10001

Reprinted 2004, 2005 by Routledge
27 Church Road, Hove, East Sussex BN3 2FA
270 Madison Avenue, New York, NY 10016

Routledge is an imprint of the Taylor & Francis Group

Typeset in Times by NWL Editorial Services, Somerset
Printed and bound in Great Britain by
TJ International Ltd, Padstow, Cornwall

This publication has been produced with paper manufactured to strict environmental standards and with pulp derived from sustainable forests.

British Library Cataloguing in Publication Data
A catalogue record for this book is available from the British Library

Library of Congress Cataloguing in Publication Data
A catalogue record for this book is available from the Library of Congress

ISBN 0-415-03924-X (hbk)
ISBN 0-415-03925-8 (pbk)

To my father
William Herbert Cornish
a man of integrity

There is no escape from philosophy. The question is only whether a philosophy is conscious or not, whether it is good or bad, muddled or clear. Anyone who rejects philosophy is himself unconsciously practising a philosophy.

Karl Jaspers

In Russell's words, 'All human knowledge is uncertain, inexact and partial.' This conclusion is a sobering one, but no education is worth anything that does not impart it.

D.J. O'Connor

Contents

Figures and tables

FIGURES

TABLES

Preface

The aim of this book is to provide a broad treatment of the main conceptual issues in psychology: to explain what the problems are, to outline the main approaches which have been taken to them and to indicate their relative merits and demerits, although my hope is that the reader will ultimately reach his or her own conclusions. The chief intention has been to provide a basic framework to guide further reading in an area which is often found difficult by students.

Chapter 1 provides an overview of most of the topics treated. The first part of the book is concerned with the more substantive philosophical questions such as free will and determinism, consciousness and the relation between body and mind, and includes a consideration of empirical work in psychology which may be relevant to these perennial problems that have interested scholars and lay people alike. This leads on to the methodological problems of introspection and sources of artefact in experimentation. The second half of the book is concerned with different theoretical approaches and types of explanation within psychology such as behaviourism, reductionism, computer modelling and purposive explanation. These are overviewed in Chapter 8 and dealt with in more detail in the subsequent chapters.

The book is aimed primarily at the student of psychology, who, it is to be hoped, will emerge with a more sophisticated understanding of the theoretical construction of the subject and in a position to give a balanced account of some of the controversies about its nature which have arisen both from within and from outside the discipline. In so far as these raise fundamental issues about the nature of human existence and conceptualisation, it is likely also to be of interest to non-psychologists.

In preparing the second edition, I have not made fundamental alterations to the structure of the book, nor have I always cited current reformulations of perennial truths. Conceptual change is slower than empirical advance, and I have tended to favour priority over recency. However, the focus of interest does shift and there have been a number of important developments since the appearance of the first edition, notably work on artificial intelligence, neuroscience, parallel distributed processing and consciousness. In the philosophy of science, the attack on traditional, empiricist views has continued, while the philosophy of mind has flourished. A number of useful books have been published in the area, such as those by James Russell, Patricia Churchland and William Bechtel. Interdisciplinary links have been fostered between philosophy, psychology, computer science and linguistics under the umbrella of cognitive science, and with neuroscience, in some cases through neuropsychology and work on neural networks. Alternatives to orthodox approaches have also increased in sophistication and popularity. The text has been thoroughly revised and updated, and new sections have been included on parallel distributed processing and Eastern psychology.

Elizabeth R. Valentine
London
January, 1991

Acknowledgements

By now it is impossible to thank everyone who has contributed to this volume, let alone to my thinking over the past fifteen or thirty years. A number of people offered help or made specific suggestions for this edition, amongst them: Rob Farr, Sean Mullarkey, Gina Pauli, Simon Pembroke, Janet Simpson, Tony Winefield and an anonymous reviewer. I would also particularly like to thank Graham Richards for getting it onto the stocks, Dave Swann who rescued me from computer crises on a number of occasions, Mark Wells for drawing figures, and John Valentine who has tolerated for too long a spouse who is 'always working'. Thanks too to the staff at Routledge, particularly David Stonestreet, Kerstin Walker and Katy Wimhurst who carried out their duties with suavity, meticulousness and *joie-de-vivre*.

I am particularly grateful to the Carfax Publishing Company Ltd and to John Rust, the editor of *Philosophical Psychology*, for allowing me to use material originally published therein, in Chapters 12 and 14. I would also like to thank the following for permission to reproduce material: Professor P.N. Johnson-Laird and Cambridge University Press (Figure 2.1); Professor M.R. Westcott and the Institute of Mind and Behavior (Figure 2.2); Professor R. Fischer and the American Association for the Advancement of Science (Figure 4.1); Dr J.H. Clark (Figures 4.2 and 4.3); Dr J.H. Crook and Basil Blackwell (Figure 4.4); Professor S.J. Tatz (Figure 6.1); Professor F.E. Goodson and Professor M.H. Marx (Figure 8.1); Professor M.H. Marx (Figure 8.2); General Systems Science Foundation (Figure 9.1); The American Psychological Association (Figure 9.2a); John Wiley and Sons Inc. (Figure 9.2b); Adams, Bannister, Cox (Figure 9.3); and Professor D.P. Schultz and the American Psychological Association (Table 6.1).

Chapter 1

Psychology as science

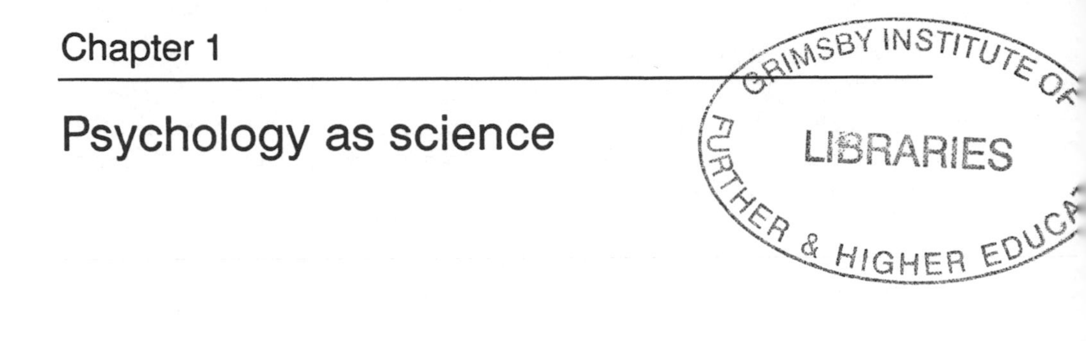

Is psychology different from other sciences? Many of its theoretical problems are based on such a belief. What particular problems does the nature of its subject matter raise and how may they be resolved? In this chapter we shall introduce a number of issues that will be dealt with in more detail later in the book and indicate the main approaches to be taken to them. Our first concern will be to consider psychology as science and what assumptions underlie such treatment. For convenience, these may be classified as: (1) metaphysical – fundamental views about the nature of the subject matter, (2) theoretical – relating to the nature of scientific theories, and (3) methodological – pertaining to observation and experimentation.

METAPHYSICAL ASSUMPTIONS

The scientific treatment of psychology assumes that its subject matter, *the behaviour of humans and other animals, is similar in relevant respects to the subject matter of other sciences*, namely, other natural phenomena. Human behaviour is indeed one of the most recently added areas of scientific investigation, partly due to theological objections: it was formerly considered sacred and not appropriate subject matter for science. (For the history of, and rationale for, the dichotomy between human beings as the possessors of a soul and reason, and other animals whose behaviour is guided by instinct, see Beach, 1955.) This dichotomy was challenged by Darwin's assertion of continuity between human and infrahuman species, which led to the 'brutalisation of Man' and the 'humanisation of animals' (Peters, 1953).

An important respect in which this similarity must be assumed is that of *determinism*, which implies that behaviour is caused and is therefore predictable in principle. This appears to raise a difficulty for free will (how can a person be 'free' if behaviour is completely determined?) and similarly for moral responsibility (how can people be held responsible for their actions or praise and blame be apportioned?). Possible resolutions of this dilemma will be discussed in Chapter 2, where it will be argued that the obverse of determinism is randomness, that free will may require rather than preclude determinism (the issue becoming one of the nature rather than the existence of determination) and that determinism does not imply compulsion, coercion or any mysterious force.

Determinism does imply *predictability*, at least in principle though not necessarily in practice. It is interesting to speculate as to whether our failures to predict are due to lack of skill on our part or the inherent nature of the subject matter. One successful prediction does not imply determinism (one might predict correctly by chance) but repeated successful prediction does imply an underlying regularity.

There are, however, a number of difficulties here, namely, areas of unpredictability. One of these is the possibility of the falsification of predictions (which has sometimes been used as an argument in favour of, or at least a test of, free will). The process of making a prediction may be subject to interfering effects which invalidate it. Attempts to take these into account lead to an infinite regress. A similar difficulty arises from Gödel's theorem, which demonstrates that within some consistent systems of logic there are propositions which can be seen to be true but which are not provable within the system. Neither of these, it will be argued, endangers determinism but both suggest that there are limits to the possible completeness of descriptions.

A discovery in quantum mechanics, namely, Heisenberg's uncertainty principle, threw doubt on the universality of determinism: at the level of subatomic physics there are certain conjugate properties such as the position and momentum of a particle which cannot be simultaneously determined. Thus, there is some evidence for indeterminism in some aspects of the universe. The implications of this micro-level for the macro-level of human behaviour are, however, remote and obscure, to say the least.

The possibility of prediction raises the possibility of *control*, and the consequent ethical problems of deciding who does the controlling, frequently held up against Skinner's Utopia (Skinner, 1948; 1971). In a symposium with Rogers (1956) the latter points out that science, and Skinner, must presuppose values. Science can investigate the determinants and effects of values and hence may provide knowledge relevant to their selection and implementation (see Day, 1976) but it cannot itself determine what they shall be (see also Heather, 1976, who argues forcefully against the notion that psychology is value free).

A fundamental problem in the philosophy of psychology has been whether laws of a different nature from those which apply to inorganic matter are required. An adequate solution to this problem may depend on advances in the philosophy of biology. Generally in science a *mechanistic model* has been preferred, which enables future events to be predicted on the basis of antecedent conditions and assumes the universal applicability of causal laws. (It is worth noting, however, that modern physics has advanced beyond causal explanations. Psychology has frequently sought to ape outdated models from other sciences.) There are a number of features of the behaviour of organisms that have raised doubts about the appropriateness of the mechanistic model. One is purposiveness, essential to survival, which involves flexibility, sensitivity to consequences and the direction of behaviour towards goals; this has tempted explanation by reference to future events. On first sight it looks as though purposive and causal explanations are diametrically opposed, and, indeed, many philosophers have taken the view that actions are intentional and fundamentally different from movements or happenings. Much heat has been generated on this question. We shall argue that the two types of explanation are compatible but different. Indeed, purposive phenomena depend on mechanistic ones. It can thus be argued that the truth of a mechanistic account is a necessary but not a sufficient condition for the truth of a purposive one. Purposive explanations are discussed in Chapter 12 and the use of cybernetic models in the explanation of behaviour in Chapter 10.

This intentionality of behaviour leads on to the issue of consciousness. What treatment it should be afforded in psychology and its relation to behaviour are considered in Chapter 4, and its relation to physiological processes as an aspect of the mind–body problem in Chapter 3. One particularly thorny issue is whether conscious processes should properly be assigned causal efficacy. This view has not found much favour amongst psychologists for a variety of reasons: (1) the difficulty of operationalisation (that is specifying observations that would be relevant to the truth of statements about a concept), (2) the difficulty of independent identification of mental states and resulting circularity of explanations in these terms, and (3) the successful prediction of behaviour without recourse to conscious states, though this does not preclude the possibility of alternative explanations in terms of mental states. Some form of double aspect theory, according to which the mental and physical are two aspects of the same underlying reality, will be considered the most acceptable solution to the mind–body problem.

A general assumption held in varying degrees of strength by scientists concerns the relation between different sciences. Many would agree that sciences can be arranged in a hierarchical order according to the size of unit or level of analysis; for example, it might be said roughly that sociology deals at the level of groups, psychology at the level of individuals, physiology with parts of individuals, biochemistry at the intra-cellular level and physics at the molecular. Hence, what is relatively molecular for a higher level science is relatively molar for a lower level science (compare, for example, a muscle twitch for psychology and physiology). The question arises as to what the relation between these different level descriptions is or should be. *Reductionism* is the view that higher level descriptions can be derived from lower level descriptions and hence in due course it might be possible to replace psychological explanations by physiological explanations. There is a covert assumption that lower level descriptions are more fundamental and hence preferable. *Emergence* is the opposite view, that higher level descriptions cannot be derived from lower level ones. The assumptions underlying reduction and the whole issue of the relation of psychology to physiology are discussed in Chapter 11. It will be argued that, as in the case of the relation of purposive to mechanistic descriptions, psychology and physiology describe different aspects of phenomena and hence are complementary, that strict reduction entailing logical identity is untenable because psychological and physiological descriptions have different meanings, and that empirical reduction which requires the establishment of bridging laws faces many difficulties.

THEORETICAL ASSUMPTIONS

Many of the characteristics of scientific laws raise potential problems for the subject matter of psychology.

A first requirement is that of *systematicity*. At the very least science must be a coherent body of knowledge. The complexity of psychological subject matter, notably the diversity and likely interactive nature of relevant variables promises trouble for psychology, a promise that has been amply fulfilled. Grünbaum (1952), however, has argued that the subject matter of other sciences, such as physics, is hardly simple, and may have seemed as complex as that of psychology at the time of its inauguration. It is unlikely that psychology can rely on youth to account for its lack of progress. Comparison with biochemistry is enough to suggest that the malaise goes deeper.

A particular difficulty is due to the *reflexivity* of psychology. Not only is it the case that the observer and the observed are often members of the same species, but also that actually doing psychology constitutes part of its subject matter. This means at the very least that psychological theories must be self-referring in the sense of explaining the psychologist's own behaviour, as Oliver and Landfield (1963) point out. Bannister (1968) has used this as an argument for the non-reducibility of psychology to physiology (see Chapter 11).

Other problems are associated with a second characteristic of scientific laws, that of *generality*. It is generally accepted that scientific laws are unrestricted in space and time. A glance at typical psychological theoretical statements indicates that this condition is not always met. Too often these statements refer to specific times and places. Of course this is a matter of degree: all statements are restricted to a greater or lesser extent, but the scientific ideal is that this should approach the latter rather than the former. The failure probably reflects a greater interest on the part of investigators in the content rather than the process of behaviour. Since the content of behaviour varies considerably, it presents much greater problems for scientific treatment than do the principles of adaptation. Social and cultural aspects of behaviour are much less amenable to a scientific analysis than are biological aspects.

Another possible challenge to generality comes from the conflicting demand to recognise the uniqueness of the individual. Since the movement of *Verstehen* psychology in nineteenth-century Germany, there have been cries to understand the individual rather than predict behaviour in general. It is frequently said that more is to be learned about human behaviour by studying literature rather than psychology. A comparison of idiographic and nomothetic approaches, which focus on the particular and general respectively, and encompass differences in subject matter, methods and explanations, is the topic of Chapter 14. They probably largely reflect differences in aims: empathic understanding as against deductive, predictive explanation, and in application they may be complementary. As far as science goes, however, nomothesis must be the rule of the day. If a clinical method works it must be covertly nomothetic and if truly unique it could not be communicated (see Holt, 1967). Nevertheless, there can be a scientific study of individuals.

Since, if not before, Popper's (1959) epoch-making work, the hallmark of scientific hypotheses has been *testability*, in this case falsifiability (further discussed in Chapter 7). This has raised problems for psychology because of the inherent difficulty in operationalising its concepts. Most of its area of interest is not directly observable. Indeed, Popper was led to formulate his demarcation principle partly as a result of noting the inadequacies in this respect of the psychological theories of Freud and Jung. The whole question of the relation of theoretical constructs to the evidence for them is thus a central one in psychology and discussed in Chapter 9.

METHODOLOGICAL ASSUMPTIONS

There may well be no definitive characteristics of science, and indeed if there were they would probably change from one time to another. Strictly, 'science' means 'knowledge' but what it has come to mean in the modern Western world is knowledge acquired as a result of employing empirical methods. If there is any one thing that characterises it more than anything else, it is probably the empirical method. Other pursuits have been systematic, such as Greek cosmology, but we would not call them science. Empiricism involves appeal to sensory experience as opposed to reliance on a priori reasoning; the criterion of truth becomes one of correspondence with the facts rather than logical coherence. Typically it involves observation, measurement and experimentation. In some sciences, such as astronomy and geology, only observation and measurement are possible but usually experimentation is regarded as the characteristic of science *par excellence*. There are some difficulties in the way of experimentation in psychology, as we shall see below, and it may be more akin to geology than has been generally recognised. The possibility of applying any of these three procedures to psychological subject matter has been doubted by many.

Observation presents problems for psychology on account of the previously mentioned fact that most of what is of interest, that which is essentially psychological – thoughts, feelings and the springs of action – is not open to direct observation. Hence, as indicated above, almost all psychological statements must be inferential. I would claim that this is true of all sciences, but the gap between data and theory is probably greater and the connection looser in psychology than in other sciences. The issue of privacy will be taken up in Chapter 5, where it will be argued that all scientific statements are based on observations of private experiences, and that the distinction between subjective and objective is not as clear cut as at first supposed.

Furthermore, it is now clear that neither the observer nor the observed are passive, non-interactive organisms in the experimental situation. The fact that observation necessarily interferes with what is observed, first discovered in physics, became the subject of experimentation in psychology with the recognition that the experiment is itself a social situation. This work is treated in Chapter 6.

Dualistic thought would suggest that quantifiability was the exclusive prerogative of the physical. Kant (1781) held that observation could be applied to psychological phenomena but that measurement and experimentation were impossible. However, since the latter part of the nineteenth century, advances in the *measurement* of psychological or mental characteristics have progressively been made and the grounds for such a belief gradually eroded. In 1861 Fechner published an account of psychophysical methods, in the vain belief that they solved the mind–body problem. They did, however, provide methods for establishing functions relating psychological values or reported sensations to physical values of stimuli, though these have since been superseded. Ebbinghaus, coming on a copy of Fechner's *Elemente der Psychophysik*, was spurred to similar achievement in devising ways of measuring memorial associations. The turn of the century saw the beginning of attempts to measure intellectual ability, or at least performance, with the Binet-Simon scale, and Galton's predominantly physical measures and development of percentile ranks and correlation. From these sprang the whole field of psychometrics and factor analysis. Scaling focuses the difficulty of measurement in psychology. One of the central questions is the arbitrariness of the scale: to what extent can the values be said to reflect fundamental realities and relations and to what extent are they a function of theoretical constructs? For further discussion of this topic see, for example, Coombs, Dawes and Tversky (1970).

Herbart (1824) believed that observation and measurement could be applied to psychology but not experimentation. Wundt (1862), the first experimental psychologist proper, thought that experimental methods could only be applied to what he considered lower order processes: thinking, judgement and language were too socially conditioned to be similarly treated. Empirical investigation of social phenomena is possible, but experimentation in the sense of isolating variables with the purpose of identifying causal factors may not be because it is virtually impossible to implement sufficient *control*. There are various reasons why this is so: the number of variables, their interaction and the history of the organism.

One reason results from the adaptability of organisms. Behaviour is a function of the past history of the organism and can only be explained by reference to it. Only the blinkered would still fail to acknowledge that behaviour is not predictable on the basis of the observable, external physical stimuli but only on the basis of the meaning of these stimuli for the organism – cf. Underwood's (1963) distinction between the nominal and the functional stimulus. In addition, there are practical and ethical limitations to the amount of control that is possible. Despite transgressions in this direction, there are limits to noxious stimuli that can be inflicted on subjects. Deprived environments and brain damage have to be taken advantage of rather than created.

In conclusion, psychology does have particular problems but generally these represent differences in degree rather than kind from those of other sciences. Most are capable of resolution to a greater or lesser extent.

Chapter 2

Determinism and free will

WHAT IS MEANT BY FREE WILL?

It was noted in Chapter 1 that one of the presuppositions of psychological science is determinism (the view that all events, including human actions, are caused) and that this appears to conflict with the notion of free will. How can responsibility for actions be maintained if they are determined by genetic constitution and environmental experience? As psychology progresses, knowledge of factors which determine behaviour increases.

But first it must be decided what is, or could be, meant by free will. Part of the problem is that it is not at all easy to give a coherent account. The lay person would probably maintain that what is required for free will is the possibility that the agent *could have done otherwise*, the situation remaining the same; that is, that the agent had a real choice. (Dennett, 1984, however, argues that this is not one of the varieties of free will worth wanting.) The problem with this interpretation, I think, is that it is untestable. It can never be known whether the person might have acted differently in the same circumstances, particularly as circumstances are never exactly repeated. What is known of the psychology of choice and decision-making leads to the surmise that it is unlikely.

Dennis Noble (oral communication) has suggested *ability to falsify a prediction about one's behaviour*, once informed of it, as a test of free will. Indeed, this possibility raises doubts about the feasibility of determinism (see pp. 16–17). Howard, Youngs and Siatczynski (1989) attempted to test this experimentally in a study where subjects successfully chose whether to follow the experimenter's instructions to modify their peanut intake or to do the opposite. My view is that this merely complicates the issue and requires meta-level predictions which take account of the subject's information and decision.

MacKay (1987) has sought justification for the subjective conviction of freedom in the logical peculiarity of propositions which are not universally valid in that they cannot claim everyone's unconditional assent. A proposition whose truth depends on the agent's believing it is a case in point; for example, an observer's prediction of an agent's behaviour on the basis of the agent's brain state. A paradox arises from the fact that, although agents might be correct to believe these predictions if they knew them, they would also be correct to disbelieve them because this would entail an alteration in their brain state and hence the invalidation of the original prediction. However, I think MacKay is mistaken in believing that the existence of logically alternative descriptions implies that the agent has a choice in determining which applies.

Another possibility might be to suppose that what is meant by an act of free will is that it is *uncaused*. Some philosophers have argued that this cannot be what is intended, on the assumption that the alternative to determinism is randomness. (For an alternative view on the relationship between determinism and randomness, see Clark, 1987.) It is supposed that, rather than *no* cause, what the libertarian (as the defender of free will is sometimes called) wants is special causation.

We must then ask what the nature of this special causation might be. One way of distinguishing special causes supposedly typical of cases of free will from other causes might be along the lines of Spinoza's (1677) distinction, within a thoroughgoing determinist system, of two types of determination: internal and external. The latter type is inferior, the result of accidental contingencies and in modern terminology would be described in terms of conditioning (see Reeves, 1965). The former is superior, logically determined, rational, acting in accordance with one's character or 'conatus' – the force according to which each individual persists in its own being or essence. Social psychologists might describe this as behaviour determined by personal rather than situational factors, and psychotherapists might see it as authenticity. It is in accord with the view that what we would call 'free' acts are moderately predictable: they lie somewhere between randomness (zero predictability) on the one hand and rigidity (perfect predictability) on the other. The 'free' person is not dictated to by the demands of the environment but acts consistently with his or her character.

This bears some similarity to the view known as *soft determinism* (see p. 18), according to which all acts are determined, but not all are constrained. Free acts on this view are those *free from coercion* or compulsion. Thus, stepping out of a window to see if one could fly and undertaking the same act at gunpoint are both determined, but the former is free and the latter constrained.

A psychologist might identify free acts with *voluntary* behaviour. There is both phenomenological and behavioural evidence for the distinction between voluntary and involuntary behaviour. A cough to attract someone's attention is different from one that results from a tickle in the throat. Penfield's (1958) patients, whose motor cortices were stimulated while they were awake, reported that they felt as if their limbs were being moved passively rather than as if they were initiating the action themselves. Voluntary eyeblinks can be distinguished from involuntary on the basis of their form and latency (Kimble,

1964). It is generally agreed that voluntary behaviour is learned, flexible (sensitive to consequences), relatively slow and that verbal processes may play a part, whereas involuntary behaviour is automatic, inflexible (independent of consequences) and may be interfered with by verbalisation (Kimble and Perlmuter, 1970; Shiffrin and Schneider, 1977). James (1890) thought that voluntary acts depended on an anticipatory image of the movement's sensible effects. However, the role of feedback in the control of voluntary behaviour has been disputed (for example, Jones, 1974). It is much more likely that, as Bindra (1976) suggests, the basis for a voluntary act is the conditioned excitation of the effective stimulus for that act.

Johnson-Laird (1983a) distinguishes three main levels in the phylogeny of automata, which he calls 'Cartesian', 'Craikian' and self-reflective. Cartesian automata are open-loop systems – for instance, bacteria and protozoa, whose behaviour is physically mediated by a direct causal link between stimulus and response (see Figure 2.1a). They lack any kind of awareness or symbolism. The behaviour of Craikian automata is guided by a representation of the external world (see Figure 2.1b); they construct symbolic models of the world in real time; for example, insects whose flight is controlled by a perceptual model of certain features of the physical environment. They possess a simple kind of awareness and symbolism. Self-reflective automata are capable of intentional behaviour, which is claimed to depend on the recursive embedding of models within models. They are self-aware in that they have at least a partial model of their operating system. Humans know that they can generate models of future states of affairs and decide to try to bring them about. Johnson-Laird (1988) argues that freedom consists in the ability to use models of ourselves to select a method of making a choice. Moreover, the range of options could include arbitrary methods of decision-making such as throwing a die. (See also the discussion of intention in Chapter 12.)

Norman and Shallice (1986) likewise identify 'will' with the highest of three modes of control. They distinguish automatic performance, contention scheduling and deliberate conscious control. Automatic performance of well-specified sequences occurs without conscious attention and is generally not susceptible to interference from other tasks. Contention scheduling involves selection from amongst competing schemas, as in the initiation of routine actions, and is probably located in the basal ganglia. Deliberate conscious control demands a supervisory attentional mechanism, which biases the selection process. It is required for the performance of novel, dangerous or difficult sequences; planning; trouble-shooting and overcoming habitual responses. It typically gives rise to slower behaviour with reduced environmental control. Neuropsychological evidence suggests that the supervisory attentional mechanism is located in the prefrontal lobes.

As Norman and Shallice note, the distinction between contention scheduling and deliberate conscious control is similar to William James's (1890) distinction between ideomotor action (where an idea leads to an action

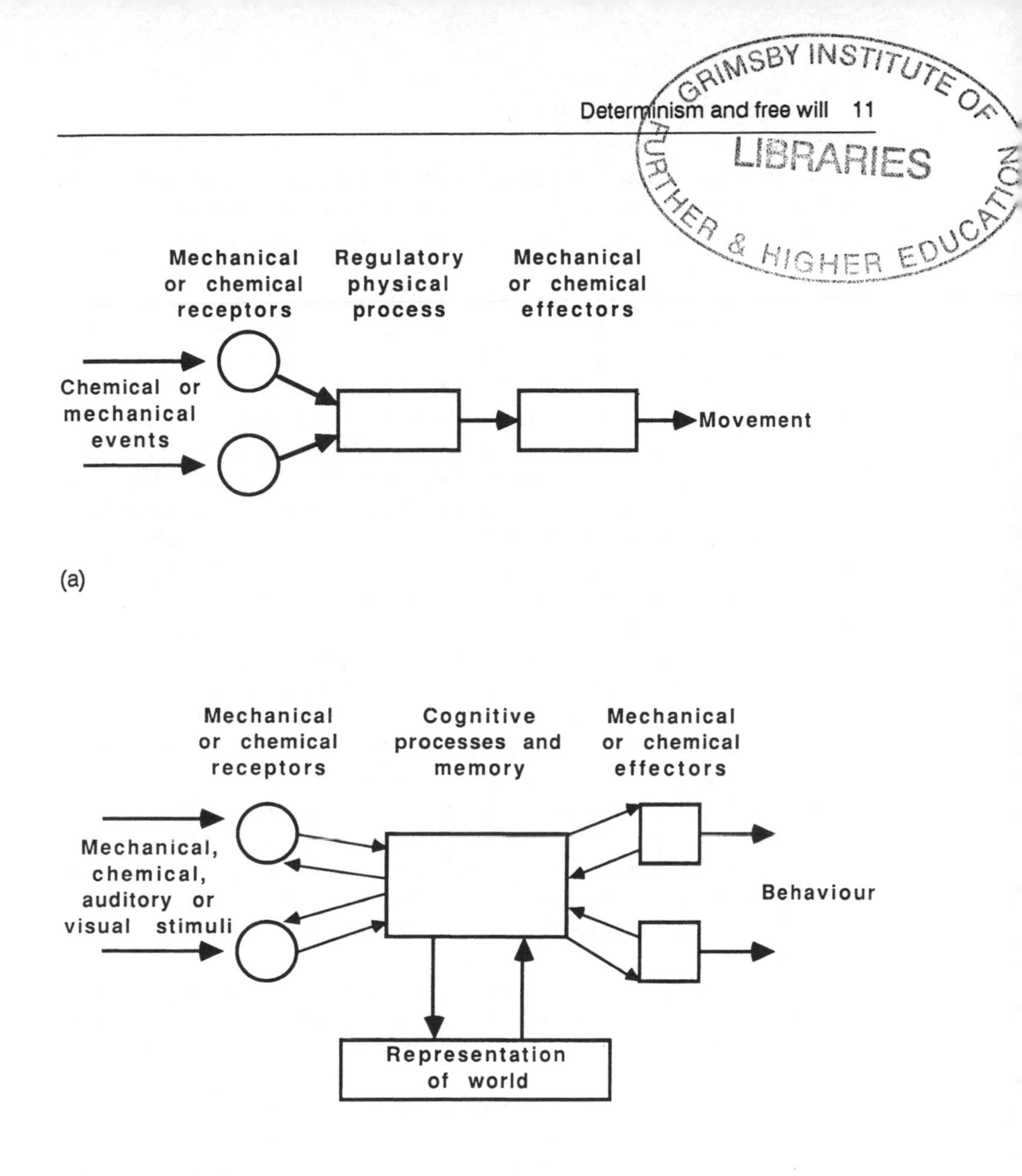

Figure 2.1 Block diagrams of (a) a Cartesian automaton; (b) a Craikian automaton
(*Source:* Johnson-Laird, 1983a)

without interruption) and will (which he went on to analyse in terms of an effort of attention). However, there are a number of problems with the interpretation of free will as actions preceded by a period of deliberation and accompanied by a special feeling, an act of will or, as James called it, a 'fiat'? One is that these cases may be the exception rather than the rule: there may be others which we would want to include as instances of free will but which are not preceded by this special act of deliberation or will. More seriously, there is no a priori reason why this act of deliberation should serve a causal function. (Indeed, there are difficulties in supposing that mental events can be the causes of non-mental events; see Chapter 3.) There are some reasons for believing that subjective experiences may be deceptive. Perhaps they are best regarded as aspects of the process. They only appear more important because they are available to consciousness. The relations of experience to behaviour and physiology are problems central to the philosophy of psychology and discussed further in Chapters 3 and 4. As O'Connor (1971) points out, it seems that the libertarian view is inconsistent with what is known about the working of the human nervous system. It can only by established by postulating a kind of cause with which we are totally unfamiliar and for whose existence there is no independent evidence. In the words of Karl Pearson (1892): 'Will as the first cause of a sequence of motions explains nothing at all; it is only a limit at which very often our power of describing a sequence abruptly terminates.'

Jones (1968) has remarked that 'the only situations which are philosophically interesting for the student of the "will" are situations of conflict'. It is true that the exercise of 'will' typically occurs in such situations. The desired effect may be either inhibitory, as in the case of resisting temptation, or excitatory, as in the case of forcing oneself to do something one doesn't want to do.

Paradoxically, others have interpreted freedom as *consistency between desire and action*. A man who is forced to marry the woman he loves may be free in this sense, although he could not have done otherwise. The same sense of freedom occurs in a religious context in the cultivation of acceptance, as in the phrase 'whose service is perfect freedom' (*Book of Common Prayer*), or see Krishnamurti (1956) for the Eastern equivalent. In theory at least, consistency may be attained by modifying either attitude or behaviour. (Compare Rogers's (1965) suggestion that the discrepancy between ideal and real self may be reduced by modifying the former if the latter is unalterable.) Voltaire was less optimistic, however, for he wrote: 'When I can do what I want to do this is my liberty for me . . . but I can't help wanting what I do want.'

Westcott (1982a; 1982b) has subjected some of these interpretations of freedom to empirical investigation. He asked Canadian undergraduates to rate how free they thought they were and how free they felt in different types of situation (see Figure 2.2). As he observes, the results might be rather different for members of another culture (and indeed somewhat different results were obtained for an Indian sample; see Westcott, 1988). Highest

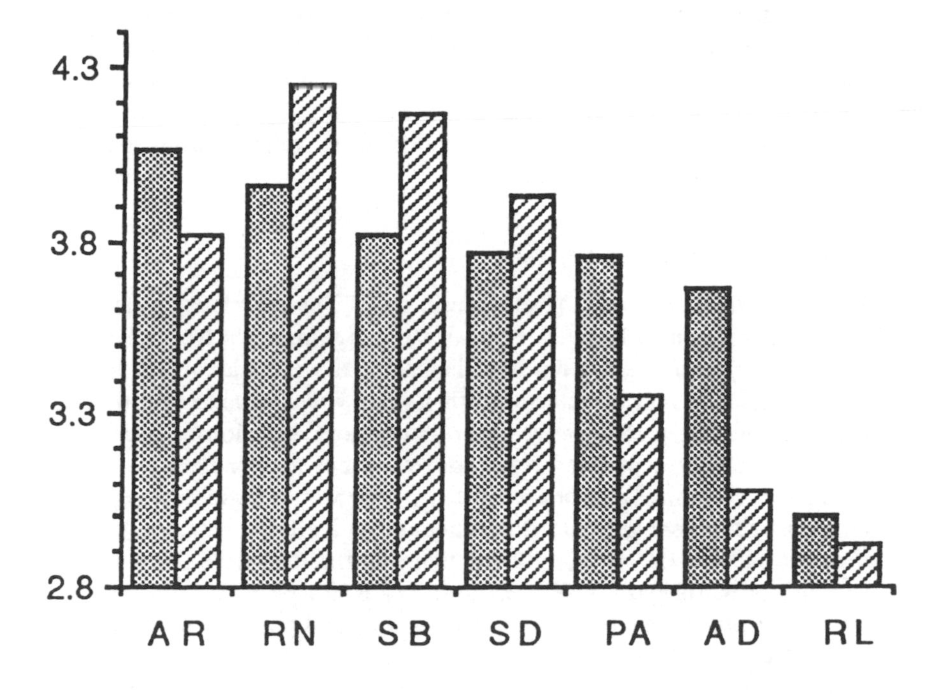

Figure 2.2 Average ratings (n = 135) on a seven-point scale of being free and feeling free for seven types of situation
(*Source:* adapted from Westcott, 1982a)
Note: ▩ = being free; ▨ = feeling free; AR = absence of responsibility; RN = release from noxious stimulation; SB = skilled behaviour; SD = self- direction; PA = presence of alternatives; AD = active decision-making; RL = recognition of limits

ratings of being free were given to situations involving absence of responsibility and release from noxious stimulation (for example, realising that a nagging headache had gone). Intermediate ratings were given to situations involving the exercise of skilled behaviour (cf. the discussion of voluntary behaviour above), self-direction, the presence of alternatives, and active decision-making (cf. 'could have done otherwise'). Clearly lowest of all were situations involving recognition of limits, such as curtailing desires to fit abilities (cf. consistency between desire and action). Absence of responsibilities, the presence of alternatives and active decision-making were rated significantly more highly on being free than on feeling free, whereas release from noxious stimulation and the exercise of skilled behaviour were rated significantly more highly on feeling free than on being free. Correlations with ratings of liking suggested that feeling free is a result of perceiving oneself as free in a situation and liking that situation. The most frequently cited opposites of feeling free were: prevention from without, diffuse unpleasant affect, and conflict and indecision. Different patterns of opposites also enabled a qualitative distinction to be drawn between active freedom, as in self-direction, the exercise of skilled behaviour and decision-making, and passive freedom, as in absence of responsibility, release from noxious stimulation and recognition of limits.

Arguments in favour of free will

'We know our will is free, and there's an end on 't.' This statement, attributed to Dr Samuel Johnson by Boswell, expresses the argument for free will based on *subjective impression*. It is hard to deny, but the trouble with it is that subjective certainty is no guarantee of truth, a point which has been clear since the time of Descartes. Subjective impressions are notoriously unreliable regardless of the degree of conviction with which they may be held.

The subjective impression of free will is, however, a legitimate topic of investigation for psychology. Its determinants and effects can be studied. Mandler and Kessen (1974) suggest that belief in free will develops with age (it is a mark of maturity to delay decision) and is more common in cultures that demand explanations for action, responsibility and personal efficiency. In their view it is caused partly by the post-decision perception of choices. An alternative view is that it results from anticipating the consequences of actions. Bindra (1976) argues that conditioned feedback, rather than being involved in the production of voluntary acts as William James thought, is the basis of the subjective experience of volition. Perceived freedom, even if illusory, has definite consequences for behaviour (see Steiner, 1970), as studies of attribution and learned helplessness show. Since it generally leads to optimisation of performance, many consider it a beneficial illusion.

The main argument in favour of free will is from *moral responsibility*. The apportioning of praise and blame, and reward and punishment, appears to be premised on the possession of free will. If we are not in control of our actions, how can we be held responsible for them? Indeed, James (1890) opted in favour of belief in freedom of the will on ethical rather than psychological grounds. The notion of responsibility may require free will but administration of reward and punishment does not. As Skinner (1971) has pointed out, the latter is compatible with a deterministic system. The aim merely shifts from the evaluation to the modification of behaviour.

Arguments against free will

The first problem facing a proponent of free will is the *difficulty of giving a coherent account* of the concept, which is adequately attested by the length of the foregoing discussion.

The second problem is that of *inconsistency with science*. The more that is discovered about factors determining behaviour, the less room does there seem to be for free will. Of particular interest is work by Libet (1985), which suggests that the role played by conscious will may be relatively limited. He observed that reported awareness of the intention to perform a voluntary act (finger or wrist flexion) occurred about 350 ms after the electrophysiological readiness potential. However, subjects could veto performance for a 100–200 ms period before a prearranged time to act. He concluded that the role of conscious will is 'permissively' to permit or prevent the motor implementation of an act which arose unconsciously: its function is thus one of selection and control rather than initiation. In general, the progress of science, premised on determinism, and all that is known about the world tend to support determinism. However, giving a coherent account of this doctrine is not without its own difficulties, to which we now turn.

WHAT IS MEANT BY DETERMINISM?

O'Connor (1971) distinguishes metaphysical from scientific determinism, the former being independent of human knowledge, the latter dependent on it. The argument for metaphysical determinism he states as follows:

1 every macroscopic physical event has a cause;
2 every human action is a macroscopic physical event;
3 therefore, every human action is caused;
4 any event that is caused could not have happened otherwise than it did;
5 therefore, no human action could have happened otherwise than it did.

Metaphysical determinism allows the possibility that the human will is not free but that we could never know this.

As a statement of scientific determinism, Laplace is quoted:

> We ought then to regard the present state of the universe as the effect of its antecedent state and the cause of the state that is to follow. An intelligence knowing, at a given instant of time, all things of which the universe consists, would be able to comprehend the actions of the largest bodies of the world and those of the lightest atoms in one single formula, provided his intellect were sufficiently powerful to subject all data to analysis; to him, nothing would be uncertain, both past and future would be present to his eyes. The human mind in the perfection it has been able to give astronomy affords a feeble outline of such an intelligence.
>
> (Laplace, 1820: 4)

Other definitions are 'by determinism, we understand the belief that the future of the whole universe, or of an isolated part of it, is determined in terms of a complete description of its present condition' (Bridgman, 1927), and 'according to determinism, the future can be completely predicted from the past' (Schlick, 1925). Thus scientific determinism requires (1) a complete description of the present state of the system, and (2) knowledge of the laws governing it, which together enable prediction of a future state of the system to be made.

Arguments in favour of determinism

The *success of science* to date is usually given as the main argument in favour of determinism, though some might claim that an optimistic extrapolation from the success of physical science is implied. However, there are a number of problems with which any proponent of determinism must deal.

Arguments against determinism

There are certain difficulties in the way of giving a coherent account of determinism. Popper (1950) has demonstrated that indeterminism extends to the realm of classical physics. If the concept of the predictability of an event is made explicit, it can be proved that not all macroscopic events can be predicted. There are limits to the extent to which a machine (which can be considered an instantiation of a formal system) can predict its own states. The Laplacean view of *universal predictability is incoherent*. Thus if determinism is accounted for in terms of predictability, determinism cannot be a defensible theory.

First, a difficulty arises from the fact that the description of the system's current state takes time to complete, so that it may be out of date by the time it is made and hence the prediction based on it invalidated.

The second argument involves an application of Gödel's theorem in mathematical logic which shows that, in any formal system of logic sufficiently complex to formulate the arithmetic of integers, there will always be propositions which are true but unprovable. A corollary is that this proposition itself is also undemonstrable within the system, and thus the system cannot be shown to be consistent within itself.

Popper's third argument concerns the fact that to pass information to a machine about its own state 'is liable to interfere strongly with that state and thereby to destroy the predictive value of the information'. I conclude from these arguments that it is unlikely that complete predictability can be attained.

It has further been argued that determinism is not identifiable with predictability in principle owing to the *limited precision* with which predictions can be formulated. Although every event must be perfectly determinate, no prediction can identify such a determinate event unambiguously. A given state of the world at an instant determines not a given subsequent state but a class of possible states, and no explanation why one rather than another of these possibilities should actually be realised. No prediction can distinguish the predicted event in such a way as to discriminate it from any of the other possible events that could fall under the same set of measurements. We are concerned with variable classes of events rather than complete descriptions of uniquely designated events. 'If anyone claims that all events, including actions, are predictable, he is saying something that is either false or empty of content' (O'Connor, 1971).

Other limits to determinism have been suggested by *Heisenberg's uncertainty principle* (1927), according to which there is indeterminism at the level of sub-atomic physics. There are certain conjugate properties which cannot simultaneously be predicted; namely, position and momentum, and energy and time. Thus, if the position of a particle is specified, its momentum cannot be. Two classes of events occur without any assignable cause: (1) the emission of alpha particles, electrons and gamma rays by radioactive material, and (2) the jump of electrons from one orbit to another within the atom. Such unpredictability in principle has worried some, including Einstein, who exclaimed that 'God does not play dice with the world'. Others have sought here a defence of free will but the implications for macroscopic phenomena are unclear. As O'Connor (1971) writes: 'The findings of quantum mechanics do not offer any clear and indisputable evidence in favour of free will.'

An objection commonly raised against determinism is that it *would make rational deliberation impossible*, an argument expressed by Haldane though later repudiated (1954): 'If my mental processes are determined wholly by the motion of atoms in my brain, I have no reason to suppose that my beliefs are true . . . and hence I have no reason for supposing my brain to be composed of atoms' (Haldane, 1927: 209). Similar objections have been raised against Skinner by those who claim that his theory that all behaviour is a function of environmental history must apply to the production of his own theory, and hence there is no reason to suppose it to be true. But the argument does not follow. Equally there is no reason to suppose that the theory is not true. The question of truth value is independent of the question of determinism. If anything, determinism favours rather than jeopardises the truth of a theory. A theory that bears some relation to evidence is more likely to be true than one that has arisen by chance. (The question of the relation between reasons and causes has been much discussed in philosophy; see, for example, Toulmin, 1970).

Finally, there is the charge concerning the logical nature of the theory of determinism, to the effect that it is *not falsifiable*. When causes are not forthcoming, it is assumed that they have not yet been discovered rather than that they do not exist. Neither is the determinist maxim integrated into a logically coherent system. Paradoxically, the uncertainty principle, by limiting its empirical scope, strengthens its logical status by showing that it can be falsified.

ARE FREE WILL AND DETERMINISM COMPATIBLE?

Attempts to reconcile free will and determinism have been variously called the 'consistency hypothesis', the 'compatibility hypothesis' or 'soft determinism' (a term coined by William James), and date from the time of Hobbes, who wrote in *Leviathan*:

> Liberty, and necessity are consistent . . . which, because they proceed from their will, proceed from liberty; and yet, because every act of man's will, and every desire, and inclination proceedeth from some cause, and that from another cause in a continuall chaine, . . . proceed from necessity.
>
> (Hobbes, 1651: 108)

Other philosophers who have taken this view include: Hume, J.S. Mill, Schlick and Nowell-Smith. It has tended to characterise those of a logical positivist persuasion, for example Ayer (1946), who argues that free will implies determinism on the grounds that the opposite of determinism is randomness, and surely that cannot be what is meant by free will. Free action is contrasted with compulsion rather than with causation. Unfortunately, soft determinism does not provide what the libertarian wants. The type of freedom which it reconciles with determinism is freedom in the sense of consistency between desire and action and not freedom in the sense that the agent could have done otherwise. Nor, as soft determinism is generally stated, is it clear how constrained and unconstrained acts can be distinguished. To the hard determinist, both compelled and uncompelled acts are caused and inevitable. O'Connor argues that compelled acts cannot be distinguished by the agent's being conscious of the constraint because it is possible to imagine counter-examples. Nor is moral blamelessness any more satisfactory as a distinguishing criterion. Responsibility is not a descriptive term and there is no way of identifying responsibility that is both consistent with the compatibility hypothesis and non-circular.

CONCLUSIONS

Few issues have been discussed so frequently or inconclusively as free will. One feature of the controversy is the extraordinary difficulty in putting forward an argument for or against free will without covertly begging the question against the other side. This is due to the fact that the libertarian and the determinist have world views so utterly opposed to each other and offering so little in the way of common ground that can serve as mutually acceptable premisses for the controversy, that the very first premisses of the arguments on one side will be unacceptable to the other. Neither can afford to make the smallest concession without rendering their own position covertly inconsistent.

The discussion may be summarised as follows: the main problems for the libertarian are the inconsistency of free will with the premisses of (successful) science, and the grave difficulty of giving a coherent account of the notion of free will in the first place. The suggestion that free acts are uncaused acts seems not to grant what the libertarian wants. The interpretation required – namely, that the agent could have done otherwise, all circumstances remaining the same – is untestable. It is possible to distinguish instances of free will phenomenologically but no causal efficacy is thereby guaranteed. It is also possible to provide behavioural criteria for distinguishing voluntary from involuntary responses. Soft determinists have sought to reconcile free will with determinism by arguing that the former implies the latter, the proper contrast being between freedom and coercion rather than freedom and causation. However, the interpretation of free will that is reconciled here is that of consistency between desire and action rather than that of 'could have done otherwise'.

Though determinism seems to have the edge in this difficult debate, it is not without problems either. There are difficulties in identifying it with predictability, and a number of discoveries show there are distinct limitations to its completeness.

Chapter 3

The mind–body problem

INTRODUCTION

It is often said (for example, Kendler, 1970) that psychology has three subject matters: conscious experience, behaviour and physiology. The mind–body problem is concerned with the relation between two of these; namely, consciousness and neurophysiological processes. Part of the puzzle is how the latter can give rise to the former when they appear to be so different in kind. As they stand, the concepts 'mind' and 'body' are probably too vague to be useful. 'Mind' is commonly used in two main senses: (1) conscious experience, and (2) the system or program that governs behaviour. Strictly speaking, the mind–body problem is concerned with the former. It is, however, sometimes discussed in terms of the latter (for instance, Fodor, 1981), where 'mind' refers to the software and 'body' refers to the hardware. Mental phenomena include sensations, images, feelings, thoughts, beliefs, intentions and decisions. 'Body' appears to be more straightforward and refers to the physical aspect of an organism, in this case particularly the brain. Described by Schopenhauer as 'the world knot', the problem, like so many others treated in this book, is a tangle of conceptual and empirical issues; both logical arguments and scientific discoveries are relevant.

The problem has existed in various forms for a long time. The Western world has found it difficult to escape the inheritance from Greek and Cartesian thought, and it must be considered as a possibility that the whole conceptual apparatus is incorrect or misleading. In the history of philosophy, the problem was phrased in terms of a general ontological question: what kinds of things can be said to exist? Are there essentially different kinds of stuff in the world? This might be called the 'furniture of the universe' question. Any account of the mind–body problem couched in these terms is likely to involve prior analysis of the notions of substance and cause, in particular whether cause can be between unlike things and whether there can be gaps in a causal chain. The questions at issue and their possible solutions are illustrated in Figure 3.1. Some have argued that there is only one fundamental reality (*monism*) and that the duality is illusory. Varieties of this doctrine are that: physical phenomena are reducible to mental (*idealism*);

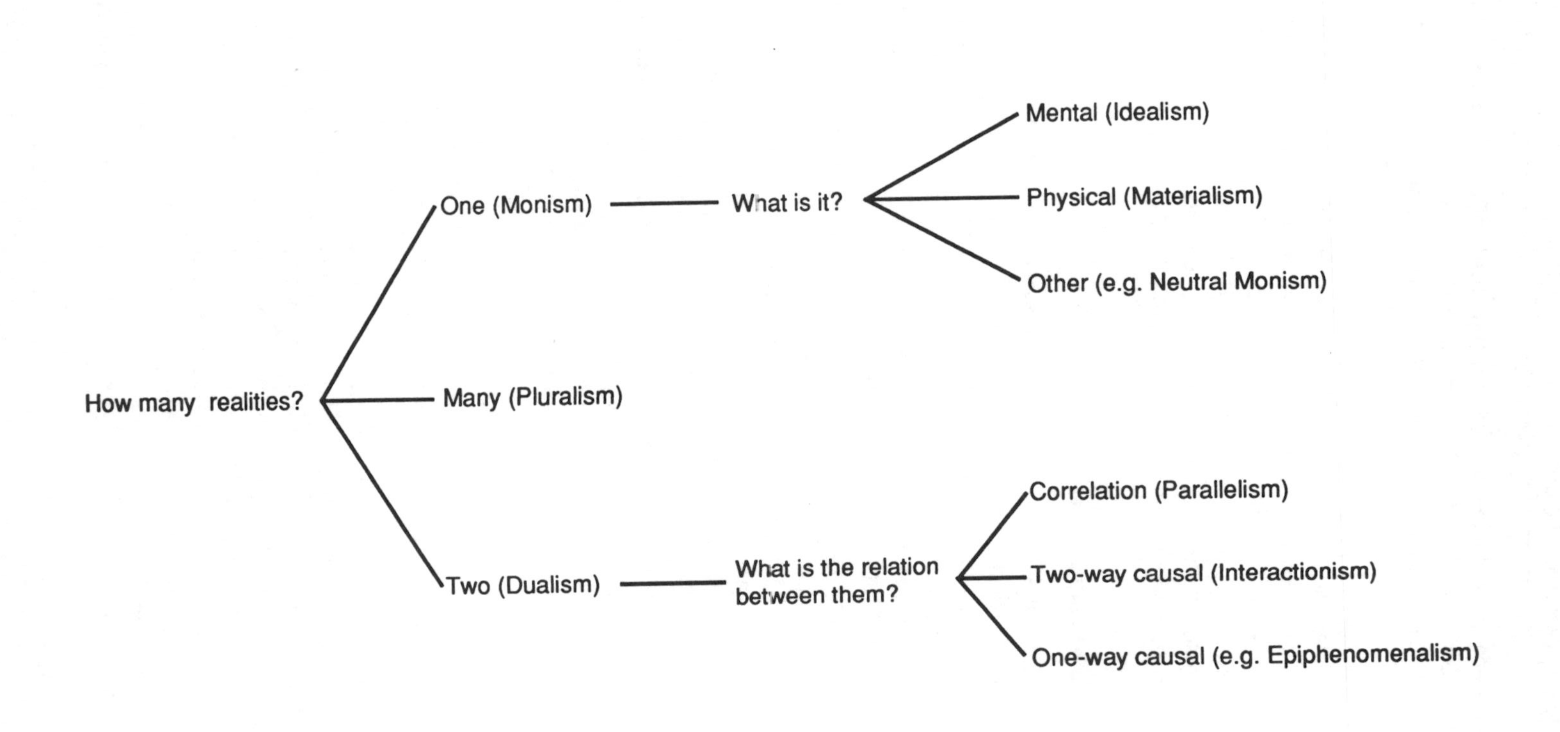

Figure 3.1 Issues and traditional solutions of the mind—body problem
(*Source:* Valentine)

mental phenomena are reducible to physical (*materialism*); or both are really something else (for example, *neutral monism*). Others have argued that there are two distinct realities (*dualism*). Then the question arises as to how they are related. Possibilities are that they are: unrelated; correlated but causally independent (for example, *psychophysical parallelism*); or causally related. Causal relations may be claimed to hold in both directions (*interaction*); or only one (such as, epiphenomenalism). In more recent times, the problem has been phrased in terms of the relation between different languages or descriptions; namely, those that refer to mental and physical events. Sometimes entangled with these ontological and semantic problems is the closely related epistemological problem of different kinds of knowledge.

Criteria for distinguishing the mental and the physical

A number of different criteria have been suggested for distinguishing the mental from the physical (see Feigl, 1958). First, there is the *qualitative character* of phenomenological experience (what philosophers call 'sensory qualia'). Colours, tastes and smells, for example, appear to have properties quite different from those of physical phenomena. Since, according to Leibniz's law of the identity of indiscernibles, two things are identical only if they have all their properties in common, some philosophers have argued for a distinction between mental and physical on the basis of qualia.

This is closely linked to an epistemological distinction in terms of the *mode of verification*. The suggestion is that mental phenomena are private whereas physical are public or intersubjectively confirmable. Thus the sort of knowledge people have of their own mental states is different from the sort of knowledge they have, or can have, of others' mental states. This distinction between the subject's and the observer's perspective is developed in Nagel's (1974) famous paper, 'What is it like to be a bat?', and in Jackson's (1982) case of the neurophysiologist inhabiting a black and white room who, although possessing perfect knowledge of the neurophysiological basis of colour vision, lacks the experience of it. However, the distinction between private and public is less clear than appears at first sight, being a matter of degree rather than kind. All knowledge is ultimately based on private experience; public knowledge is merely that on which we can reach agreement (see Chapter 5 and Valentine, 1978). Furthermore, the existence of different types of knowledge may not be sufficient to justify different kinds of entity (Churchland, 1985).

Others have claimed *intensionality* as a distinguishing feature of the mental. Brentano (1874) claimed that psychological activities had mental objects, which might or might not exist in the external world: one can imagine or hope for things that never materialise. In modern parlance these psychological activities are labelled 'propositional attitudes'. The content of a mental state can be expressed in the form of a proposition (for example, what one hopes for or believes). This approach has been popular amongst cognitive psychologists who have adopted the computational model of mind, who see it as a way of dealing with representation and meaning. (However, it is to be noted that most cognitive psychologists consider their position compatible with materialism.) A weakness of the approach is that not all mental states are of this logical form.

In similar vein, Descartes (1641) suggested that the distinctive feature of the mental realm was thinking ('res cogitans'), being particularly impressed by the capacities for reasoning and language. In contrast, the distinctive feature of the physical realm was held to be *spatial extension* ('res extensa'). However, this analysis is probably no longer acceptable. Some mental phenomena – for example, images – might be said to have spatial properties; conversely, it is to be doubted whether the entities of modern physics, such as energy and forces or electrons and neutrons, are inherently spatial. Such a division would also of course be rejected by identity theorists (see pp. 29–31). Some (such as Shaffer, 1965; P.S. Churchland, 1986) have suggested that these descriptive properties are conventions which may come to be abandoned in time: scientific discoveries may lead to the revision of our conceptual framework.

Descartes suggested another criterion for physical phenomena; namely, that they were *subject to the laws of natural science*. In contrast, he believed that mental phenomena were not subject to deterministic, mechanistic laws but were 'free' or undetermined. It is for this reason that most scientists have rejected dualism. Psychologists cannot accept the view that mental phenomena are undetermined (see Chapter 2).

We shall now turn to a consideration of the main solutions to the mind–body problem which have been proposed and will consider both logical arguments for or against each view and confirming or disconfirming empirical evidence. These solutions will for convenience be divided into three categories:

1 substance dualism, which accepts the common-sense view that both mental and physical processes have reality and is then faced with the problem of their relation;
2 monism, which claims that there is only one reality and that some kind of reduction of mental or physical phenomena is possible;
3 other more recent solutions, which generally accept substance monism but often allow property or theory dualism; on this view there is one fundamental reality but it may exhibit different attributes which require different kinds of description.

DUALIST SOLUTIONS

The common-sense or lay answer to the problem is *interaction*, made famous (or perhaps infamous) by Descartes, who espoused a two-way causal interaction between what he conceived of as two distinct substances: mental and physical (see p. 23). One motivation for postulating mind as a non-physical substance is religious belief in an immortal soul. The place of interaction between these two realms was deemed by Descartes to be the pineal gland, on the grounds that this was the only feature not known to be duplicated in each cerebral hemisphere. He had, however, the 'peculiar merit of being so clearly and distinctly confused that the difficulties of this position became apparent' (Reeves, 1958). Dualist interaction has been espoused more recently by Popper and Eccles (1977; see also Eccles and Robinson, 1984). Popper postulates the existence of three worlds: world 1, containing physical objects which conform to physical laws; world 2, containing mental states and subjective experiences; and world 3, containing products of the human mind – abstract, cultural objects, objective knowledge, such as numbers, theories or books, which are governed by normative principles, such as the rules of logic. World 3 objects can also belong to world 1 but are partially autonomous. Eccles postulates that the self-conscious mind exercises a superior interpretive and controlling role on neural events by virtue of a two-way interaction across the interface between world 1 and world 2. Popper holds that world 3 interacts with world 1 indirectly via world 2. These views have not found much favour (see for instance, P.S. Churchland, 1986, who argues that Popper has not shown that thought is non-physical but only that it is necessary for technology, and asks why, if world 3 can influence world 2, can it not also influence world 1 directly?). Humanistic psychologists wish to attribute a genuinely causal role to mental processes, a view commonly known as 'mentalism'. Psychophysiology might be thought to be based on the same premisses, if it is concerned with the effect of psychological states on physiological variables (Johnson, 1977).

Dualist interaction is in accord with common sense and ordinary language, which attributes causal efficacy to mental and physical events. On the other hand, it offends against parsimony, according to which the simplest possible explanation is to be preferred. There are a number of other serious objections too. Descartes's followers have found it difficult to see how there can be causal relations between two things defined as distinctively different, namely, spatial, mechanistic and deterministic as opposed to non-spatial, non-mechanistic and non-deterministic. How, in particular, could bodily causes produce mental effects if the latter are supposed to be non-determined? Those impressed by the success of science, based on assumptions of the efficacy of solely physical explanation and the laws of conservation, have found it difficult to see how there is room for mental causes. If physical causes are sufficient, mental causes can hardly be necessary. How could they break into a closed system? The explanatory power of dualist interaction is unimpressive: the arrows in Eccles' diagram of the liaison brain seem no advance on Descartes's animal spirits in the pineal gland.

However, there are many pieces of evidence which are in practice interpreted within this framework. Examples of apparent mental causes of physical effects are psychosomatic disorders and voluntary behaviour. Psychical research and psychokinesis, if established, would constitute confirming evidence. Examples of commonly supposed physical causes of mental effects are almost too numerous to mention, most of neuroscience demonstrating the dependence of mental activity on neural function, but brain damage and neurotransmitters may be cited as examples.

If dualist interaction is in error, the whole of psychophysiology may be metaphysical nonsense, or at least psychosomatics may be a logical howler. My own view is that it can only be salvaged by appeal to psychophysical parallelism or some form of double aspect theory (see pp. 26–8 and 29 respectively). All descriptions are to some extent arbitrary. It could be argued that in cases of apparent interaction we simply choose to focus attention on one aspect of the cause and the other aspect of the effect. This does not preclude the existence of the other correlated aspect. For example, we may choose to say that a psychological stress caused a physical ulcer; this does not preclude there being some unmentioned physiological state correlated with the stress (indeed, any conventional scientist assumes this). Shaffer (1965) discusses another possibility, dual causation theory, according to which mental and physical events could each be sufficient but not necessary causes. (See also Place, 1988, for discussion.)

Emergence claims that mental phenomena are not reducible to physical, and cannot be explained in terms of them. (This is to be distinguished from what Dennett calls 'innocent emergence', the demonstration of properties by a whole system which are not possessed by its component parts.) It tends to be held by interactionists, such as Eccles and Sperry. Sperry (1980) holds all these views, arguing that consciousness is a dynamic, emergent property of cerebral activity; it is higher order and holistic; that is, more than the sum of its neurological parts; it supervenes and exercises directive, causal control. This is reminiscent of William James, who described consciousness as just what would be expected in a nervous system grown too big to direct itself (see Chapter 4). Cognitive psychologists who subscribe to a functionalist philosophy claim that psychology is autonomous with respect to neuroscience.

Such a view may be good for morale (see Chapter 2) and is in accord with common sense. Descriptions of mental phenomena are different in meaning from, and hence cannot be logically reduced to, descriptions of physical phenomena. Demonstrations of multiple and/or variable localisation of function ('multiple instantiation') tend to support it, whereas demonstrations of systematic correlations between mental and physical phenomena tend to go against it.

Epiphenomenalism, while attributing reality to mental states, refuses to allow them causal efficacy. On this view mental processes or experiences are non-causal by-products of physical processes; they are caused by but do not themselves cause physical events. A famous exponent was T.H. Huxley, who wrote

> The consciousness of brutes would appear to be related to the mechanism of their body simply as a collateral product of its working, and to be as completely without power of modifying that working, as the steam-whistle which accompanies the work of a locomotive engine is without influence upon its machinery.
>
> (Huxley, 1874: 575)

According to radical behaviourism, behaviour can be explained without recourse to mental states.

The main arguments in favour of epiphenomenalism are parsimony and consistency with scientific explanation: no mysterious mental causes are postulated. In attributing more importance to physical than to mental processes it is in accord with the intuition that only some physical systems have mental properties. On the other hand it is counter-intuitive in denying that conscious experience can have any effect on behaviour. It leaves us with functionless 'mental danglers' (Feigl, 1960). Another problem is that it is untestable: since mental events are always accompanied by physical events, the exclusive efficacy of the former cannot be demonstrated.

Neuroscience has demonstrated the dependence of mental states on brain states. Recently Libet (1985) has argued that the electrophysiological readiness potential precedes the conscious intention to perform a spontaneous voluntary act by about 500 ms. Psychologists from the time of James and Freud have argued that conscious experience is often the result rather than the cause of behaviour. Whether it is justifiable to extrapolate from these cases to the assertion that it never is, is more difficult to establish. The existence of voluntary behaviour appears to be counter-evidence.

One way of escaping the objections to interaction is to accept that mental and physical processes both have reality, but to reject the notion that either is causally dependent on the other. Causal relations are only allowed to hold within each realm. This view of independent correlation known as *psychophysical parallelism* was held by Leibniz (1714), who proposed that there was a pre-established harmony set by God at the beginning of the universe such that mental and physical events occurred simultaneously like two synchronised clocks or orchestras. The view was satirised by Voltaire, who raised the question of the need for a conductor. Malebranche (1675) introduced the amusing variation known as 'occasionalism', which required God to leap into action every time an event of one type occurred in order to implement the appropriate event of the other type. Many early psychologists based their work on a parallelist framework; for example, Fechner, Wundt and the *Gestalt* psychologists, who postulated an isomorphism between psychological and physiological processes.

Such a view certainly meets objections to the notion of cause in general

(Russell, 1913) and causal relations between unlike substances in particular. However, postulating two distinct substances militates against parsimony, and many have sought to avoid this solution (see p. 27 ff.). A necessary but not sufficient condition for psychophysical parallelism is the existence of empirical correlations between mental states and neurophysiological conditions. Much of physiological psychology has been aimed at establishing such correlations. Early work on aphasia, emotion and the motor theory of thought suggested that such correlations were elusive. In the first case, the same psychological dysfunction appeared to be associated with a number of different physiological locations or patterns, and in the last two cases great variety at the psychological, experiential level seems to be represented by much cruder differentiation at the physiological level. Failures to find correlations may be due to technical or conceptual ineptitude and do not preclude the possibility of subsequent discoveries with further advances. More recently, neuroscience has provided many successes (see, for example, P.M. Churchland, 1986). However, these are often the prelude to attempts at causal analysis. Nor does it seem possible to distinguish psychophysical parellelism from identity theory (see pp. 29–31) on purely empirical grounds.

Overall, dualism is not a currently popular view. It is unparsimonious, appears to be inconsistent with science and faces the problem of explaining the relationship between two distinctive realms. Most scientists and philosophers have opted for some form of monism, to the consideration of which we now turn.

MONIST SOLUTIONS

There are three traditional versions of monism: (1) idealism, which claims that only mental phenomena are real; (2) materialism, the opposite view that only physical phenomena are real; and (3) dual aspect theory, according to which both are aspects of some more fundamental reality.

Idealism is commonly associated with George Berkeley (1710), who put forward the doctrine of *esse* is *percipi*, to be is to be perceived, whereby the universe was considered to be occupied only by minds and ideas, physical objects being entirely dependent on these and existing merely as ideas in someone's mind. The permanence of physical objects was explained by appeal to God's omnipresent perception, hence the limerick attributed by Bertrand Russell to Ronald Knox:

> There was a young man who said, 'God
> Must think it exceedingly odd
> If he finds that this tree
> Continues to be
> When there's no-one about in the the quad.'

To which the reply was

Dear Sir: Your astonishment's odd:
I'm always about in the quad
And that's why the tree
Will continue to be
Since observed by Yours faithfully, God.

The doctrine was taken one step further by Hume (1739), who eliminated minds from the universe, these being reduced to bundles of ideas.

Indeed, there is something fundamental about experience and it can plausibly be argued that all our concepts are constructions or inferences based on it (see, for example, Pearson, 1892; Mach, 1897, for an idealist epistemology). The phenomenologists are right to stress the dependence of our knowledge of the external world on our conceptual apparatus. On the other hand, the belief that only mental phenomena have real existence and that everything outside our experience has none goes against common sense. It seems highly unlikely that our intersubjective agreement about the outside world would be as good as it is, if the latter had no causal effect on our perceptions.

Empirical traditions which perhaps have not gone as far as to deny the existence of physical objects but have stressed the importance of experience are those influenced by phenomenology, which argue that behaviour is determined by, and hence can only be explained by reference to, the meaning of the situation for the organism. Opposing them is the behaviourist tradition, which claims to have been successful in predicting behaviour without reference to the experience of the organism.

Materialism claims that only physical phenomena have real existence, and that everything can be explained in physical terms. This view was held by Democritus and Lucretius in classical times, was developed by Hobbes, Gassendi and La Mettrie in the seventeenth and eighteenth centuries, and rose to favour at the beginning of this century under the name of 'physicalism', associated with Neurath and Carnap. It is held by a number of philosophers, for instance, Quine and Quinton, identity theorists (see pp. 29–31) and most scientists, many of whom have also favoured reduction (see Chapter 11). Amongst psychologists, those who come closest are the behaviourists. Watson's classical behaviourism attempted to reduce mental phenomena to the publicly observable evidence for them. Logical behaviourists, such as Ryle (1949), attempted to analyse mental concepts in terms of dispositions to behave. Skinner's radical behaviourism merely asserts that behaviour can be accounted for without recourse to mentalistic terms.

Such approaches are frequently motivated by parsimony and the desire for a unified science. It is true that the only knowledge we can have of others' experience is through that which is publicly observable – that is, their behaviour and physiology – and the materialist may argue that science has achieved considerable success by relying on these sources. On the other hand, common sense does attribute reality to our experiences and one of the weaknesses of materialism is how to account adequately for them, especially those of other people, which on a materialist account are identical with their underlying physical causes. Watsonian and logical behaviourism are false: a headache is not merely or necessarily a disposition to take aspirins. In fact, dispositional analyses of mental states turned out to be impossible to carry out. On the other hand, radical behaviourism has had a measure of success. The existence of disembodied spirits would militate against materialism. In contrast, many believe that the progress of science makes materialism increasingly probable.

Double aspect theory gives credence to the reality of mental and physical processes but claims that these are merely aspects of the same fundamental underlying reality. Such a view was held by Spinoza, who was a panpsychist. He believed that the whole universe had mental and physical attributes. This compromise position has the attraction of acknowledging the intimate connection between mental and physical while admitting their logical difference. It admits the existence of mental and physical phenomena while avoiding the problem of their relation. The main objection to it is that the underlying reality remains basically metaphysical and unknowable, nor is it clear exactly what it is to be an attribute. Similar views have been formulated more recently in linguistic terms. Russell (1927) adopted a position known as 'neutral monism'. He likened 'mind' and 'matter' to the lion and the unicorn fighting for the crown, considering them to be simply heraldic inventions or logical constructions. On this view, mental and physical are two sets of relations or theories for ordering phenomena. Ryle (1949) argued that the mind–body problem was a pseudo-problem resulting from a category error or failure to distinguish logically separate systems, as in the sentence 'She came home in a sedan chair and a flood of tears'. He suggested that the distinction between body and mind is merely grammatical, matter usually being described in terms of nouns or pronouns, and mind in terms of verbs, adverbs or adjectives. Thus, for example, one should speak of 'behaving intelligently' rather than of 'intelligence'. This view appears to rule out of court the possibility of any language for describing relations between mental and physical events.

We turn now to current views of the mind–body problem. Most of these have adopted substance monism, generally materialism, but opted for some form of property or theory dualism.

CURRENT VIEWS

A view which has been popular amongst philosophers is *identity theory*, variously known as 'mind–brain identity theory' or 'central state identity theory' (Place, 1956; Smart, 1959; Feigl, 1958). This states that consciousness *is* a brain process, in the sense that 'a cloud is a mass of water droplets or other particles in suspension', 'heat is mean kinetic energy' or 'a gene is identical with a section of a DNA molecule'. It is made clear that what is claimed is *contingent identity*. Hence, it is weaker than logical identity (which is true by definition and does not require empirical verification) but stronger than correlation (where the two phenomena are independent). The two descriptions have independent means of verification (there are different ways of finding out about them), but one description gives a more adequate explanation of the phenomenon than the other. Feigl (1960) employs Frege's distinction between sense and reference: the two descriptions have different meanings but refer to the same thing, as in the case of the morning star and the evening star which both refer to Venus.

Advocates of the theory urge parsimony in its favour. By claiming identity, the puzzle of otherwise irreducible and inexplicable psychophysical bridging laws is avoided: such 'nomological danglers' are eliminated. Another advantage is that, in accordance with common sense, mental states can be assigned a genuinely causal role. If mental states are identical with brain states, then the former as much as the latter can be said to be causes of behaviour.

However, there have been difficulties with the intelligibility and plausibility of the theory. It appears to violate Leibniz's law, according to which two objects are identical if and only if they have all their properties in common. As we saw (pp. 22–3), a number of features have been suggested by which mental and physical phenomena might be distinguished. (Some of these depend on the confusion of epistemological with ontological questions: different types of knowledge do not necessarily imply different types of existence; see Smart, 1959; Lewis, 1983.) Kripke (1972) argued, against identity theory, that identity cannot be contingent but must be necessary because it holds only between what he calls 'rigid designators' (terms which pick out the same referent in all possible worlds). However, one difficulty with this argument is that it depends on the problematical concept of possible worlds. In defence of identity theory, Cornman (1962) argued that such cross-category identities do not require common properties. Another respect in which the term 'identity' may be misleading is that identity theory is a form of materialism. Its goal is the reduction of mental states to brain states. The symmetry quickly dissolves into asymmetry, in which priority is given to neurophysiological accounts.

As originally formulated by Place (1956), the theory applied to mental states such as sensations and images. However, others, such as Armstrong (1968), extended it to cover propositional attitudes such as believing and hoping (see Place, 1988). The theory is more plausible in its original than in its extended form. It has also been generally assumed that the theory implies 'type identity', that is, that certain types or classes of mental event will be shown to be identical with certain types or classes of brain events. (Lewis, 1969, denies that this assumption is implied.) Against this, many functionalists and cognitive psychologists have favoured *token identity*: the view that every mental state is identical with a particular brain state but it may not be possible to construct general statements identifying classes of mental events with classes of physical events. The same mental state may be instantiated by different brain states on different occasions or in different individuals (Putnam, 1975). For example, binocular disparity is realised by different structures in the owl and the cat (Pettigrew and Konishi, 1976). Such 'multiple instantiability' is demanded by artificial intelligence, if computers are to be attributed mental states. Conversely, the same brain state may correspond to different psychological states, since the interpretation of the latter depends on the relation of the organism to its environment (Putnam, 1978; 1983). There is no reason to suppose that concepts which are useful for describing mental processes will map onto concepts which are useful for describing neurophysiological processes in a one-to-one fashion (Fodor, 1974). They may well cross-classify, psychological categories mapping onto an indefinite number of arbitrarily related neurophysiological categories.

The whole programme of course depends on the successful establishment of psychophysical correlations. In this sense identity theory is what Popper, in Popper and Eccles (1977), calls 'promissory materialism'. The theory was originally motivated by work such as that of Penfield (1955), who elicited autobiographical memories and a variety of other responses by stimulating specific regions of the cortex. Although the picture has since become more complicated, major advances have been made in determining the neurophysiological basis of sensory experience (see for example, P.M. Churchland, 1986). However, the existence of empirical correlations between mental and neurophysiological states is not sufficient to establish the stronger claim of identity. It is not clear that identity theory can be distinguished from psychophysical parallelism on the basis of purely empirical evidence. However, Bechtel (1988a) argues that if, by employing identity theory as a working hypothesis, our knowledge of mental processes can be used to generate confirmable hypotheses about neural processes and vice versa, then a claim of identity may be justified and preferred to correlation.

Evidence against the thesis would be demonstrations of one-to-many relationships between mental and physical states (see pp. 26–7), as would extra-sensory perception, if established. If temporal displacement between corresponding mental and physical events could be demonstrated (for example, Libet *et al.*, 1979), this would also cast doubt on the theory.

One version of token identity is *anomalous monism* (Davidson, 1970). On this view every mental event is a physical event: the same event can be described differently. According to Davidson, laws do not hold between events themselves but only apply to events described in a particular way, relative to a particular, conceptual framework. He claims that there are causal laws pertaining to events described physically. Because of the identity between mental and physical events, physical events can be caused by mental events as well as by physical events. However, Davidson holds that there are no laws pertaining to events described psychologically: psychology is anomalous (lacking in laws). This is because he believes that psychological descriptions are to be given in terms of reasons, desires and beliefs. Since this involves a radically different conceptual framework (see Chapter 14), there can be no laws relating mental and physical descriptions. However, it is to be noted that this conclusion depends on a particular interpretation of the nature of psychological events, as propositional attitudes. The prospects for relating other types of mental events, such as sensations and images, may be very much better.

According to *eliminative materialism* (Feyerabend, 1963; Rorty, 1970; Churchland, 1981), the explanation of behaviour in terms of beliefs and desires, deemed 'folk psychology', is to be replaced by accounts in terms of neuroscience, on the grounds that common-sense accounts are an inadequate basis for science. Why folk psychology is the only candidate to be considered is difficult to understand. Eliminative materialism is an extreme reductionist theory, which appears to discount the possibility of a scientific psychology.

The dominant theory of mind in current cognitive psychology is *functionalism* (Putnam, 1967; Fodor, 1975; Dennett, 1978; Lycan, 1981). In this view mental states are defined in terms of causal relations to environmental stimuli, other mental states and behavioural responses. For example, pain results from tissue damage, gives rise to distress and produces attempts to escape from it. Functionalism is similar to behaviourism but differs from it in allowing the existence of mental states. Although this need not be the case, as adopted in cognitive psychology it tends to be part of a package (Pylyshyn, 1980; 1984). Thus functionalists usually subscribe to token physicalism and claim that psychology is autonomous. The appropriate level of description for mental states is in terms of abstract functional organisation, independent of any particular physical realisation. Mental states exhibit 'multiple realisability' or 'multiple instantiability': they may be implemented in Martians or computers as well as human beings. Functionalists have generally adopted the computational model of mind (see Chapter 10), according to which cognition is computation: mental life consists of operations performed on symbolic representations. Functionalism thus favours the pursuit of cognitive psychology independently of neuroscience and allows artificial intelligence, either of which may be seen as an advantage or a disadvantage, according to one's point of view. P.S. Churchland (1986) makes the point that we do not yet know at what level the neurophysiology is irrelevant. There are problems with some current formulations of functionalism in cognitive psychology: not all thinking is rational, nor is all of mental life a matter of sentence crunching. Perception, learning and memory, the central topics of psychology, tend to be neglected.

One serious objection to functionalism is that it ignores the quality of experience (Nagel, 1974; 1986), even on the admission of its own adherents (Fodor, 1981). For this reason it can hardly be considered a solution to the mind–body problem. One form of the argument levelled against it is the inverted spectrum thought-experiment (Block and Fodor, 1972). It is possible to imagine – even though Hardin (1988) has shown that it is empirically unlikely – that there are people whose experience of the colour spectrum is systematically inverted with respect to our own; for instance, they may have the experience of red in situations where we have the experience of green and vice versa. Their behaviour will not be distinguishable from ours because the inversion is systematic. Since it is impossible to distinguish these cases on a functionalist account, the conclusion is that functionalism is inadequate. (For attempts to rebut this argument, see Shoemaker, 1975; Churchland and Churchland, 1981.)

CONCLUSIONS

As we noted at the beginning of this chapter, the mind–body problem has appeared in various guises. Over its long history, metaphysical and ontological problems have given way to semantic issues. Epistemologically, the subject's perspective can be distinguished from the observer's perspective. This is illustrated by the case of a neurophysiologist who might have complete knowledge of the physiological basis of colour vision but lack the experience of seeing colour, or John Locke's example of the studious, blind man who thought that scarlet was like the sound of a trumpet. However, the idealist is right to point out that public knowledge is a construction based on private experience.

In some cases empirical evidence may be insufficient to decide between competing views. It is widely believed that epiphenomenalism is untestable since mental events seem always to be accompanied by physical events. Hence, it is difficult to distinguish this position from interaction. Likewise, it may be difficult to decide on the basis of purely empirical evidence between psychophysical parallelism and identity theory. However, conceptual considerations can be brought to bear. Thus substance monism is now generally preferred to substance dualism on the grounds of parsimony and consistency with science. This view is usually held to be materialism but, in view of the fact that our conception of matter has changed radically (see Zukav, 1979), this may no longer be appropriate.

Although substance monism has generally been accepted, most current positions incorporate some form of theory dualism. The most popular view of the relation between mental and physical is token identity, according to which every mental event is a physical event but there may be no general psychophysical laws relating the two. There has been confusion over the interpretation of mental states: identity theorists have focused on sensations whereas functionalists have concentrated on propositional attitudes. Perhaps paradoxically (in view of the generic nature of experience) the prospects for establishing the neurophysiological basis of sensations are much better than they are for propositional attitudes.

Chapter 4

Consciousness

PROBLEMS

'Consciousness is both the most obvious and the most mysterious feature of our minds' (Dennett, 1987). Part of the problem arises from its privacy, and part from the fact that at present it is a pretheoretical term (Johnson-Laird, 1983a). Indeed, Gray (1971) suggests that these two issues are related, in that the reason why psychology lacks a theory of consciousness is that consciousness has arisen as a datum from our own experience and has been generalised to others inductively by analogy. Explanatory links are missing between conscious and other processes. We are therefore unable to specify its nature or its relations to behavioural and physiological processes.

Some of the main questions which might be asked about consciousness are as follows:

1 What *status* should it be afforded in psychological theory? Can consciousness form part of the subject matter of psychological science? Is it possible to provide a theory of consciousness? What particular problems are raised by its nature? How are they to be solved? What is the status of verbal reports and their relation to conscious events?
2 What is the *nature* of consciousness? Is it an all-or-none process for which there is a cut-off point, or does it represent a continuum? Are there degrees of consciousness? What are its defining properties? Do its criterial features lie in biological tissue, behaviour or the organisation of the system? Is consciousness restricted to organic matter or can computers be said to be conscious? Is there anything which distinguishes processes accompanied by consciousness? What, if any, analysis of consciousness can be given in terms of neurophysiological and ultimately physical processes?
3 What is the *function* of consciousness? What is its evolutionary advantage? What is its relation to, and role in, behaviour? Are they unrelated? Or correlated? Are they aspects of the same or different processes? Is consciousness merely epiphenomenal to behaviour, or does it have causal efficacy in determining behaviour?

THE STATUS OF CONSCIOUSNESS IN PSYCHOLOGY

Historically the fate of consciousness in psychology has followed a curious course. For the structuralist school, usually regarded as the first experimental psychologists, the subject matter of psychology was virtually coextensive with consciousness. The aim of psychology was held to be the analysis of mental experience. For a variety of reasons, both theoretical and practical (see Chapter 5), the approach adopted by this school fell into disuse: large portions of the processes underlying behaviour are inaccessible to consciousness and there were methodological difficulties in investigating those that were. The rise of behaviourism demanded the removal of consciousness from the psychological arena. However, since the 1960s there has been a resurgence of interest in conscious processes, attributed by Holt (1964) to a variety of causes (substantive, for example, contemporary political interest in subjective phenomena; theoretical, for instance, dissatisfaction with strict behaviourist formulations; and methodological, such as improved techniques, both behavioural and physiological).

The confused state of consciousness in psychology is partly the result of misunderstandings of the behaviourists' methodological prescription which insisted on public data. Consciousness is private in the sense that each individual has immediate access to his or her own experience but that of other people can only be inferred by analogy. In a celebrated passage, Wittgenstein used the analogy of a beetle in a box: 'No-one can look into anyone else's box, and everyone says he knows what a beetle is only by looking at *his* beetle . . . it would be quite possible for everyone to have something different in his box . . . the box might even be empty' (1953: para. 293). Consciousness is peculiar in that one has special access to one's own, but this does not detract in any way from the possibility of studying it scientifically. Conscious processes of others, unconscious mental processes and the external world all have the same epistemological status; namely, that of inferred constructs. Conscious experience provides data of the observer's own consciousness immediately and directly, and of that of others mediately and indirectly through the observation of their behaviour, both in the form of what might be called 'performance responses' as well as by means of verbal reports, and of their neurophysiology. These observations are themselves part of consciousness. Thus consciousness provides data for all sciences but its status as subject matter in psychological science is that of an inferred construct. So far as psychology is interested in the processes underlying behaviour, this is true of all its subject matter. The use of introspective reports is discussed in Chapter 5.

THE NATURE OF CONSCIOUSNESS

What is consciousness?

Consciousness has the paradoxical quality of being intuitively obvious, everyone having immediate knowledge of it, yet extremely difficult to *define*. Miller (1964) has drawn attention to the range of meanings it has had for different people: 'a state of being, a substance, a process, a place, an epiphenomenon, an emergent aspect of matter, or the only true reality'. The most basic sense of consciousness is in terms of experience or awareness. Many have emphasised this *phenomenal* aspect, for example Titchener (1899), for whom consciousness was 'the sum total of a person's experiences as they are at any given time'. An important distinction is that between consciousness in the sense of sensory experience – which Jackendoff (1987) terms 'primary awareness' – and a higher order self-consciousness in which one is aware of being aware ('reflective consciousness'). The reader should be warned that many writers have focused exclusively on the latter, presumably because of its pre-eminence in humans. Reflective consciousness is closely related to language and social functions and is typically 'intensional' or propositional. Whereas the contents of primary awareness are essentially sensory, reflective consciousness is dominated by inner speech (what Buddhists refer to as the chatter of the mind), a constant rehearsal of scenarios. It is debatable whether the mind can ever be content-free, although the subjects of the Würzburg psychologists sometimes reported impalpable awareness and some meditational techniques aim to empty the mind. It is notable that the contents of consciousness are the results of activity rather than the process itself (in William James's simile, the contrast between the perchings and the flights of thought): as Lashley (1956) remarked, 'No activity of mind is ever conscious.' Knowledge of which one is aware is typically declarative rather than procedural: 'knowing that' rather than 'knowing how'. This is highlighted in amnesic patients who can learn a variety of skills but report no recollection of having performed the task on previous occasions (Cohen and Squire, 1980; Squire and Cohen, 1984).

We have already noted the close relationship between primary awareness and sensory processing. However, it is important to emphasise the *distinction between discrimination and awareness*. The behaviourist identification of consciousness with the behavioural evidence for it is mistaken. This is clearly demonstrated by such phenomena as subliminal reception and blindsight. Studies of subliminal reception are reviewed by Dixon (1971; 1981). Marcel (1983a) found that reliable semantic judgements about words could be made in conditions which prevented their detection (tachistoscopic presentation followed by a pattern mask): subjects were able to make decisions about the meaning of words which they reported being unable to see. Similarly, in the case of blindsight (Weiskrantz *et al.*, 1974; Weiskrantz, 1980; 1986), patients with damage to the occipital lobe, who are blind in certain areas of their visual field on conventional perimetric testing, can point to a target and make various discriminations significantly above chance level in a forced choice situation. Thus, although they report no experience of seeing, they can 'guess' at high rates of accuracy. This residual capacity has been attributed to a midbrain visual system routed through the superior colliculus and concerned with detection, orientation and location, as opposed to the cortical route through the lateral geniculate responsible for identification. Here we have a clear dissociation between discriminative capacity and acknowledged awareness. Weiskrantz points out that the distinction is not between verbal and non-verbal responding but rather between monitoring and reacting. Equally interesting are cases of anosagnosia, where patients are unaware of deficits such as cortical blindness and aphasia. They deny their incapacity (they are unaware that they are unaware), often confabulating.

Although the contents of consciousness can normally be reported, this is not necessarily so. Not all experiences can be put into words. A striking example is provided by split-brain patients who are unable to report verbally on stimuli presented to the left hemisphere which it is clear, from other behavioural responses such as mimes or emotional reactions, that they have comprehended (Sperry, 1968).

A number of writers (for example, James, 1890; O'Keefe, 1985) have provided intuitive accounts of the *characteristics of consciousness*. First, it is *private* and personal, confined to the individual. Items within one person's consciousness belong to their owner and are separated from those of others. It is experienced as a constantly *changing* sequence. This seems to be an essential feature and may be explained by its role in dissonance detection as some have suggested. For example, Crook (1987a) claims that the key element in making a representational process conscious is 'the temporal continuum of the detection of dissonance which maintains and updates the integrity of the model and its coherence'. O'Keefe (1985) suggests that the reason why it is difficult to maintain attention on an item is that it becomes incorporated in the model and thus the mismatch signal is terminated. Despite its changing nature, consciousness is *sensibly continuous*. 'Consciousness, then, does not appear to itself chopped up in bits', wrote James; 'it flows. A 'river' or a 'stream' are the metaphors by which it is most naturally described.' Temporal continuity is maintained across gaps, as in sleep. There is also integration of information within and between modalities, perceived simultaneously, giving rise to the *unity* or holistic nature of consciousness. 'Whatsoever things are thought in relation are thought from the outset in a unity, in a single pulse of subjectivity' (James, 1890). This 'singularity of interpretation' (Jackendoff, 1987; see also Marcel, 1983b) is closely related to the *selective* nature of consciousness. In Jackendoff's view, short-term memory is 'regulated by a selection function that at each moment designates one of the sets [of representations] as most coherent or salient'. In James's words: 'The mind is at every stage a theatre of simultaneous possibilities. Consciousness consists in the comparison of these with each other, the selection of some, and the suppression of the rest by the reinforcing and inhibiting agency of attention.' James went on to distinguish the substantive parts (containing sensory images) from the transitive parts (the relations between these ideas in the margin of attention), using the simile of the perchings and flights of a bird. Thus some items may be in the focus of attention, while others are in the fringe. Focused attention is strictly limited in capacity.

Descriptive approaches

There is a good deal of empirical evidence relevant to consciousness, but until recently relatively few attempts had been made to integrate what Newcombe (1985) describes as 'the labyrinth of speculation and uncoordinated data' into a coherent theory. In this section we shall consider phenomena, additional to the characteristics considered above, which any adequate theory of consciousness would have to account for.

Much early work in psychology was concerned with an analysis of the *contents* of consciousness and its qualities. Using introspection, Wundt concluded that the elements of mental life consisted of sensations, images and feelings. Titchener later attempted to reduce images and feelings to sensations, and suggested quality, intensity, extensity and protensity (temporal duration) as dimensions. Work in the *Gestalt* tradition was aimed at describing the phenomenal characteristics of perception and in particular its independence of the physical stimulus; for example, the phi phenomenon where the perception of apparent motion results from specific patterns of stationary stimuli. Imagery has been the subject of much recent work. The main dimensions have been established as vividness (Sheehan, 1967), control (Gordon, 1950) and spatiality (Baddeley and Lieberman, 1980). With respect to feelings, Wundt suggested that these could be described by reference to three dimensions: pleasantness of quality, strength of intensity and suddenness of mode of occurrence. These bear a striking resemblance to Osgood's semantic differential dimensions – namely, evaluation, potency and activity – of which it has been claimed that they measure affect rather than meaning.

A variety of evidence suggests that it is reasonable to postulate a *continuum of consciousness–unconsciousness*. The notion of levels of functioning in the nervous system has been familiar since the time of Hughlings Jackson (1878). Medical practitioners distinguish the following states on the basis of largely behavioural evidence but relate them to levels of functioning in the central nervous system: normal wakefulness, representing cortical activity; drowsiness and confusion, characterised by responsivity to words, representing subcortical activity; semicoma, characterised by responsivity to pain, representing brain-stem activity; and coma, characterised by a lack of responsivity to pain, representing spinal activity. A reliable coma scale has been developed by extending these principles (Jennett *et al.*, 1981).

Electroencephalographic (EEG) recordings generally enable the distinction of states of alertness, relaxation and four stages of increasingly deep sleep to be made. Decreasing arousal is associated with increasing amplitude and synchrony, and decreasing frequency and voltage of brain waves. These states do not have sharp boundaries but rather represent points on a continuum, which is consistent with the behavioural evidence of decreasing sensitivity to environmental stimulation. One exception to this is the point at which consciousness is lost: a study by Dement (1972), in which subjects were asked to tap a key to a strobe, showed a sudden cessation of tapping when they fell asleep, in the absence of any corresponding discrete change in the EEG. REM sleep, in which dreaming occurs, is considered to be qualitatively different from slow wave sleep. It is distinguished largely on the basis of rapid eye movements (hence 'REM') and is paradoxical in that cortical arousal is accompanied by loss of muscular tonus. Moreover, the two types of sleep are controlled by different neural structures, the raphe system in the lower brain stem in the case of slow wave sleep and the pons in the case of REM sleep.

An interesting question is the relation between different states of consciousness and unconsciousness. They may interact, as in cases of creative writing – see, for example, the study of dramatists by Binet and Passy (1895) – or they may appear independent and ignorant of each other, as in fugue states and hypnotic trances – see, for instance, the study of Huxley by Erickson (1965). Any theory of consciousness would have to account for such cases of *dissociated consciousness* as occur in multiple personality, hysteria and possession – see, for example, Prince (1905); Thigpen and Cleckley (1957). One relevant piece of empirical work is the study of split-brain patients. Sectioning of the corpus callosum results in structural and apparently functional independence of the two hemispheres (Sperry, Gazzaniga and Bogen, 1969; Gazzaniga, 1970; Dimond, 1972). Although these patients behave normally in everyday life, experimental testing conditions reveal certain anomalies. Such patients cannot tell whether two spots presented independently to the two visual half-fields (and hence exclusively to each hemisphere) are the same or different in colour. They are typically unable to perform tasks requiring the processing of linguistic information (located in the left hemisphere) if either input or output involves the use of the right hemisphere. Thus, they are unable to name objects presented to the left visual field, or to the left side of the body, when blindfolded; or to carry out verbally given commands with their left arm or leg. Cases of potential rivalry have also been reported, where the right hand grabbed the left correcting its false choice, or the left side of the body twitched at the mistakes of the right. These findings have tempted conclusions such as 'two rather separate streams of conscious awareness' (Sperry, 1974), 'double consciousness' (Gazzaniga and LeDoux, 1978) and 'two free wills . . . inside the same cranial vault' (Sperry, 1966). Such claims have been disputed by MacKay (1981) who, after careful analysis of the evidence, suggests that such 'twoness of will' is confined to the executive rather than the normative level and that the higher levels of the evaluative supervisory system have their neural basis in the undivided depths of the central nervous system. Other potentially relevant cases with implications for theories of consciousness could be the possibility of transplanting one person's brain into another's, or of one person receiving another's sensations; but these are perhaps more germane to questions of identity.

Other abnormal phenomena, which a theory of consciousness would need to encompass, are *altered states of consciousness* (see Tart, 1969; Wolman and Ullman, 1986), for example, dream, hypnagogic, hypnotic, meditational, trance and drug-induced states. Classic studies of hallucinations induced by drugs such as mescaline, LSD and those in peyote and datura include those by Huxley (1954) and Castaneda (for example, 1968). Reported phenomena include distortions of space and time. James (1890) reports a case of loss of consciousness of self as a result of taking chloroform. Many of the 'mystical' phenomena resulting from meditational techniques can be explained in terms of perceptual mechanisms and alterations in attention (Valentine, 1989a). Early studies suggested that different brain states were associated with different meditational states. Normal subjects show a blocking of alpha rhythm to stimulation, a response which subsequently habituates; yogis, whose aim in meditation is to transcend the phenomenal world, showed no response to a variety of stimuli (Anand *et al.*, 1961); whereas Zen monks, whose aim is to attend to the here-and-now of immediate experience, showed a blocking of alpha to auditory stimuli which did not habituate (Kasamatsu and Hirai, 1966). However, Becker and Shapiro (1981) failed to replicate these results. Experienced practitioners of Zen, yoga and transcendental meditation all showed initial alpha suppression to clicks, followed by habituation at about the same rate. Nor were there any differences between groups in the P300 component of the average evoked potential, which would be more likely to reveal attentional differences. Fenwick *et al.* (personal communication) obtained evidence for delayed blocking, failure of conditioning and a number of other abnormalities of cognitive functioning in a Zen master tested while not meditating.

Several attempts have been made to provide maps of the mind, covering normal, drug-induced, psychopathological and mystical states. Fischer's (1971) cartography of inner space (see Figure 4.1) proposes a perception–hallucination continuum of ergotropic, noradrenergic hyperarousal, characterised by EEG desynchrony, and interpreted as creative, psychotic and ecstatic states; and a perception–meditation continuum of trophotropic, serotonergic hypoarousal, characterised by EEG synchrony, and interpreted as various meditative states. However, progression along either of these continua is accompanied by decreasing variability in EEG amplitude, an increased sensory-to-motor ratio and increased stereotypy. Hence, it is not surprising to find that rebounds can occur between the states of ecstasy and samadhi (the ultimate mystical state).

Clark's (1972; 1983) model is in the form of a double cone (see Figure 4.2)

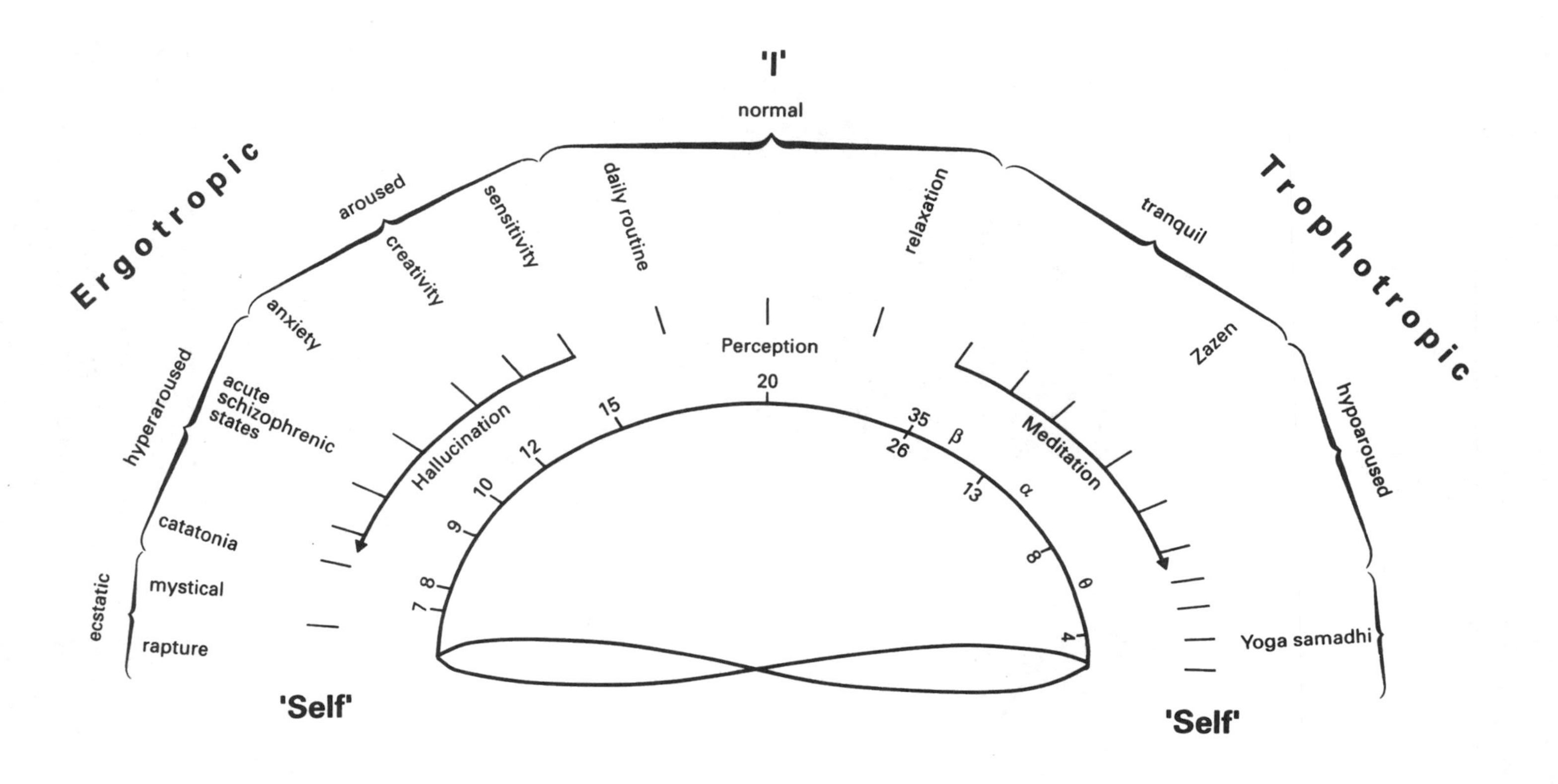

Figure 4.1 Cartography of inner space
(*Source:* Fischer, 1971; copyright 1971 by the American Association for the Advancement of Science)

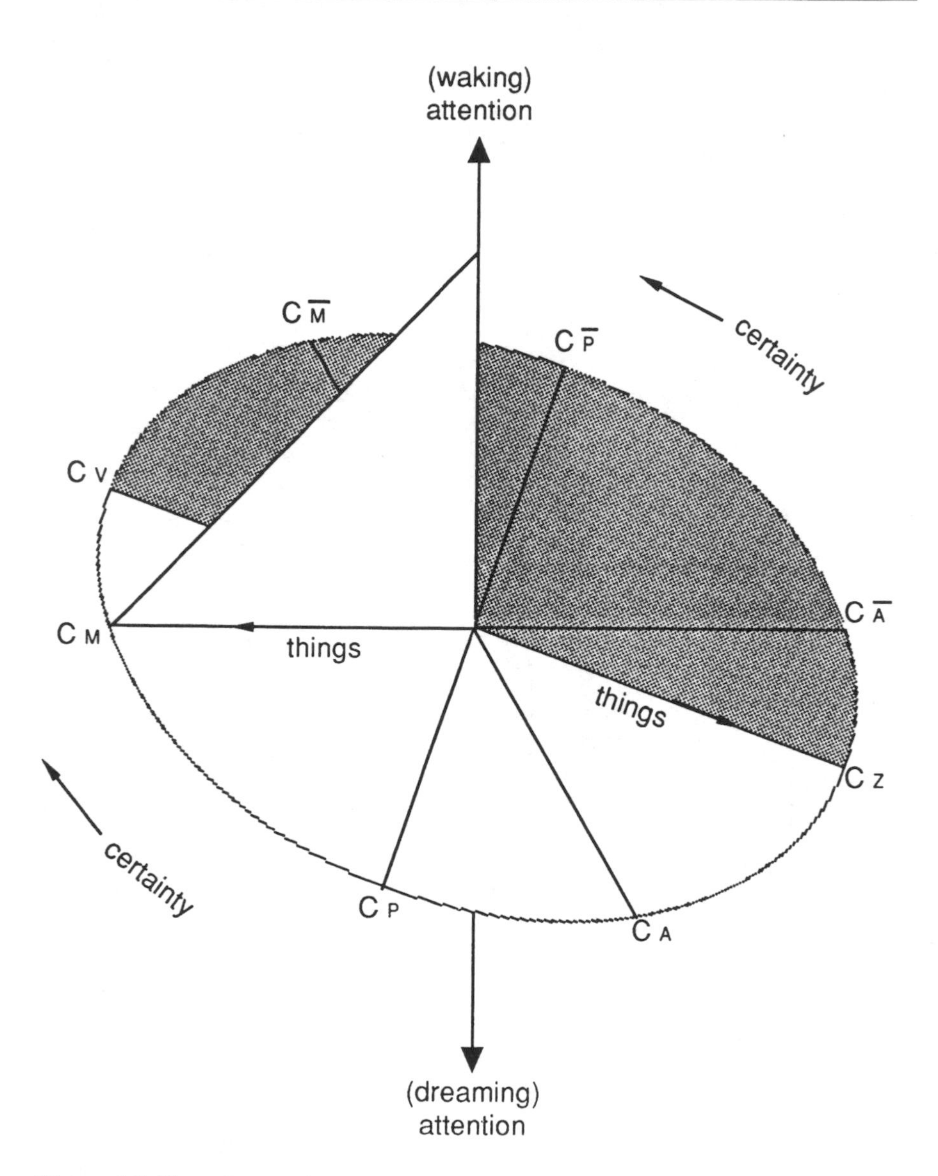

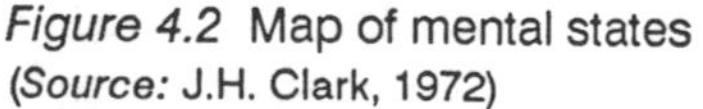
Figure 4.2 Map of mental states
(*Source:* J.H. Clark, 1972)

with subjective dimensions of attention on the vertical axis ranging from waking to dreaming; certainty, an angular dimension in the horizontal plane, an intensity factor ranging from zero at Z to 100 at V; and things, a radial axis in the horizontal plane, the number of things attended to increasing with distance from the central origin O. 'Mindwork' (attention + things) can be

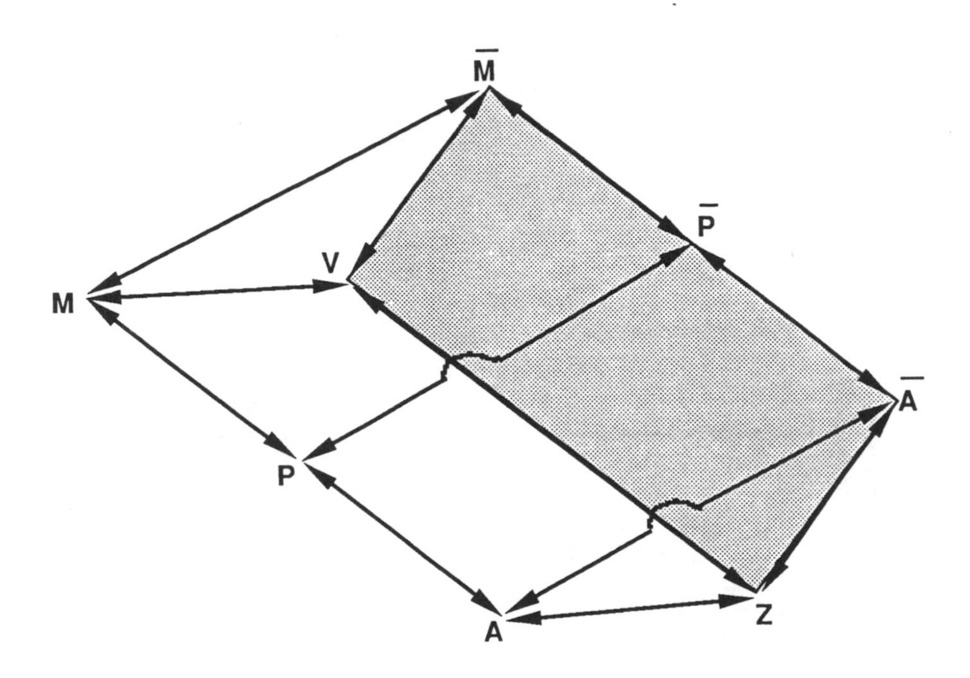

Figure 4.3 Flow diagram of possible inter-state transitions
(*Source:* J.H. Clark, 1972)

represented by the size of the cone. The concentration ratio (attention/things) enables the contrast to be made between concentrated and diffuse attention. The shaded half is negatively evaluated, the unshaded side positively evaluated. Arranged on it are the following states: Ā (average everyday slightly optimistic state), A (mild depression, as after influenza), P (euphoric states, as in peak experiences or mania), P̄ (severe, clinical depression, as in manic depressive psychosis), M (mystical states proper), M̄ (what is described in the mystical literature as 'the dark night of the soul'), Z (the Zen or zero state), and V (the ineffable void). Clark has also proposed a flow diagram to indicate possible transitions between the various states (see Figure 4.3).

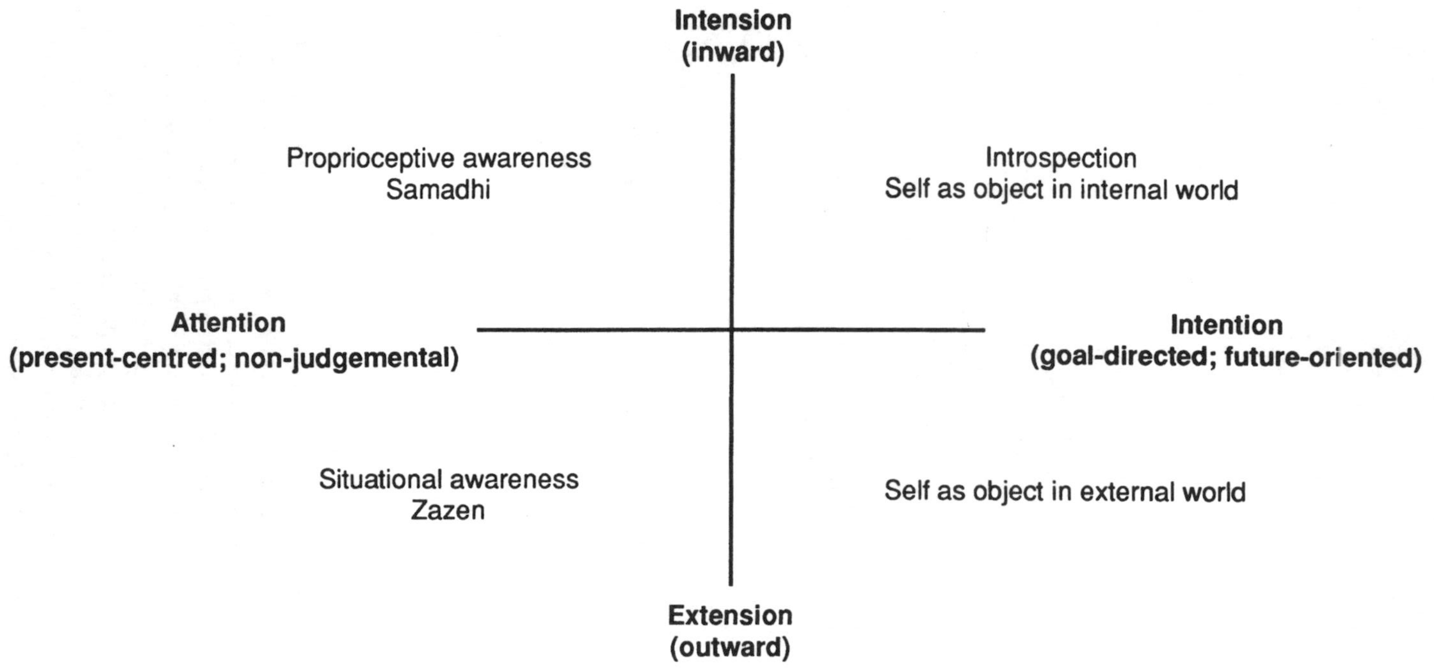

Intension
(inward)

Proprioceptive awareness
Samadhi

Introspection
Self as object in internal world

Attention
(present-centred; non-judgemental)

Intention
(goal-directed; future-oriented)

Situational awareness
Zazen

Self as object in external world

Extension
(outward)

Figure 4.4 Two dimensions of self-awareness
(*Source:* Crook, 1987a)

Crook (1987a; 1987b) has drawn attention to two dimensions of self-awareness (see Figure 4.4). Extension is looking outwards at the external world; intension is looking inwards at one's mental states. Intention is goal-directed and future-orientated, usually involving the evaluation of alternative courses of action, whereas attention is present-centred and non-judgemental. This distinction is similar to that drawn by Apter (1989) between telic (goal-directed) and paratelic (intrinsically rewarding) states, and by Duval and Wicklund (1972) between objective self-consciousness, involving the reification of the self as an agent whose performance is experienced as socially evaluated, and subjective self-consciousness where attention is focused on the activity itself. See also Gallwey's (1975) 'inner game' and Csikzentmihalyi's (1975) concept of flow. Examples of attention directed inwards are proprioceptive awareness or certain meditative trance states; for instance, 'samadhi'. Attention directed outwards is a relaxed but alert openness to the environment, as in zazen and the martial arts. Intention directed inwards is typified by introspection. Intention directed outwards is concerned with problem-solving in the external world, with planning and reviewing activities.

The mechanism of consciousness

Clinical data suggest that consciousness in humans depends on the preservation of the mesencephalon and the diencephalon. Newcombe (1985) aptly remarks that the putative neural substrate of conscious activity is dependent on its operational definition. Thus any or all of the structures subserving arousal, perception, attention and voluntary action may be invoked. O'Keefe (1985) – see also O'Keefe and Nadel (1978) – has identified consciousness with the activation of the theta system which organises neocortical and entorhinal inputs into the hippocampus, and which synchronises all three structures for the construction, correction and manipulation of maps of the environment. He argues that the system is analogous to a hologram in that it consists of a reference beam of non-movement theta direct from the brain stem to the hippocampus, and a carrier beam of movement theta from the brain stem via the entorhinal cortex to the hippocampus. This hypothesis is based on observed parallels between introspectively derived characteristics of consciousness and the anatomy and physiology of the rat septo-hippocampal system. Thus, the unity or holistic character of consciousness is accounted for by the fact that the record is distributed across the entire surface of the hippocampus: each neurone participates in many different representations. The multi-modal nature of consciousness can be accommodated by the fact that the hippocampus integrates information from different modality-specific sensory areas in the neocortex. The distinction between the focus and the background fringe of attention is mirrored by the contrast between the mismatch signals generated by the hippocampus compared with normal activation direct from the brain stem. The two modes of controlling consciousness (internal and external) are represented by two modes of activating the theta system: one driven by the brain stem, the other being the mismatch system in the hippocampus itself. The function of consciousness in accessing long-term, narrative memory is met by the fact that the theta system accesses, organises and codes information stored in the hippocampus. Finally, the fact that some behaviours are accompanied by consciousness but others are not finds a parallel in the distinction between flexible and rigid control of the motor system, as in the contrast between place and non-place learning. This theory is based on work on the cognitive mapping system of the rat. O'Keefe admits that a theory of human consciousness will need to accommodate additional features such as language and self-consciousness, and speculates that in humans the left hippocampus may be involved in these functions.

Valentine (1982) has noted parallels between certain important features of consciousness and the quantum mechanical behaviour of electrons in a bound state (see also Haldane, 1963). The unity of consciousness – that is, the simultaneous integration of items both within and between different sense modalities in a single observer – might be accounted for by the fact that in such systems particular electrons are indistinguishable and non-localisable. Since each electron is equally likely to be found in any nucleus, the observer is, as it were, in the presence of all details at once. The privacy of consciousness could be accounted for by the fact that electronic events within separate quantum systems are independent of each other, since the wave function comes to zero at the system's boundaries. If, as is hypothesised, mental events correspond to quantal electronic transitions within currently connected networks in the sensory nervous system, then, since very small and hence precise amounts of energy are involved, the time-energy uncertainty principle dictates that their timing will be less precisely specified. The resulting gradual transition from one state to another, given a sufficiently high rate of occurrence of events, could account for the fact that the psychological present is extended in time and for the experience of continuity and change in mental life.

THE FUNCTION OF CONSCIOUSNESS

The possible role of consciousness in behaviour has been the subject of much debate but few firm conclusions. Some authors have focused on consciousness in the sense of sensory awareness, others on reflective self-consciousness. Some have emphasised perception, others action.

Marcel (1983b), on the basis of a series of experiments on the effect of pattern masking on word perception (Marcel, 1983a), offers an account of the relationships between conscious *perception* and unconscious perceptual processes. He argues that non-conscious perceptual processes automatically redescribe sensory data into every representational form and to the highest levels of description available to the organism. Such processes: (1) provide records of each resultant representation, (2) produce perceptual hypotheses in different domains, (3) activate related structures, and (4) affect analogue aspects of actions. He rejects the assumption that phenomenal experience is identical to, or a direct reflection of, perceptual processing, asserting that it requires a constructive act whereby perceptual hypotheses are matched against information recovered from records, thereby serving to structure and synthesise information from different domains. Thus consciousness is an attempt to make sense of as much data as possible at the most functionally useful level. This is somewhat similar to Wilks's (1982) view that consciousness is at the uppermost level of mental representation, and to Baars's (1988) that it provides the organism with a global workspace, whose contents are widely distributed throughout the system (see also Crook, 1987a).

Jackendoff (1987) admits failure to find a function for consciousness, but offers a solution to what he calls the 'mind–mind' problem; that is, the relation between conscious experience (the 'phenomenological' mind) and information processing systems (the 'computational' mind), or how computations can result in experiences. In contradistinction to those who suggest that consciousness is a high level process, Jackendoff offers an intermediate level theory, stressing that conscious awareness lies between 'bottom-up' peripheral, sensory processes and 'top-down' central, thought processes: in his view, it is a way-station between perception and understanding. He speculates that it may be an early warning system for comprehension (perhaps a throwback to an earlier stage of evolution when conceptual structures were less developed), which compares what is detected with what is understood, so that attention can be directed to problematic portions of the field. After considering perception, language and music processing in some detail, his final formulation is as follows:

> The distinctions present in each modality of awareness are caused by/ supported by/projected from a structure of intermediate level for that modality that is part of the matched set of short-term memory representations designated by the selection function and enriched by attentional processing, plus the features of affect associated with the set. Specifically, phonological structure is responsible for the form of linguistic awareness; the musical surface for the form of musical awareness; the $2\frac{1}{2}$D sketch for the form of visual awareness; and the affects for the 'feel' of phenomenal entities.
>
> (Jackendoff, 1987: 310)

However, the purpose of this representation is action: consciousness is 'conditional readiness' (Crook, 1987a). Many cognitive psychologists have discussed the role of consciousness in the *control of action*, attributing to it an executive function. Shallice (1972; 1978), noting that consciousness is assumed by many concepts in cognitive theory such as attention and short-term memory, has attempted an information-processing account, according to which consciousness is identified with aspects of the operation of action systems. In his view it corresponds to an intermediate level of control, being isomorphic with strong inputs to the dominant action system, having the properties of assisting in the control of action, being retained in memory and being capable of being spoken about. Shallice (1988) suggests that awareness is related to four sub-systems: the supervisory system, the language system, contention scheduling and episodic memory, which normally operate in an integrated way. He makes the interesting point that when these control systems operate in an uncoordinated fashion – for example, in certain neuropsychological cases or absent-mindedness – it may not be possible to determine whether a person is behaving consciously or unconsciously. Mandler (1975; 1984; 1985) considers consciousness as a mode of information-processing affecting structures governing actions and suggests that it may play a role in the following: choice and selection of action systems, modification and interrogation of long-range plans, retrieval of programs from long-term memory, storing representations of activity and trouble-shooting.

It is noteworthy that *consciousness only accompanies certain aspects of actions*. Penfield (1969) observed, as a result of his work with neurological patients, that consciousness was required for starting and stopping skilled behaviour which otherwise ran off automatically. Thus consciousness seems to be involved with *goal-setting and monitoring* behaviour. Conscious attention appears to be necessary for the acquisition of *novel* sequences of behaviour but not for the performance of well-learned skills, where it may actually interfere. It extends the application of existing operations to new contexts (Rozin, 1976). It is plausible that consciousness is invoked where behaviour on the basis of automatic reactions is inadequate. It implies *flexibility* of behaviour, being associated with controlled processes which are slow but modifiable as opposed to automatic processes which are fast but unmodifiable (Shiffrin and Schneider, 1977). Reason (1984) attributes absent-mindedness to the failure to switch from an open-loop mode of behaviour to a closed-loop mode.

Some have attributed to consciousness a *trouble-shooting* function. Bruner (1983) describes it as 'an instrument for the analysis of necessity and trouble'. This notion is a key feature of Johnson-Laird's (1983a; 1983b) functionalist account of consciousness in terms of mental models. In his view, consciousness is a high-level operating system which monitors hierarchically organised parallel processors. 'The contents of consciousness are the current values of parameters governing the high-level computations of the operating system' (Johnson-Laird, 1983a). He suggests that it may have evolved for the purpose of overriding pathological configurations; for example, conflicting instructions, or deadlocks where two processors are mutually dependent on the output of the other for their continued operation. Craikian automata, which construct internal, symbolic models of the external world, would be capable of simple awareness. Self-reflective automata, which have the ability to embed models recursively, could possess a model of their own operating system (including options available to it) and thus embody self-awareness and intentionality (in both senses: propositional knowledge and the use of knowledge to influence action). However, he argues that consciousness is a property of (a class of parallel) algorithms rather than of functions. If behaviour depends on the function computed rather than the method of computation, then there may be no behavioural criterion of consciousness which could be applied to an organism or a computer. Self-deception, which depends on the division between a conscious and an unconscious part of the mind, may be a suggestive diagnostic. Another indication may be the ability to engage in discourse concerning self-reflective judgement.

Consciousness is likely to be invoked where what is immediately present in the external world is inadequate to determine adaptive behaviour. It enables past experience and future plans to be brought to bear on the situation. Bruner (1983) describes it as a 'vehicle for making present the absent'. Consciousness is associated with deliberation and thus appears to be involved in choice and *decision-making*. MacKay (1981), believing evaluation to be the crucial feature of consciousness, distinguished two functions of a supervisory nature which might be expected to have correlates in conscious experience: (1) perception, the evaluation of sensory input in terms of its implications for the conditional organisation of action; and (2) decision-making, involving the determination of current goals and the running assessment and ordering of priorities. Mandler (1984) argues that consciousness serves to enable delay and reflection to take place, thus increasing the likelihood of the selection of relevant behaviour patterns: possible actions can be considered and their outcomes compared and evaluated covertly without the risk that overt testing would entail. This gives rise to the phenomenal experience of choice, although the actual mechanisms are unconscious.

Others have focused on *self-consciousness*, usually interpreted as having a social role. Jaynes (1976) has speculated that consciousness is a relatively late cultural development, having evolved out of auditory images which were interpreted as voices of the gods and served as forms of social control. As society became more complex these voices of authority became internalised, providing imagery and a language for deliberating about action, in which people could describe themselves and their reasons for acting. Jackendoff (1987) makes the interesting point that if, as Jaynes supposes, these changes were culturally learned, then studies of the way in which children learn to interpret experiences as internally or externally determined and to distinguish between imagination and reality (for example, Olson, 1986) may be relevant to testing the theory. Jaynes claims that this self-reflective consciousness has the following characteristics: (1) 'spatialisation' (even time may be thought of in spatial terms), (2) 'exerption' (selection and interpretation), (3) 'narratisation' (events are explained and set in context), (4) an 'analogue "I" and a metaphor "me"' (we imagine ourselves doing things), and (5) 'conciliation' (resulting in a consistent account). Like Mandler, he argues that consciousness provides a sophisticated strategy for making decisions, since it facilitates internal, vicarious planning without commitment. (Despite different terminology, Baars's (1988) necessary conditions for conscious experience bear similarities to Jaynes's characteristics: (1) perceptual or quasi-perceptual coding, (2) global broadcasting – the contents are widely distributed throughout the system, (3) informativeness – that is, adaptation is demanded by other parts of the system, (4) access to a self-system, and (5) internal consistency – from which he believes limited capacity and seriality follow.) Humphrey (1983) suggests that reflexive self-consciousness is a form of 'natural psychology', supplying subjective reasons for behaviour. It provides social animals with an explanatory framework which, when extended by means of empathic perception, enables them to understand and predict the behaviour of other members of the group.

The relation between consciousness and behaviour

Possible relations between consciousness and behaviour are that they are consistently correlated; that consciousness causes behaviour; that consciousness is the result of behaviour, behaviour causing consciousness; or that they are unrelated. These possibilities are considered below.

Mentalism, which asserts that *experience causes behaviour*, is the common lay view, the belief that ideas determine actions (see Chapter 2). Plato's ethics depended on such a view: knowledge automatically led to action; hence, in order for people to behave well it was necessary merely to inform them of what was good. Right knowledge led to right action. James (1890) also held that it was the norm, as expressed in his ideo-motor theory of action. Other traditions which attribute a dominant role to conscious experience are phenomenology and existentialism (discussed in Chapter 13) and certain approaches in social and clinical psychology. Intuitively, conscious experience affects behaviour through perception (behaviour being a function of the interpreted stimulus) and plays a role in voluntary action. It appears to allow deliberation and flexible responding.

However, there are conceptual difficulties in postulating causal relations between items from different universes of discourse (as was discussed in Chapter 3), an alternative view being that mental states guide rather than cause behaviour (see Boden, 1972). Moreover, there are empirical objections to the view that experience plays a causal role in behaviour.

The accompaniment of behaviour by conscious experience is the exception rather than the norm. Much behaviour occurs without conscious awareness. Particularly striking cases are provided by blindsight and subliminal reception, where discrimination occurs without awareness. Zajonc (1980) has shown that repeated exposure of stimuli can lead to the development of preferences in the absence of conscious recognition. Amnesics can learn skills without any recollection of having performed the tasks. Indeed, it is difficult to find examples of behaviour for which consciousness is essential (Velmans, 1989).

In other cases consciousness may be present but relatively unimportant in the control of behaviour. Emotional experience may be felt after a behavioural adjustment to the situation has been made. One has taken one's hand out of the hot water by the time the pain is felt. Other examples come from studies of thinking and problem-solving which show that it is the products (the results or partial solutions) rather than the process which are available to consciousness (for example, Hayes, 1973; Maier, 1931). Further evidence comes from skills where behaviour may become automatic and performed without consciousness (indeed, conscious attention may even be detrimental to performance), even though conscious verbalisation may have been beneficial in its acquisition. Kimble and Perlmuter's (1970) work illustrates the way in which the role of consciousness alters at different stages in the development of a skill.

Other evidence is indicative of discrepancies between experience and behaviour. A number of studies have shown a poor correlation between measures of the subjective experience of imagery such as vividness, and performance measures such as the recall of visualisable material (Sheehan and Neisser, 1969; Neisser, 1970). Other examples come from the study of attitudes, where there is frequently a lack of convergent validity. As Fishbein and Ajzen (1975) point out, failures to obtain correlations between attitudes and behaviour may be the result of taking measures at inappropriate levels of specificity or ignoring the effect of intervening events. Attitudes are merely one factor in a complex network of situational factors, beliefs and intentions, which determine behaviour.

Finally, there are cases where experience occurs after behaviour and it may well be argued that *behaviour causes experience*. James (1890) argued that emotional experience was the result, not the cause of action: 'We feel sorry because we cry, angry because we strike, afraid because we tremble.' Experimental work by Laird (1974) tends to support this. He manipulated the facial expressions of subjects. Those who were made to 'smile' rated their mood as significantly more positive and laughed more at cartoons than did those made to 'frown'. Much of the evidence on attitude change is consistent with such an interpretation; for example, cognitive dissonance and role playing. Active participation (being forced to take the role of someone holding a view and to attempt to persuade others to favour it) leads to greater attitude change than does passive participation (merely being required to listen) (Janis and King, 1954). Other evidence which suggests that consciousness may be epiphenomenal (that is, a non-causal by-product of behaviour) is found in demonstrations of rationalisation of the kind described by Freud, who distinguished the subject's reason from *the* reason, and are exemplified in cases of post-hypnotic suggestion (where the reasons subjects give appear to be rationalisations of behaviour determined by suggestions made under hypnosis of which they are not conscious). A similar theme has been developed by Bem (1972) in the context of attribution theory, Wason and Evans (1975) to explain the results of reasoning experiments, and LeDoux, Wilson and Gazzaniga (1979) for split-brain patients. In each case it is argued that conscious verbalisations are rationalisations based on observing one's behaviour.

CONCLUSIONS

What answers, then, can be given to the questions posed at the beginning of this chapter?

The status of consciousness in psychology has had a chequered history. Consciousness is peculiar in that everyone has immediate experience of their own. But this privileged access neither provides a scientific hypothesis that would enable predictions about relevant observations to be made nor does it preclude the scientific study of it. Consciousness, as one of the phenomena which form the subject matter of psychology, is an inferred construct imperfectly indexed by observations of behaviour and physiology. Verbal reports generally provide primary validation but measures of performance and physiology may also be employed as converging operations.

'Consciousness' is still a pretheoretical term, although many relevant data exist and there have been a number of speculative attempts at integration. The term is used to refer to both sensory awareness and reflective consciousness. Early work concentrated on describing the contents of consciousness and the dimensions on which they may be categorised. More recently, rich resources in this respect have been discovered in Eastern psychologies (Valentine, 1991) and some of these have been incorporated in maps of mental states. There is phenomenal, behavioural and physiological evidence for levels of consciousness. Discriminative capacity exists independently of awareness, which in turn may be verbalisable. Good agreement has been reached on the characteristics of consciousness: privacy, unity, continuity and selectivity. Recently, there have been a number of attempts to use these features of phenomenal experience to guide the development of neurophysiological and physical accounts. Progress in this direction is necessary for the solution of the problem of the criteria for consciousness. However, an ultimate account may prove impossible: if consciousness is indeed quantal, the appropriate investigations cannot be carried out, since only the state of the system induced by the measurement can be known and not the prior state (see Valentine, 1982).

Many functions have been suggested for consciousness. Its role in perception appears to be temporal integration, event perception (Marcel, 1983b), the detection of novelty and the provision of the organism with a coherent account. Its role in the control of action appears to be strictly limited to goal-setting and monitoring flexible behaviour, which has led some to suggest it plays a role in deliberation, decision-making and trouble-shooting. It has been argued that self-consciousness provides an explanatory framework for the behaviour of oneself and others. However, the paradoxical fact remains that conscious experience is the subjective aspect of functions which could and frequently do take place without it. There is also evidence that consciousness is often the result rather than the cause of behaviour.

Chapter 5

Introspection

WHAT IS INTROSPECTION?

William James saw no problem: 'The word introspection need hardly be defined – it means, of course, the looking into our own minds and reporting what we there discover' (James, 1890). For Wundt it was the observation of the contents of consciousness, self-observation (*Selbstbeobachtung*), as distinct from self-perception or inner perception (*innere Wahrnemung*). Natsoulas (1970) describes it as 'a relatively neutral term for the process(es) whereby one arrives on the spot at introspective awareness . . . process(es) whereby one acquires on-the-spot beliefs or convictions concerning his mental episodes'. Essentially, introspection is noting, and being in a position to report on, mental states and processes.

A number of attempts have been made to distinguish different types of introspection. McKellar (1962) notes the following sources of variance in the method: the circumstances in which the reports are obtained (for example, laboratory, clinic or everyday life), and whether they are normal or special (as in the case of hypnosis, sensory deprivation or drug-taking); whether or not the procedure is systematic; the training of the subjects and the experimenter; and the purpose for which the reports are required (for instance, for oneself or another). Radford and Burton (1974) distinguish self-observation (which might be called introspection proper), in which subjects aim to observe and report on their experiences; self-reports, in which experiences, perhaps of an unusual kind, are described without trying to be particularly objective; and thinking aloud, in which an attempt is made to provide a running commentary on some on-going mental activity. Evans (1980) distinguishes reporting an experience and reporting a strategy.

Pilkington and Glasgow (1967) distinguish five kinds of verbal report in terms of the extent to which they can be checked by other methods. These range from descriptions of subjective experiences such as dreams and images, through reports about phenomena which have behavioural components, such as personality traits, to explanations of behaviour and experiences. These differences have important implications for the validity of introspection. In this connection it may be useful to distinguish reporting: the content of experience, the process of behaviour and the determinants of behaviour.

HISTORY

A study of the use of introspection in the history of psychology highlights the different ways in which verbal reports can be treated. Introspection was the prime method used by the structuralists, other methods being considered supplementary. In their case, strictly controlled conditions were employed and subjects were highly trained. It is not quite clear of what the training consisted but one of its aims appears to have been avoidance of the 'stimulus error': subjects were instructed to exclude previous knowledge of the stimulus items, to eliminate meaning from their descriptions and to report only 'pure' sensations. These reports provided the data for a theory of the structure of the mind in which the contents of consciousness were analysed into sensory components.

The Würzburg psychologists attempted to extend this approach to the higher mental processes of thinking and judgement. Subjects, having completed such tasks as word association, answering questions or deciding which of two weights was heavier, were asked to describe what had gone on in their minds. A relatively free technique was used, in which the experimenter might question the subject if the introspection was unclear. Two problems arose. The first was the discovery of imageless thought: the Würzburg subjects were frequently unable to give a coherent account of the contents of their consciousness while reaching their judgements. The conclusion was inescapable: mental processes could occur without conscious accompaniment. The second problem was the apparent disagreement between the results of the structuralist and Würzburg schools (the former challenging the existence of imageless thought), which contributed to the discrediting of introspection as a method. The inconsistency appeared to be at the level of data. Some thought that the privacy of introspection made it unclear how the argument could be resolved. With hindsight it seems likely that the problem of inaccessibility has more serious implications for the method of introspection than has the problem of privacy. These are discussed below.

The immediate result, however, was that the behaviourists rejected introspection as unreliable. Watson, influenced by the positivist aim of basing all science on objective methods and public data, dismissed introspection as follows:

> Psychology as the behaviorist views it is a purely objective, experimental branch of natural science. Its theoretical goal is the prediction and control of behavior. Introspection forms no essential part of its methods, nor is the scientific value of its data dependent upon the readiness with which they lend themselves to interpretation in terms of consciousness.
>
> (Watson, 1913: 158)

Later behaviourists were prepared to listen to what their subjects said, but not to take it at face value. Verbal reports were treated in exactly the same way as any other responses, as data which required interpretation.

The *Gestalt* psychologists, opposed to the structuralists' theoretical analysis, encouraged a more naïve attitude in their subjects who, in the phenomenological tradition, were instructed to report experience as it immediately appeared to them. Other traditions where introspective reports are taken at face value include those of Kelly (1955), who considered people the best authority on themselves, and Rogers (1965) for whom unconditional acceptance, empathy and positive regard were attitudes of the therapist towards the client necessary for successful therapy.

Psychoanalysis represents a paradoxical, interesting intermediate case, where the subject is instructed not to censor material but is 'constrained' to be 'free'. An interpretation is then imposed by the analyst. In this sense psychoanalysis takes a behaviourist attitude to verbal reports. Thus constraint, and hence bias, can enter in either at the stage of production, as a result of the conditions imposed, or at the later stage of interpretation, in the form of the theoretical framework used. The increase in interest in conscious experience as part of the subject matter of psychology in recent years has led to a number of papers which have sought to reassess the role of introspection (for example, Pilkington and Glasgow, 1967; Lieberman, 1979; Ericsson and Simon, 1980).

THEORETICAL PROBLEMS

Is introspection different in kind from other methods, and if so, in what way? Considerable debate has centred on the nature of introspection and the status of introspective reports. On the one hand, it has been suggested that it confers privileged 'access', and that it can supply unique data which could not be obtained in any other way; on the other hand, it has been rejected as a scientific method on the grounds of subjectivity. According to the mentalist, the subject has direct access to inner states, which are observed as if on a private cinema screen. These determine and are referred to in verbal reports. According to the behaviourist, the experimenter observes verbal responses, which are the product of, and provide indirect evidence for, underlying processes.

Ayer (1959) has distinguished a number of different senses in which mental states might be considered to be private. On the most stringent interpretation, introspective reports would provide the only possible evidence for the existence of a mental state. This is more plausible for images than for motives but is generally untrue. In most cases other behavioural and/or physiological observations can be made which are relevant to determining its existence.

According to a second interpretation, the subject is the only person who has this particular type of evidence. This appears to be true of our current situation. People do have special knowledge of their sensations. Whether anyone in the future could have the same kind of evidence of another person's mental states would depend on technological advances and the conceptual analysis of personal identity (that is, how we chose to describe such advances should they occur).

Thirdly, are mental states private in the sense that introspective reports of them are subjective? The distinction between subjective and objective is less clear cut than at first appears. On the one hand, as we have seen, there are usually alternative public sources of evidence; private experiences can be made public by communicating them; and descriptions of private events are derivative from public ones. The impossibility of private languages has been demonstrated by Wittgenstein (1953), and the social origin of descriptions of inner states has been discussed by Skinner (1953). On the other hand, all so-called 'objective' observations depend on subjective experiences. 'Strictly speaking, every first hand observation is necessarily "private" ' (Burt, 1962). As Schrödinger (1958) pointed out of physics, 'All this information goes back ultimately to the sense perceptions of some living person or persons, however many ingenious devices may have been used to facilitate the labour. . . . The most careful record, when not inspected, tells us nothing.' Observations are necessarily private and particular; the scientific statements inferred from them are necessarily public and general (Perkins, 1953). Thus the distinction between subjective and objective is a matter of degree.

If verbal reports are allowable as scientific data, how are they to be treated? Can they be accepted at face value? Or do they have the same status as data from other methods, simply providing a basis from which inferences can be made? Some have argued that they carry special authority, perhaps even being incorrigible; others that they are particularly prone to artefact.

It might be claimed that the final authority for descriptions of mental states lies with the subject. This may be defensible with respect to experience but appears not to be so with regard to behaviour. Subjects may be in a privileged position due to greater familiarity with their own biographies. As Skinner (1953) observed,

> Because of his preferred position with respect to his own *history*, he may have special information about his readiness to respond, about the relation of his behavior to controlling variables, and about the history of these variables. Although this information is sometimes erroneous and . . . may even be lacking, it is sometimes useful in a science of behavior.
>
> (Skinner, 1953: 278–9)

The results of psychological experiments clearly show that introspective reports are not infallible. In many cases subjects may be in no better a position to make observations about their behaviour than other observers, and there is evidence that introspective reports are susceptible to various kinds of bias (for example, Sheehan and Neisser, 1969; Nisbett and Wilson, 1977). But 'because one sometimes makes mistakes . . . it does not follow that one always makes them or even that one makes them frequently' (Kelvin, 1956). Harré and Secord (1972) support a balanced view, espousing what they call an 'open souls doctrine', according to which introspective reports are authentic but revisable; a special case must be made out if they are to be rejected.

Introspection provides data like any other method, from which inferences are made. The behaviourist is incorrect in denying that subjects have privileged access to their experiences and in assimilating introspective reports to ejaculations such as 'ouch!' (Hebb, 1968); they are conceptually different in that they make referential claims. The mentalist is incorrect in attributing to them superior validity.

PRACTICAL PROBLEMS

Some have suggested that introspection is actually impossible. Kant claimed that introspective acts could not themselves be introspected. Comte argued the point explicitly:

> As for observing in the same way *intellectual* phenomena at the time of their actual presence, that is a manifest impossibility. The thinker cannot divide himself in two, of whom one reasons whilst the other observes him reason. The organ observed and the organ observing being, in this case, identical, how could observation take place? This pretended psychological method is then radically null and void.
>
> (Comte, 1842, vol. 1: 37–8)

That the thinker cannot divide himself in two, and that the organ observed and the organ observing are the same, are assumed rather than demonstrated. Parallel processing does occur, but to the extent that the processes involved are dependent on conscious attention there are likely to be severe capacity limitations. An extreme case of impairment would be attempting to make reports while in a state of heightened emotion.

J.S. Mill's reply was as follows:

> It might have occurred to M. Comte that a fact may be studied through the medium of memory, not at the very moment of our perceiving it, but the moment after: and this is really the mode in which our best knowledge of our intellectual states is generally acquired.
>
> (Mill, 1882: 64)

The following dilemma arises as described by De Groot (1965), who has provided one of the most thorough discussions of the topic, having used the method of thinking aloud to study the making of moves in chess. If subjects delay their report until after they have completed the task, they may forget what has happened and *memory errors* may creep in. If, on the other hand, they attempt to introspect at the same time as performing another intellectual task, there is likely to be mutual *interference* and alteration of the process.

> Verbalising one's thoughts unequivocally adds *an extra burden* to the subject's task. On the one hand, the added instruction to think aloud, necessarily influences the thought process to some degree; on the other, concentrated thinking on the problem itself must somewhat hamper its reporting.... Quite often *thoughts move so quickly* that the spoken word cannot keep up with them. The subject is then either forced to skip steps or to deliberately slow down his thinking (if possible) which thereby disturbs the thought process.
>
> (De Groot, 1965: 81–2)

Ericsson and Simon (1980; 1984) argue that the effect of verbalisation depends on the task demands, and review evidence that is consistent with their hypotheses that recoding of information from non-verbal to verbal form has the effect of slowing down performance, whereas tasks that require selection and inference may result in an alteration of the thought process. For example, Gagné and Smith (1962) found that instructions to state reasons for each move in the Tower of Hanoi problem improved efficiency of performance, the suggestion being that this encouraged more deliberate planning.

Another effect De Groot's subjects reported was abnormal formalisation of thinking.

> With some subjects gaps and pauses in reporting are frequent and of such duration that they cannot be assumed to result from actual pauses in thinking. He may just temporarily forget his second task (to think aloud), or he may not be able to verbalize adequately what he is or has been doing mentally.
>
> (De Groot, 1965: 379)

Thus the nature of the difficulty may lie in *communication*, in the translation of thoughts into words. Skinner has frequently remarked on the ambiguities associated with labelling private states. Part of the problem may lie in trying to force parallel processes into a sequential mode. De Groot found that there were individual differences with respect to the ease with which subjects were able to describe their mental processes, intuitive thinkers finding the most difficulty. Thus, introspective reports are likely to provide a distorted account of such processes.

Deception may be either *intentional* (some of De Groot's subjects suppressed strategies of which they were ashamed), or *unintentional*. A venerated case of the latter is rationalisation described by Freud, who distinguished the subject's reason from the reason, which might be an unconscious motive. A simple demonstration is post-hypnotic suggestion, where subjects construct a reason for behaviour which is in fact determined by instructions of which they are unaware given under hypnosis. More recently, Wason and Evans (1975) (see also Evans and Wason, 1976) have argued that protocols given by subjects in reasoning tasks are sometimes rationalisations. These appear to be determined by the situation and their behaviour in it, rather than being expressions of the causes of the behaviour, which are known from an analysis of performance in other experiments to be discrepant with the subjects' reports; see also data from Nisbett and Wilson (1977) discussed on pp. 67–9.

There is in fact evidence that introspective reports are particularly prone to experimental artefacts. For example, Sheehan and Neisser (1969), in a study which failed to demonstrate a relation between reported vividness of imagery and memory for patterns, found effects due to the experimenter (Sheehan obtaining higher vividness ratings than Neisser) and demand characteristics (vividness ratings increased after an enquiry which focused attention on imagery). As Orne (1962) observed, the more ambiguous the situation for the subject the greater the likely resulting variability in interpretation. It is perhaps ironical that Orne recommends pre- and post-experimental enquiry as methods of attenuating the effect of demand characteristics.

The most serious objection to introspection as a method in psychology, however, is the fact that most of the relevant data are *unavailable* to consciousness. Conscious processes are the tip of the iceberg (Miller, 1964). Most of mental life and behaviour proceeds unconsciously (as we saw in Chapter 4). Discrimination can occur without awareness, concepts can be formed and problems solved without subjects being able to report on the critical features. The Würzburg psychologists made this discovery when they attempted to apply the structuralists' method to thinking and judgement, and their findings were soon confirmed by Binet (1903) and Woodworth (1906). It is the perchings (the static images) rather than the flights (the relations in the margins of attention) (James, 1890) that are in consciousness, the products rather than the processes of thinking (Lashley, 1956). One example is the storing of running totals in mental arithmetic (Hayes, 1973). Ericsson and Simon (1980) propose three causes of incompleteness of verbal reports:

1 Information may be unavailable to short-term memory, for example, in fast, automatic processes in contrast with slow, controlled processes (Kellogg, 1982), as is often the case in perceptual encoding, retrieval of familiar items from long-term memory, and perceptual-motor tasks.
2 There may be failure to report the contents of short-term memory, such as in cases where there is a high cognitive load or where a task is interrupted. In Maier's (1931) experiment, subjects were more likely to report the hint if they described the solution to the problem as emerging in several steps rather than one. The suggested explanation (although others are possible) is that in the latter case the hint was only transiently available in short-term memory, being quickly obliterated by other information (possibly the appearance of the solution, White, 1988). Ericsson and Simon (1980) suggest that periods of thinking during the incubation period in creative

problem-solving may be forgotten because they are frequently interrupted.

3 Retrieval from long-term memory may be incomplete. For example, the content of daydreaming may be difficult to retrieve subsequently because appropriate cues are lacking in the external environment.

Nisbett and Wilson's (1977) paper is devoted to showing that subjects are only able to give correct reports on the determinants of their behaviour when the stimuli are salient and plausibly related to the responses, these judgements resulting from a priori causal hypotheses rather than direct access to mental processes. Furthermore, introspection cannot be used with animal subjects and presents problems in developmental and abnormal psychology. Unfruitfulness rather than subjectivity was the reason for its decline.

At best introspective reports are likely to lead to an account which is incomplete, at worst to one which is misleading. What is required is an analysis of the conditions which determine such reports so that their reliability and validity can be assessed. Ericsson and Simon (1980; 1984) have attempted to produce just such an account. In a re-examination of verbal reports as data, they argue that what is required is a theory of the measuring instrument, a model of how verbal reports are generated, which will permit the prediction of situations where they are likely to be reliable as distinct from those where they are not. They claim that 'verbal reports, elicited with care and interpreted with full understanding of the circumstances under which they were obtained, are a valuable and thoroughly reliable source of information about cognitive processes' (Ericsson and Simon, 1980). Four relevant factors are considered:

1 The relation of the verbalisation to the task-directed process. The verbalisation may be unrelated to, dependent on, or may modify the task-directed process.
2 The time interval. The verbalisation may be concurrent or retrospective.
3 The existence and nature of any intermediate process. Verbalisations may come direct from short-term memory; they may require recoding; or they may require selection and inference; for example, being asked to supply reasons for behaviour or answering personality questionnaire items which involve consideration of hypothetical states.
4 The form of the probe, which may be specific or general. Their thesis is that verbal reports will be most reliable when the information to be reported is attended to, or heeded (that is, stored in short-term memory and therefore directly accessible).

Any of the four factors above may have the effect of weakening the relation between the verbalisation and the heeded information.

THE USE OF INTROSPECTION IN CURRENT PSYCHOLOGY

An examination of the use of introspective reports in current psychology may illustrate some of its advantages and disadvantages, and ways in which the problems of reliability and validity can be tackled.

The content of experience

Introspective reports can provide useful information in a variety of circumstances and in some cases may be superior to either behavioural or physiological measures. Verbal descriptors have been found useful in the measurement and diagnosis of different pain syndromes. Dubuisson and Melzack (1976) found that syndromes could be accurately predicted on the basis of pain descriptors from the McGill pain questionnaire, and Leavitt and Garron (1980) found that functional pain disorders could be distinguished from organic ones in this way. Thayer (1970) argued that self-report scales provided a more integrative and representative estimation of general states of bodily activation than did four physiological measures, which inter-correlated poorly.

One of the most obvious areas for the use of introspection, and one in which systematic sources of error have been extensively investigated, is psychophysics. Fechner's methods may not have solved the mind–body problem as he had hoped, but they enabled a start to be made on the investigation of sensory experience and an examination of the validity of sensory judgements. Few would hesitate to use verbal reports in the study of perception, but much has now been learned about their limitations (see Woodworth and Schlosberg, 1954). One discovery that was made was that more accurate results were obtained if subjects were not allowed to use a 'don't know' category. In this case subjects may know more than they are aware of. Other systematic sources of bias such as time errors and series effects were also revealed.

The study of perception also illustrates one of the advantages of introspection. Although discriminative capacities can be studied by other means – for example, by instructing subjects to adjust a comparison stimulus to match a standard or by operant conditioning (as must perforce be done in the case of animals, cf. Stretch, 1966) – verbal report may be a much more convenient method, avoiding the necessity of setting up elaborate apparatus and training schedules. Asking can save a great deal of time and trouble.

An extension of sensation and perception, posing even more challenging problems for experimental investigation, is imagery. A number of innovative techniques have been developed. Haber and Haber (1964) introduced the criteria for eidetic imagery of accuracy, scannability, positive colour and persistence, thereby increasing the stringency of claims for its existence. Accuracy can be objectively checked against the presented stimulus, scannability probably by observing the subject's eye movements, and positive colour perhaps by getting subjects to superimpose their images on differently coloured backgrounds and observing the results. Persistence is more dependent on the subject's report but might be checked by observation of eye movements or a superimposition technique.

An extension of this last was used in an ingenious experiment by Stromeyer and Psotka (1970), employing identical Julesz random dot stereograms. On these a figure was superimposed, slightly displaced between the stimuli for the two eyes, such that it stood out in depth when viewed stereoscopically. The stimulus for one eye was presented to the subject, who was instructed to form an eidetic image of it. After an interval of up to twenty-four hours the appropriate stimulus was presented to the other eye and the subject instructed to combine the two. Their eidetic subject was able to point to the corners of the figure. The likelihood of such a result occurring by chance is extremely remote. However, no other subject has been found to equal this performance.

A related case is the study of dream imagery, which is particularly interesting with respect to the use of multiple measures. Stoyva and Kamiya (1968) have documented the way in which the study of the subjective state of dreaming became respectable with the discovery of a correlation between rapid eye movements (REM) and dream reports (DR) by Aserinsky and Kleitman in 1953. This raises the question of whether the increase in respectability is justified. Is one measure superior to the other or is it the correlation that is important? In what way can a correlation strengthen an inference? They suggest that, in this case, verbal reports provide primary validation, and behavioural and physiological measures corroborative evidence. REM by themselves tell us nothing about dreaming; their usefulness is dependent on their having first been validated against verbal reports. We take it on trust, arguing by analogy that when other people report dream experiences these are similar to our own.

The corroborative value of the correlation between physiological measures and verbal reports was strengthened by establishing what might be described as gradations of correlation. Qualitative and quantitative improvements were made by making the correlation more fine grain. A nominal correlation (the co-occurrence of REM and DR) was raised to a quantified one by the following demonstrations: (1) a correlation between the time elapsed prior to awakening and the estimated length of dream (Dement and Kleitman, 1957); (2) a correlation between the density of REM and the amount of physical activity reported in the dream (Berger and Oswald, 1962); (3) a relation between the direction of REM and the visual activity reported in the dream – for example, horizontal movements for watching tennis matches (Dement and Kleitman, 1957) – although this has not been confirmed by all subsequent work. These 'extensions of the empirical network' strengthen the corroborative validation.

Stoyva and Kamiya claim (rightly) that the mental state of dreaming is indexed imperfectly by both verbal report and physiological measures (namely, DR and REM). This raises the very interesting question of what inferences are made when the measures conflict, and we may take this example as a case study.

Here we have two indices (DR and REM) of a hypothesised mental state (dreaming). Logically there are four possible empirical situations: DR and REM, DR in the absence of REM, REM in the absence of DR, and neither DR nor REM. For each of these, logically, there are two possible conclusions: the existence or non-existence of the hypothesised state of dreaming. It is instructive to consider how the conclusion might be reached in each case.

1 *Co-occurrence of DR and REM* This is represented by Aserinsky and Kleitman's (1953) original demonstration. Here researchers seem to be in agreement that the appropriate conclusion is that dreaming took place. This inference is strengthened by the refined correlations with respect to duration, density and direction described above. However, it should be noted that it is logically possible that dreaming did not occur. Is the fact that this conclusion has been ignored an instance of verification bias?
2 *DR in the absence of REM* Here opinions differ. Those who take DR as the sole criterion of dreaming (for instance, Malcolm, 1959) conclude that dreaming occurred; those who take REM as the ultimate criterion (for example, Dement, 1955; Wolpert, 1960) deny that dreaming occurred and conclude that the DR was a fabrication. And indeed such reports might be considered suspect because of the lack of physiological corroboration; there is a sense in which they are less convincing than cases where both indices are present. There are a number of instances of this situation and they may perhaps warrant different conclusions. We shall consider them in turn. Foulkes (1962) obtained reports from non-REM periods. However, these were qualitatively different from reports from REM periods, being more thought-like. Distinctive verbal reports correlated with distinctive physiological measures might give credence to a conclusion of different mental states and hence non-existence of dreaming. Reports are sometimes also obtained from hypnagogic states (Foulkes and Vogel, 1965). In the absence of further evidence, the choice is perhaps equally divided between a conclusion of dreaming on the basis of the similarity of verbal report, or not dreaming on the basis of a difference in physiological measure. Other cases of mental activity in non-REM periods, such as sleep-talking and sleep-walking, being so different from verbal reports of dreaming, might best be interpreted as indicative of non-dream states. And indeed this is confirmed by their occurrence in stage 4 rather than stage 1 sleep (where REM occur). Finally, subjects deprived of sleep often come to report dreams outside REM periods. As these might be thought to be abnormal and dream-deprived a conclusion of dreaming might be appropriate.

3 *REM in the absence of DR* In this case also opinions diverge and opposite conclusions may be reached. Those who define dreaming in terms of REM conclude that dreaming occurred; those who opt for DR as the sole criterion conclude that dreaming did not occur. There are a number of empirical instances of this situation: 15–20 per cent of times where subjects are awakened from REM periods they do not report dreams. Are these cases of recall failure or did dreaming not occur? Cases of non-report where it may be plausible to argue that the subject has forgotten the dream are those where there is a delay before wakening (evidence for interference or decay theory could be brought in support). In this latter case, the argument is supported by the knowledge that had the sleeper been awakened there is a high probability that a dream would have been reported. Here REM are preferred to DR as the criterion and, if this argument is accepted, it shows that DR are not always the sole or best indicator. Another difficult case is that of neonates, in whom REM periods form about 50 per cent of their sleep. Some have queried whether they dream. Here other theoretical ideas might help to make the situation less ambiguous. For example, if dreams are thought to have the function of organising experience, then a verdict of dreaming would be plausible. That DR are not the sole index of dreaming is shown somewhat trivially by an experiment of Antrobus *et al.* (1965), in which human subjects were taught to indicate dreams by pressing a switch, the frequency of such presses increasing during REM periods; and more intriguingly perhaps by one in which monkeys were taught, in an avoidance conditioning paradigm, to press a bar whenever a visual image appeared on a frosted screen (Vaughan, 1964). High rates of bar-pressing in REM periods were taken to indicate dreaming. This is noteworthy as an attempt to demonstrate dream imagery in animals but hinges on the verbal report validation in humans and the argument from analogy.
4 *Neither DR nor REM* An example is the failure to give dream reports when awakened in non-REM periods. It would probably be concluded that dreaming did not occur, and indeed anyone who holds either index as the sole criterion must conclude this. It might also be taken to confirm the correlation of DR and REM. However, it is logically possible that a dream experience did occur. If this were so then dreaming would not be a necessary condition of either DR or REM and neither would be an infallible index.

What can be concluded from this discussion? An examination of these situations has shown that a complex network of data and theory is involved. It appears that verbal reports are necessary for initial validation but that the physiological measure turns out to be slightly more reliable.

In a final example, also involving sleep, three measures were compared. Birrell (1983) examined the relationships between physiological, behavioural and self-report measures of sleep onset latency and sleep duration. The behavioural measure (pressing a button switch in response to a chime) correlated well with EEG stage 2 sleep and is a cheaper and more convenient method. By contrast, stage 1 EEG gave a significantly shorter estimate of sleep onset latency and one which was behaviourally very similar to EEG stage 0 (81 per cent as against 100 per cent response rate); the self-report measure gave a significantly longer estimate of sleep onset latency. The pattern was reversed for sleep duration. In comparison with the behavioural and stage 2 EEG measures, stage 1 EEG provided an overestimate and self-report an underestimate. Sixty-five per cent of subjects awakened from EEG stage 3 reported that they had not been asleep!

The process of behaviour

Introspection is an obvious method for studying the content of experience. When it comes to the processes underlying behaviour, however, its use is much more questionable. Nevertheless, there have been some reports of the superiority of introspection over other measures. Kroll and Kellicutt (1972) found that subsequent recall could be predicted much better on the basis of self-reported rehearsal of the material (indicated by pressing a button) than on the basis of performance on another task undertaken during the retention interval. Introspection may provide more detailed information about methods used – for example, mnemonic techniques (Gordon, Valentine and Wilding, 1984) – than could be obtained using purely behavioural methods. A number of classic studies employed the technique of asking subjects to think aloud. Duncker (1945) hoped to reveal the processes of problem solving in this way. One of the most extensive investigations of this type has been De Groot's (1965) study, in which he aimed to infer the macroscopic structure of processes involved in chess-playing, an activity he considered to be goal-directed and hierarchically organised. Shallice (1972) has suggested that this work provides some of the best evidence for serial processing in thinking.

A particularly interesting case of the application of introspection to the study of thinking is that of Newell and Simon (1972), who used protocols both as an initial starting point from which to develop a theory and a final validation. They asked subjects to think aloud while solving symbolic logic and other problems, and used the descriptions of the operations employed as the basis for the construction of computer programs to model the thought process. The resulting simulations were accepted as psychological theories if they generated behaviour which adequately matched that of the subjects; see Valentine (1978) for a fuller discussion of the contribution of introspection to the study of thinking.

As a final example, consider the case of personality questionnaires. These employ a type of introspection, in that self-reports of feelings or behaviour are elicited. However, there is no necessity to take these reports at face value: a behaviourist approach is perfectly possible. It may merely be concluded that a particular pattern of responding (for example, 'neurotic introversion') is predictive of a particular pattern of behaviour in another situation (such as taking fewer involuntary rest pauses in tapping tasks).

The determinants of behaviour

Nisbett and Wilson (1977) make it abundantly clear that subjects are often unreliable informants with respect to the determinants of their behaviour. Evidence is reviewed from subliminal perception, learning without awareness, problem-solving, complex decision-making, cognitive dissonance, attribution and helping behaviour, in addition to a number of experiments of their own, which demonstrates that subjects are, in general, unable to report accurately on the effects of stimuli influencing their behaviour. It is argued that subjects have little or no introspective access to higher order cognitive processes. They may be unaware of the stimuli – as in the case of subliminal perception or Maier's (1931) experiment, where the majority of subjects failed to report the usefulness of the hint which helped them solve the problem; they may be unaware of the responses – subjects in studies of attitude change may report their pre-experimental opinion inaccurately and thus be unaware that a change has occurred, as in experiments by Bem and McConnell (1970) and Goethals and Reckman (1973); or they may be unaware of the relation between stimuli and responses.

On the one hand, subjects may fail to report influential stimuli. There is now an increasing body of evidence where an experimental manipulation is demonstrated to have an effect on behaviour but whose efficacy is denied by subjects. For example, Storms and Nisbett (1970) anticipated that insomniac subjects given placebo pills said to produce arousal would report getting to sleep earlier than controls (because they would attribute their symptoms to the pill rather than their internal state), whereas those given pills said to produce relaxation would report getting to sleep later (because they would infer that they must be particularly aroused if they had their usual sensations despite having taken a 'relaxation' pill). These predictions were borne out, but when asked to account for their behaviour subjects did not report that the pill had had any effect on it. In the bystander effect, subjects deny the influence of the number of people present on the likelihood of their helping (Latané and Darley, 1970), perhaps to avoid moral embarrassment. In one of Nisbett and Wilson's own experiments, evaluative judgements concerning the quality of articles of clothing showed a marked position effect, right-most objects being over-chosen; not surprisingly subjects denied any such influence. These last two cases provide instances of phenomena which are dependent on subjects' ignorance for their existence. It seems unlikely that people would continue to behave in these ways if they were fully cognisant.

On the other hand, ineffective stimuli may be reported, as in Maier's (1931) experiment where some subjects reported the efficacy of a useless hint, or one of Nisbett and Wilson's experiments where subjects incorrectly reported that the inclusion of a 'reassurance' phrase in the instructions increased their willingness to take electric shocks. In this latter case, in common with many others, subjects' reports correlated very much more highly with the predictions of observers or control subjects not actually run in the experiment, but asked to say what they thought the effect would be, than with what actually happened. This led Nisbett and Wilson to argue that subjects' reports have the same basis as observers' reports, namely, a priori causal theories, which may have as their source cultural rules, implicit causal schemata, assumed covariation or connotative similarity between stimuli and responses. (There is evidence that people's judgements of covariation are based on conceptual similarity rather than empirical observations, see, for example, Shweder, 1977.) Subjects' reports will sometimes be correct, but only incidentally and not as the result of direct introspective access. Conditions where they are likely to be correct, it is argued, are those where the influential stimuli are available, the connection between the stimuli and responses plausible, and where there are few plausible non-influential factors available. One case where these conditions obtain is in learning without awareness paradigms (Dulany, 1962). Another is where rules are overtly checked, as in the complex judgements made by stockbrokers and clinicians (Slovic and Lichtenstein, 1971). Reports will be likely to be inaccurate when either the relevant stimuli are unavailable or non-salient – for example, if they are contextual rather than in the focus of attention, non-verbal, removed in time, or where the non-occurrence of events is significant; or where the connection between stimuli and responses is implausible, as for instance in the case of discrepant magnitudes between cause and effect. Other known factors which militate against the accuracy of verbal reports are what Nisbett and Wilson label the 'mechanics of judgement', such as order, anchoring, contrast and position effects.

It remains to explain the illusion of introspective access. People do have privileged knowledge of their sensations and personal biographies. Three factors which may help to maintain the illusion are the confusion of products or intermediate outputs with process; the fact that disconfirmations are relatively hard to come by, negative instances being easily explained away; and self-esteem, people preferring to feel they are in a position of superior knowledge and control.

Nisbett and Wilson (1977) have been criticised on theoretical and methodological grounds by Smith and Miller (1978) and White (1980; 1988). They argue that the thesis is not formally stated and depends on unjustified assumptions about the relations between conscious awareness, internal processes and verbal reports. (Indeed, until these relations are specified precisely, there can be no adequate theory of introspection.) It is also asserted that the case is overstated and that there is evidence that verbal reports can be accurate in certain circumstances. Ericsson and Simon (1980) contend that the unreliable reports described by Nisbett and Wilson are obtained in exactly those conditions which their model would predict; namely, in retrospective reports or generalised probes, where information is required which was never in memory or which can be generated without consulting it.

VALIDATION

Pilkington and Glasgow (1967) argue that the use of introspection may be more difficult than other methods but that it is not substantially different in kind. Conditions can be specified in which statements about subjective experiences can be intersubjectively confirmed and their truth checked. As they point out: 'Statements subjects may make about their subjective experiences are not unique in being difficult to confirm' and 'introspective reports are not unique in achieving only high probability'. Approaches to the validation of introspective reports have also been discussed by Natsoulas (1967).

Internal validity can be improved by ingenious exerimental design, as in the case of Stromeyer and Psotka (1970). Schoenfeld and Cumming (1963) are of the opinion that discrimination training might improve the control of perceptual responses over verbal responses.

External validity can be obtained by the application of a public criterion as a check on the accuracy of reports, as suggested by Natsoulas (1967), who comments that autonomic responses are often favoured. Behavioural measures can also be employed, as was discussed in connection with the experiment on eidetic imagery by Haber and Haber (1964). That this is not a simple matter became clear from the examination of indexing the state of dreaming. Broadbent (1961) takes the view that 'amongst responses, it is perfectly legitimate to include the statements made by human beings, as long as the differences between such responses correspond to differences between other stimuli or other responses,' implying that these other responses are somehow more respectable or more reliable. This leads to the paradox that if verbal reports correlate with other measures then they are redundant; if they do not correlate, the problem arises of deciding which are valid. The example quoted by Natsoulas is an instance of a discrepancy between verbal and autonomic responses. In an experiment by Gunter (1951) on the binocular fusion of colours, a galvanic skin response (GSR) was conditioned to binocular presentation of yellow spectral light. In one of the test conditions, red was presented to one eye and green to the other. The autonomic responses indicated fusion (a large GSR occurring) whereas the verbal responses indicated rivalry (subjects reporting that they experienced red and green rather than yellow). Our discussion of dreaming illustrated both the way in which the validity of verbal responses could be strengthened by corroboration from other measures and how cases of conflict might be resolved by judicious theorising and experimentation.

Another possibility is to make *verbal reports the object of investigation* and examine their determinants. What is required is the discrimination of cases where they can be taken at face value from those where they cannot. Ericsson and Simon's (1984) model, discussed above, provides important guidelines towards this end. They also review empirical studies on verbalisations. Pilkington and Glasgow (1967) note, as general kinds of test, that it is possible to search for intra-subject consistency, and evidence of the subject's honesty and reliability in situations where these can be checked. Warshaw and Davis (1984) found that subjects who reported themselves as having high self-understanding were better at self-prediction than were subjects who reported themselves as low in self-understanding.

On the one hand it may be possible to distinguish different types of verbal report. Carlson (1960) tested the implications of hypotheses concerning subjects' errors in size constancy experiments. Empirical confirmation of these enabled conditions where phenomenal matches were obtained to be determined with some certainty. A possible technique is to obtain subjects' comments on their introspections. Joynson (1958) asked subjects, after participating in constancy experiments, to comment on the nature of their judgements, thus acquiring evidence, supplementary to that obtained by manipulating the instructions, on the distinction between judgements of apparent shape or size ('looking the same') and analytic judgements of 'real' shape or size ('being the same').

On the other hand it may be possible to uncover systematic sources of error. Pilkington and Glasgow refer to the elimination of motives for deception, artefacts such as suggestibility and demand characteristics. An experiment by Natsoulas and Levy (1965) suggests conscious monitoring of verbal reports: subjects who knew that tapes they heard were of repeated material were less likely to report transformations than subjects not so informed. Other examples are provided by the work on the 'mechanics of judgement' in psychophysics, and other evidence cited by Nisbett and Wilson (1977).

Most of these approaches involve *embedding reports in a theoretical network* (Dulany, 1962) and testing the implications (Natsoulas, 1967). Hypotheses may either be confirmed or disconfirmed. Platt (1964) and Garner, Hake and Eriksen (1956) have argued that inferences can be considerably strengthened by systematic formulation and elimination of competing hypotheses. However, two points should be made. First, the number of possible alternative hypotheses is unlimited. All scientific hypotheses are revisable. The possibility of a better one always exists. Second, there is no algorithm for formulating alternative hypotheses. The *elimination of alternative hypotheses* may be effected either statistically or experimentally (Natsoulas, 1967). An example of the former is an experiment by Landauer and Rodger (1964) in which the hypothesis that apparent brightness judgements were composed of a combination of judgements made under 'reflectance' or 'luminance' instructions was disconfirmed by demonstrating that the variance for apparent judgements was lower than would be predicted on this basis, thus favouring the conclusion that distinct kinds of judgement were involved. Empirical elimination of alternative hypotheses is likely to involve the use of *convergent operations* (Garner, Hake and Eriksen, 1956). They write:

> Convergent operations are any set of experimental operations which eliminate alternative hypotheses and which can lead to a concept which is not uniquely identified with any one of the original operations, but is defined by the results of all the operations performed. Thus converging operations can lead to concepts of processes which are not directly observable.
>
> (Garner, Hake and Eriksen, 1956: 158)

They illustrate the use of convergent operations to distinguish perceptual from response effects. For example, the demonstration that increasing the response set improves discrimination suggests that response factors may be involved in subception (Bricker and Chapanis, 1953). Stoyva and Kamiya (1968) consider the use of DR and REM to be another example of the use of convergent operations, permitting the rejection of the hypothesis that DR from REM periods reflect inaccurate recall and fabrications, and acceptance of the alternative hypothesis that they represent dream experiences reasonably accurately. Natsoulas (1967) gives as an example an experiment by Wallach, O'Connell and Neisser (1953) in which, in order to check that the three-dimensional perception of shadows cast by stationary wire figures was not due to knowledge that the shadows were of three-dimensional figures, a control condition was introduced in which subjects were not exposed to the wire figures rotating. Alternatively, competing hypotheses may be shown to be incapable of producing the effects, as in an experiment by Haber (1965), in which the hypothesis that experimental results were due to differential knowledge of the stimulus materials was eliminated by showing them to all subjects before the experiment.

All these methods involve the collecting of more data in a variety of theoretically linked situations, the progressive elimination and confirmation of hypotheses and the strengthening of inferences.

EVALUATION

Introspection was first overrated and then underrated. The structuralists thought it provided a royal road to the contents of the mind. The behaviourists rejected it as unscientific on the grounds of subjectivity and privacy.

It has both advantages and disadvantages. Some of its advantages have been listed by Pilkington and Glasgow (1967). Introspection may provide important information on phenomena such as imagery, and in disciplines such as psychiatry and sociology. In clinical psychology it may additionally facilitate empathy. Reports by subjects or experimenters (perhaps themselves as subjects) may generate new hypotheses to test, or suggest modifications to experimental designs. They may aid in the interpretation, control and elimination of artefacts. Finally, it has the advantage of convenience, providing a method which is very much quicker and easier than most. Introspection as a method is not unique but it may be useful.

The disadvantages have already been discussed in detail. We have seen that introspective reports are particularly prone to distortion but that the problems raised are not different in kind from those of other methods. No methods guarantee certainty and all can be validated in the same ways by theorising and experimentation.

Introspection has been underrated because it was once overrated. With hindsight we are in a better position to come to a balanced view. With regard to the contents of experience, introspection provides primary data which can be supported with other measures. With respect to the process of behaviour, introspection is of relatively little use because most of the relevant data are unavailable to consciousness. Subjects have a reasonable chance of telling an experimenter what they experienced or did, but not how they did it. Products are available and these can be used as an aid in the reconstruction of the process. As to the reasons for behaviour, the evidence suggests that introspective reports are not generally a reliable guide to the stimuli influencing responses. Subjects may be able to report strategies and goals, and may sometimes be correct about the causes of their behaviour, but these judgements have the form of inferences and are not the result of privileged, direct access.

Finally, verbal reports are themselves behavioural responses. They provide data and are themselves in need of explanation. With the excesses of introspectionism and behaviourism in the past, a start can be made on their investigation. They can indeed be reinstated as part of the subject matter of psychology.

Chapter 6

Sources of artefact

Most of the problems for psychological science dealt with in this book have arisen from fundamental philosophical objections. However, there is also a body of experimental evidence – namely, research on research – to be considered in this chapter, which has contributed to the debate on the appropriateness of the application of scientific methods as used in the physical sciences to psychology. Starting from the assumption of the experiment as itself a social situation, it has cast doubt on the traditional picture of an objective experimenter investigating an inert subject. Following similar discoveries in physics, it has demonstrated that non-interference and independence of the observer and observed are scientific myths. (It is perhaps worth noting in passing that the models of the physical sciences which psychologists have studiedly aped have usually been outdated.) Westland (1978) has drawn an important distinction between objections to psychological science which are of a fundamental, philosophical nature, suggesting that the whole enterprise is misconceived, and those which are merely tactical, implying deficiencies in its actual practice. It is with the latter that this chapter will be primarily concerned. Much of the work has been carried out and reviewed by Rosenthal (see Rosenthal, 1966; Rosenthal, 1967; Rosenthal and Rosnow, 1969), using such methods as reports of experimenters' behaviour by subjects and films of experimenter–subject interactions. We shall begin by considering some of the least plausible candidates for factors influencing the experimental situation.

THE PHYSICAL ENVIRONMENT

Rosenthal (1967) cites evidence from Mintz that subjects judged others to be less happy when the judgements were made in an 'ugly' laboratory; and from Haley that experimenters took the experiment more seriously in disorderly, uncomfortable laboratories. Moreover, experimenters assigned to more professional-appearing laboratories were perceived by their subjects as more expressive in voice, face and gesture.

EXPERIMENTER ATTRIBUTES

Perhaps Rosenthal's main contribution has been to demonstrate characteristics of the experimenter which may influence the outcome of an experiment. Subjects' behaviour may be affected by the experimenter's sex, race, religion, status, intelligence, likeability, warmth, anxiety, adjustment, hostility, authoritarianism, acquiescence, need for approval and prior acquaintance with the subject (Rosenthal, 1963).

Rosenthal *et al.* have shown complex effects due to the *sex* of experimenter. Male experimenters were more friendly than female, as shown by their behaviour in films and by subjects' ratings. Most of the effects, as one might guess, are interactive between sex of experimenter and sex of subject. Female subjects evoked more smiling from their experimenters (data from Friedman cited in Rosenthal, 1967). Rosenthal (1967) described the pattern of behaviour that female experimenters show towards male subjects as 'interested modesty'. Citing data from Katz, he reports that they did not lean as close to male as to female subjects; they were friendly in the visual but not the auditory channel towards female subjects, whereas they were remarkably friendly in the auditory but not the visual channel towards male subjects. The pattern of behaviour shown by male experimenters towards female subjects, however, is described as just plain 'interested'. They took significantly longer in preparing stimulus material for presentation to female subjects.

Experimenter effects of principal investigators may be mediated through research assistants. One study suggested that principal investigators may transmit bias through their research assistants (Rosenthal *et al.*, 1963). In another, research assistants whose behaviour had been given more favourable evaluations by their principal investigators were described by their subjects as more casual and courteous, and obtained more positive results in a verbal conditioning experiment (Rosenthal *et al.*, 1966).

There are effects due to *practice* and *fatigue*. Rosenthal's films showed that experimenters read the instructions faster to later than to earlier subjects and became more bored as the experiment progressed. That there are individual differences in these respects, and that these factors may have an effect on the experimental results, are suggested by the finding that subjects of experimenters who showed such changes rated people pictured in photographs as less successful (Rosenthal, 1967).

In particular, Rosenthal's name has become associated with the phenomenon known as the *experimenter bias effect*, the way in which an experimenter's expectancy can determine the experimental outcome, serving as a self-fulfilling prophecy. Such effects have been demonstrated in a wide variety of experiments – for example, reaction time, psychophysics, animal learning, verbal conditioning, personality assessment, person perception, learning and ability, as well as everyday life situations (Rosenthal and Rubin, 1978). In one experiment, experimenters who were told that their rats were bred for maze brightness on the one hand or maze dullness on the other obtained results in accordance with their expectations; namely, 'maze bright' were perceived to perform significantly better than 'maze dull' rats despite being drawn from the same population (Rosenthal and Fode, 1963). In this experiment certain cases of cheating were observed (namely, experimenters prodding subjects to run the maze) but whether such effects are sufficient to account for the results has not been demonstrated. In another study, the 'Pygmalion' experiment, children whose teachers were told (arbitrarily) that they would show unusual intellectual development within the next academic year, showed significantly greater gains in IQ than children for whom such predictions were not made (though these children showed substantial improvements too), the effect being more marked in the youngest groups (Rosenthal and Jacobson, 1966). Some of the technical defects of this study have been exposed by Thorndike (1968), and it has been subjected to detailed methodological criticism by Elashoff and Snow (1971).

Since Pfungst's (1911) study of Clever Hans, it has been known that experimenters can unintentionally communicate their expectations to their subjects. Pfungst showed that Clever Hans's apparent ability to count was due to his responding to minimal movements that his owner, Herr von Osten, made when the correct number had been tapped out, cueing the horse to stop. Rosenthal (1967) argued that unintended covert communication from the experimenter to the subject, which affects the subject's response, is the norm rather than the exception. He suggests that experimenters learn to communicate their hypotheses to their subjects covertly. It is obviously rewarding to have one's expectations confirmed, so experimenters are likely to be reinforced for, and repeat, behaviour which produces such results. That subjects' behaviour may affect experimenters' behaviour was suggested by one of Rosenthal *et al.*'s (1965) experiments, where confirmation or disconfirmation of the experimenter's hypothesis by initial stooge subjects differentially affected the responses in the experimental task and the personality test scores of subsequent subjects.

Analysis of films has led Rosenthal to claim that whether experimenters will be successful in learning to influence the subject to respond in accordance with the hypothesis can be predicted from their non-verbal behaviour during the first thirty seconds of the experiment. Experimenters of whom this was true were more likeable, personal, relaxed, dominant and important acting, and showed less leg movement. Later in the experiment, professionalism of manner became a predictor (Rosenthal *et al.*, 1960).

The work of Rosenthal has been criticised – for example, by Barber and Silver (1968) – on the grounds that many of his findings are based on the results of *post hoc* tests, without adjustment of critical values appropriate for multiple comparisons. Results are reported which do not reach conventionally accepted levels of significance. Contradictory effects have been obtained and failures to replicate reported. Barber and Silver conclude that the experimenter expectancy effect is more difficult to demonstrate and less pervasive than is implied by Rosenthal. Even where the experimenter bias effect has been demonstrated, the mode of its operation is not clear. It may be mediated by subtle paralinguistic and kinesic cues which influence subjects' responses, as Rosenthal suggests, but it is also possible that the mode of operation is independent of subjects' responses and may be intentional. Barber and Silver claim that, in the majority of experiments, misjudgement or misrecording of responses and fabrication of data have not been ruled out. There is no guarantee that these experiments on experiments are themselves free from the kind of biases they seek to demonstrate. In some cases, for example, expectancy was confounded with desire: experimenters were told that they 'should' expect certain results or were paid more for obtaining them. However, Rosenthal and Rubin (1978) claim that interpersonal expectancy effects have been obtained in studies instituting special safeguards against intentional or recording errors.

Such bias, if and when it does occur, becomes serious when it is differential rather than systematic. However, a thorough study of it may enable us to (1) correct for its effect, and (2) learn about communication in other dyadic relations. Methods of minimising these biases include double-blind techniques, automation of experimental procedures and the use of expectancy control groups (where experimenters are informed of the hypothesis but the treatment manipulation is not implemented). Another approach is to employ non-reactive methods. Webb *et al.* (1966), having surveyed the disadvantages of reactive methods (experiments, interviews and questionnaires) – such as response bias, social desirability and the Hawthorne effect (awareness of being a subject in an experiment alters behaviour) – recommend the complementary use of non-reactive methods. Measures of behaviour may be obtained from

1 physical traces: for instance, wear on steps, tracks, the contents of garbage containers;
2 records: for example, library withdrawals, retail sales, unemployment figures;
3 unobtrusive observations, such as of pupil dilation, or seating position.

SUBJECT ATTRIBUTES

In a similar way, both long-term and short-term characteristics of the subject may influence the results of an experiment. We have already seen that sex is one of these.

Another factor is the amount of *experience* a subject has from previous experiments. Holmes (1967) found that continued participation in verbal conditioning experiments increased the probability that subjects would become aware of the reinforcement contingency. Experienced subjects professed a higher level of intended cooperation and produced a greater number of conditioned responses in subsequent experiments. They also tended to see the experiment as more scientific and more valuable. (This could be a reason for their continuing to act as subjects.)

Subjects may also vary considerably with respect to their attitude towards an experiment. Gustav's (1962) investigation of attitudes of students towards compulsory participation revealed that 40 per cent expressed unfavourable attitudes ranging from irritation and apprehension; the remaining subjects reported positive attitudes including eagerness, curiosity and great interest. Of the group, 37 per cent said that they would not have participated voluntarily (but this is probably a good thing from the point of view of scientific methodology). Argyris (1968) reports that the majority of a large sample of American undergraduates were 'critical, mistrustful, and hostile' to the course requirement of research participation. Jackson and Pollard (1966) asked subjects to give their reasons for volunteering for an experiment on sensory deprivation. Fifty per cent gave curiosity as the reason, 21 per cent money, and a mere 7 per cent a desire to help science. The motivations lying behind an attempt to discover the experimenter's hypothesis may be similarly various and aimed at validating it (Orne, 1962), presenting oneself in the most favourable light (Riecken, 1962), or fouling up the experimenter's research, termed the 'screw you effect' by Maslow (1966).

This active participation of the subject in the experiment has been particularly stressed by Orne, who has suggested that the reasons for the lack of reproducibility and ecological validity of psychological experiments may be due to the failure to consider the role of *demand characteristics* in the experimental situation. These he defines as 'the totality of cues which convey an experimental hypothesis to the subjects'. They include 'the rumors or campus scuttlebut about the research, the information conveyed during the original situation, the person of the experimenter, and the setting of the laboratory, as well as all explicit and implicit communications during the experiment proper'. He goes on to point out that the experimental procedure itself may be a source of cues for the subject; for example, if a test is given twice with some intervening treatment, even the dullest college student is aware that some change is expected. Demand characteristics will vary with the sophistication of the subjects and the ambiguity of the experimental cues. It is likely that the demand characteristics which are most potent in determining subjects' behaviour are those which convey the purpose of the experiment effectively but not obviously.

The experiment, as has now been pointed out, is a special type of social situation with clearly defined rules and expectations. As Orne reports, people asked to do five push-ups as a favour will ask 'why?' but if the request appears in the guise of an experiment they will ask 'where?'. Also reported is an experiment in which subjects, instructed to add sheets of random digits and then tear up the sheets, worked for several hours with relatively little sign of overt hostility, apparently imbuing the task with meaning, perhaps construing it as an endurance test. The experiment is a problem-solving situation in which subjects have to work out what the experimenter's hypothesis is (they have one clue: it will not be what the experimenter says it is because 'psychologists always lie'), so that they can act appropriately. Orne argues that the subjects in psychological experiments are active, unlike the passive, inanimate objects of the physical sciences, and that this demands modifications in experimental methodology. Demand characteristics cannot be eliminated, because subjects are bound to impose meaning on tasks, but they can be studied. Attempts can be made to identify them so that their importance as determinants of behaviour in experiments can be assessed, by correlational means; for example: do subjects' perceived demand characteristics predict behaviour better than the experimental variables do?

Orne has suggested three experimental techniques for the study of demand characteristics:

1 *Post-experimental enquiry* In this case it is necessary to proceed from general to specific questions, and difficult to get valid answers on account of the 'pact of ignorance' between subject and experimenter, by which the subject's naïvety is tacitly agreed. There are a number of difficulties, of which one is that subjects' perception of the experimenter's hypothesis may be determined in part by their own experimental behaviour rather than being a relevant determinant of it, a distinction which would be obscured by merely establishing a correlation between them. This problem may be dealt with by the second method.
2 *Pre-experimental enquiry* In this case subjects are interrogated after being given as much information as real subjects in the experiment would have but are not allowed actually to make any responses. Both these procedures, (1) and (2), are of course subject to demand characteristics, which may be mitigated somewhat by using independent experimenters.
3 *Use of simulating subjects* This is an attempt to keep demand characteristics constant while eliminating the experimental variable. The behaviour of subjects not exposed to the experimental variable but instructed to behave as if they had been is compared with that of normal subjects.

Orne (1959) first discussed demand characteristics in connection with his work on hypnosis, but he has also used the third technique mentioned above to demonstrate sensory deprivation effects without sensory deprivation. Significant differences in the expected direction were obtained between a group of subjects given all the accoutrements of a sensory deprivation experiment (such as careful screening, release forms and a panic button) but no actual sensory deprivation, and a group who were told that they were controls for a sensory deprivation experiment, who had identical treatment except for the absence of the panic button (Orne and Scheibe, 1964).

A considerable body of data is now available on the characteristics of an important sub-section of the subject population, *volunteers*. Rosenthal (1965), reviewing a variety of studies, concluded that volunteers differ significantly from non-volunteers in the following respects: they tend to be more intelligent, younger, less conventional, less authoritarian, more sociable and show a greater need for social approval. These matters would not be serious perhaps but for the fact that such a high proportion of subjects are in fact volunteers.

SAMPLES

Beach (1950), in a famous paper entitled 'The snark was a boojum', estimated that 50 per cent of studies in comparative psychology during the first half of this century were carried out on 0.001 per cent of the extant species, namely, the Norway rat (see Figure 6.1). Lurking doubts about the *representativeness* of samples of human subjects have now also been amply documented. Smart (1966) examined the *Journal of Abnormal and Social Psychology* between the years 1962 and 1964 and the *Journal of Experimental Psychology* between the

Figure 6.1 Position of many experimental psychologists
(*Source:* from Beach, 1950, drawing by S.J. Tatz)

Table 6.1 Percentages of papers in American Psychological Association journals using given categories of subjects

Subjects	*JEP Smart*	*JEP Schultz*	*JASP Smart*	*JPSP Schultz*
Introductory psychology	42.2	41.2	32.2	34.1
Other college	43.5	42.5	40.9	36.1
Pre-college	7.0	7.1	16.9	18.5
Special adult	7.3	5.6	9.4	10.1
General adult	0	0	0.6	1.2
All male	22.3	19.3	33.6	26.7
All female	6.0	6.0	10.8	10.6

(*Source:* Schultz, 1969) (copyright 1969 by the American Psychological Association)

years 1963 and 1964. Schultz (1969) examined the *Journal of Personality and Social Psychology* and the *Journal of Experimental Psychology* from 1966 to 1967. Their results are shown in Table 6.1, from which it can be seen that between 75 and 80 per cent of studies are conducted on students and that virtually none are carried out on the general adult population. Furthermore, Schultz found that in 3.6 per cent of the papers in the *Journal of Experimental Psychology* the nature of the subjects was not specified. The predominance of college students means that in the United States 80 per cent of research is performed on 3 per cent of the population, a group which is unrepresentatively young, intelligent, upper-middle class, literate, introspective and male. Any forlorn hopes that things are better in Britain are dashed by Cochrane and Duffy's (1974) survey of the *British Journal of Psychology* and the *British Journal of Social and Clinical Psychology* from 1969 to 1972, which showed that 76.4 per cent of non-clinical studies using adults were conducted on samples of students, in many cases introductory ones. Over half reported using volunteers; 28 per cent did not report how their subjects were obtained, some of which we may guess used volunteers. Fewer than 15 per cent clearly did not use volunteers and most of these used clinical or school groups.

Of the papers, 75 per cent did not report information about response rate; that is, what proportion of potential subjects approached actually agreed to participate. When it was reported, however, it was usually satisfactory. Fewer than 15 per cent used a *sampling procedure* which was considered adequate; namely, either a generally accepted method, or some demonstration that the sample was representative in appropriate respects. Most failed to provide information on this matter and it was concluded that 85 per cent probably used inadequate methods. Of these, only 5 per cent discussed these deficiencies and their possible implications.

Another cause for concern was the *size of sample*. One quarter of the studies were based on $n < 25$. Cochrane and Duffy concluded: 'Only 1–2 per cent of all the studies reported in these two journals over the past four years based their findings on a true sample of the general adult population.' The use of small samples may be related to misconceptions about their nature. Tversky and Kahneman (1971) have shown that psychologists are not immune from the common bias they call belief in the law of small numbers, in which the characteristics of large numbers, representative of the population from which they are drawn, are held to apply to small numbers too. Thus random samples are considered representative regardless of their size. Questionnaires administered to psychologists at conferences, including experienced researchers and members of the mathematical division of the American Psychological Association, showed that they overestimated the likelihood of replicating an experimental finding. They had exaggerated confidence in the validity of conclusions based on small samples. According to Tversky and Kahneman, believers in the law of small numbers practise science as follows. First, they gamble research hypotheses on small samples without realising that the odds against them are unreasonably high; they use tests that are too weak in power. Secondly, they have undue confidence in, and overinterpret, early trends (for example, the data from the first few subjects) and the stability of the observed patterns (such as the number and identity of significant results). Thirdly, they overestimate the replicability of results and underestimate the breadth of confidence limits. Fourthly, they construct causal explanations for deviations from expectations and hence never discover their errors. Cohen's (1962) survey of seventy articles in the *Journal of Abnormal and Social Psychology* for 1960 showed them to be low in power: on average they had a less than 50/50 chance of obtaining a significant result given that a medium-sized effect existed. This problem could be remedied by increasing (doubling or trebling) sample sizes. Overall (1969) has drawn attention to the dangers of using small samples and low-powered tests in research areas where the a priori probabilities of real treatment effects are small: many results judged to be statistically significant by classical methods may in fact be due to chance – as many as two-thirds according to one estimate. Bayesian theory makes possible the calculation of power and sample size required for a given, chosen probability of error.

STATISTICAL ANALYSIS

Baloff and Becker (1967) draw attention to the *fallacy of the aggregate* or mean learning curve. They adduce both mathematical arguments and empirical evidence to demonstrate that aggregating functions of one form may yield functions of a quite different form; for example, convex functions may become concave or exponential, exponential functions may become sigmoidal. Summing individual stepwise functions typical of insight learning might produce a smooth negatively accelerated curve. Thus a mean function may represent no individual case and hence be quite meaningless and misleading, merely serving to obscure individual differences which need systematic investigation.

Wolins (1962) reported an alarming case in which raw data were requested from thirty-seven authors. Five failed to reply; twenty-one reported that the data were misplaced, lost or inadvertently destroyed; and two offered data on condition that they had control over what was done with them. Of seven re-analyses made from the remaining authors, three contained errors so gross as to change the outcome of the results reported.

Cochrane and Duffy scrutinised a random sample of fifty of the papers in their survey for various kinds of statistical error. Apart from random sampling, parametric tests assume a normal distribution and homogeneity of variance. One third of the thirty-seven studies using significance tests made some basic *error in the application of the test*. None reported testing the assumptions nor discussed the implications of ignoring them. More than six – that is, 26 per cent – seriously violated the assumptions of the test used. In most cases insufficient data were available for such an evaluation to be made. Nunnally (1960) observes that small samples make it impossible to assess the validity of assumptions.

Null hypothesis testing has come in for a good deal of criticism. A radically different alternative is offered by Bayesian statistics, which takes into account the prior probability of the alternative hypothesis. Eight authors in Cochrane and Duffy's survey appeared to have misinterpreted the results of their hypothesis testing, usually by inferring that rejection of the null hypothesis implied acceptance of the experimental hypothesis. As Savage remarks, 'Null hypotheses of no difference are usually known to be false before the data are collected; when they are, their rejection or acceptance simply reflects the size of the sample and the power of the test, and is not a contribution to science' (1957: 332–3). Nunnally (1960) remarks that 'in the real world the null hypothesis is almost never true, and it is usually nonsensical to perform an experiment with the *sole* aim of rejecting the null hypothesis'. This is merely a first step. The size of the difference and confidence limits should also be specified.

No one in Cochrane and Duffy's survey discussed the *strength of the relation* reported, as distinct from its statistical significance. Of the results for which it was possible to estimate this, 56 per cent showed a relatively weak relationship. In 25 per cent of cases, the results accounted for less than 10 per cent of the variance in the dependent variable. Likewise, a study by Hakel (cited in Dunnette, 1966), in which F and t values in a range of papers from four journals were converted to correlation ratios in order to estimate the strength of association between independent and dependent variables, found nearly one-third failed to reach a value of 0.3 and that the tone of the conclusions was unrelated to the strength of association.

It was estimated that twelve of the papers in Cochrane and Duffy's survey *confused psychological with statistical significance*. Bolles (1962) distinguishes statistical from scientific hypotheses. Rejecting a statistical hypothesis may be a relatively clear-cut mathematical matter; acceptance of a scientific hypothesis depends not only on the appropriateness of the statistical model employed but also on rejection of alternative scientific hypotheses, and hence on confirmation by other data and incorporation within a theoretical network. Bakan (1967) distinguishes statistical, material and practical significance. It is not only statistical significance that matters, but the theoretical and practical implications of results. Cochrane and Duffy's general conclusions detail a depressing list of deficiencies, and they suggest that until these can be remedied 'it appears that most of our research efforts into human behaviour will be essentially trivial'.

PUBLICATION

It is easy to criticise publication practices in the current climate of 'publish or perish'. Armstrong (1982) cynically describes the successful author's formula in terms of the following prohibitions. Don't: pick an important problem; challenge existing beliefs; obtain surprising results; use simple methods; provide full disclosure; or write clearly. Fears are voiced that publication outlets are controlled by the psychological establishment, that pressure on space militates against publication of negative results, and that obeisance to statistical significance means that the published papers represent the 5 per cent that are significant by chance.

The unreliability of reviewers has been the focus of considerable attention. Inter-reviewer reliabilities of about 0.2 are typical (Whitehurst, 1982). Mahoney (1976a) found that reviewers were more likely to recommend papers for publication when the evidence supported their own positions: when the data contradicted their opinions, they criticised the method and interpretation and recommended against publication. Peters and Ceci (1982) resubmitted twelve articles by investigators from prestigious departments published in reputable journals but with the names of the authors and the institutional affiliations changed to fictitious ones. Certain 'cosmetic' alterations to the title, abstract and initial paragraph were also made, such as changing a word, reordering sentences or converting graphs to tables, in order to prevent automatic detection. Despite this, three of the articles were detected. However, of the remaining nine articles, eight were *rejected* on resubmission. The reviewers recommended against publication on grounds such as serious methodological flaws. The results were interpreted as indicating bias in favour of high status authors and prestigious institutions. Apart from the dubious ethical nature of this study, further work is needed in which the quality of the paper and the status of the author and the institution are systematically varied.

Dunnette (1966), in a paper entitled 'Fads, fashions and folderol in psychology', attributes the failures of psychologists to insecurity resulting from inability to predict the course of research; publication, grant and 'visibility' pressures; and the system of graduate education which encourages narrow tutelage. Remedies, he suggests, will require greater commitment to problem-solving, honesty and eclecticism. Specific deficiences of current journal publication practices are detailed by Standing and McKelvie (1986), together with methods of improving quality and efficiency. It is to be noted that a number of journals have taken steps in these directions in recent years; for example, by employing blind refereeing, but there is still a long way to go.

CONCLUSIONS

The term 'ecological validity' was introduced by Brunswik (1947) to refer to appropriate generalisations from the laboratory to non-experimental situations. The cry of lack of ecological validity in psychological research has been heard in a number of quarters both inside and outside the discipline. For example, Neisser (1976) has suggested that it applies to much of cognitive psychology, and Baddeley (1976) has discussed it in connection with specific research paradigms, such as Sternberg's high-speed memory search (see also Chapter 13). Chapanis (1967), in an interesting paper, discusses some of the reasons for the lack of ecological validity in psychological experiments. There may be hidden variables and/or interactions. Independent variables in the laboratory differ from those in real life. Some features are peculiar to the laboratory; for example, the presence of an experimenter, a test-taking set or responding to verbal instructions. Conversely, some real life variables, such as threat, are difficult to recreate in the laboratory. Dependent variables also differ between the two situations. In the laboratory these are chosen for convenience and ease of measurement; for instance, time and errors. In real life the important criteria may be, say, cost and safety. The effort to achieve statistical significance leads to artificial inflation of effects by imposing conditions such as random presentation, speed constraints or distraction. Similarly, attempts to reduce error variance are likely also to reduce applicability to real world situations.

In this chapter we have discussed two factors in particular which contribute to a lack of ecological validity; namely, unrepresentativeness and smallness of samples, and ignoring demand characteristics. However, we have mainly been concerned with technical incompetence. More alarming is the charge of irrelevancy and insignificance concerning the content of research. To some extent there is a conflict between the demands of science and those of the general public, though it is still true that some of the best theoretical advances come from applied research. What is scientifically important may not always be what is of greatest interest to members of the general public. The concern of the former is the establishment of fundamental general principles: the interest of the latter lies in the particulars of individuals. Thus the lay person may wish to predict a specific piece of behaviour, whereas the scientist is only interested in the mechanisms governing the underlying processes. We shall consider some of these issues in Chapter 14.

The cause of significance is not helped by unrepresentative sampling nor by ignoring demand characteristics; much less is it served by tackling problems that are theoretically and/or practically unimportant in the first place. The execution of psychological research that is significant in all senses of the word is one of the most difficult but worthwhile challenges.

Chapter 7

Determinants of scientific advance

In this chapter we shall consider some of the factors contributing to the development of science. First the relative contributions of cultural and personal factors will be considered. To what extent are discoveries the work of particular, outstanding, individual scientists and to what extent are they a product of the spirit of the times? In what ways do these factors interact?

Next we shall consider how far discoveries are dependent on conceptual frameworks and how far on the development of techniques. To what extent do they depend on asking the right questions and to what extent on the possession of appropriate equipment? What is the relation between these factors: is one dependent on the other?

This will lead on to a discussion of the relations between data and theory. To what extent are theories constrained by the data and to what extent are the data dictated by the theory? Does this vary from theory to theory and between theorists? What is the role in science of induction (inferring general laws on the basis of particular observations) and of deduction (deriving specific predictions from generalised hypotheses)? There are two aspects of the process to be considered: what Reichenbach (1938) termed the 'context of discovery' and the 'context of justification', and two types of question to be answered: (1) the psychological one of the way in which scientists actually proceed, and (2) the logical one of the valid inferences between theory and data, which specifies how they should proceed. How do logical and non-logical factors (such as intuition, imagination and creativity) interrelate?

A number of views in the philosophy of science will be discussed and their applicability to psychology considered. Changes in the prevailing view will be noted and particular attention given to the questions of whether science can be considered a cumulative or rational process.

CULTURAL AND PERSONAL FACTORS

The relation between cultural and personal factors in the determination of scientific development was the theme of much of Boring's work in the history of psychology. He formulated it in terms of the relative merits of the 'Great

Man' theory, according to which exceptional individuals direct the course of scientific advance, and the *Zeitgeist* theory, according to which people are merely the instruments of cultural influences. The former stresses psychological and the latter sociological factors. A similar theme of the transcendence of the will and decisions of people by greater natural forces occurs in literature in Tolstoy's *War and Peace* and was common in classical Greek tragedy (for example, Sophocles' *Oedipus Tyrannus*). After discussion of the topic in a number of papers, Boring (see Watson and Campbell, 1963) concluded in favour of a dialectical relation between them. Great scientists he saw as agents of progress, rather than simply cause or symptom, their ideas as events in the space–time field of history. Personal egoism provides the driving force which motivates scientific research but narrows perspectives: the constraining force of the *Zeitgeist* acts as a corrective check but may impede progress (Boring, 1954). Kuhn (1963) refers to the essential tension between the iconoclastic force of innovation and the conservative force of tradition, arguing that, contrary to popular belief which focuses exclusively on divergence at the expense of convergence, both are necessary for scientific progress.

Evidence for the influence of cultural factors comes from a number of sources. One is case studies in the history of science. Hyman (1964) has discussed the variety of influences which led Pavlov to his work on the conditioned response. These include the intellectual climate of the time, particularly positivism (which stressed objectivity) and materialism (which espoused physiological reduction). As is so often the case, the idea of the conditioned response was not new. It had been expressed by many before; for example Whytt's (1751) description of 'psychic secretion'. There were also more specific influences in the form of teachers and books. Pavlov acknowledges his debt to G.H. Lewes's *Physiology of Common Life*, which included a discussion of work by Bernard, who in 1855 had suggested an experiment to investigate psychic secretion in a horse using a salivary fistula exactly analogous to that Pavlov used on dogs. Pavlov was also influenced by Darwin's *Origin of Species*, particularly with respect to the notion of adaptation, and Sechenov's *Reflexes of the Brain*, which gave central importance to the reflex and its cortical inhibition.

Another particularly well-documented example is that of Freud (see Whyte, 1960; Reeves, 1965). In this case the idea of unconscious mental processes can be traced back to classical Greek times but was dominant in nineteenth-century German philosophy and literature. Freud claimed to have avoided reading Nietzsche for this very reason. More specific influences came from his clinical experience, especially with Charcot and Janet (with whom he studied hysterical patients) and Breuer (with whom he first tried out the 'talking cure' on Anna O.); from his attendance at Brentano's lectures on Aristotelian logic (from which he may have gained the ideas of hierarchical levels and multiple causation); from his association with Brücke (a member of a group of 'physicalistic' physiologists committed to a reductionist programme, which also numbered among its members Helmholtz, who had recently revived the notion of the conservation of energy); and from reading von Schubert's *Die Symbolik der Traumes*, which described many of the ideas later adopted by Freud, including several of the defence mechanisms.

A second source of evidence is that of simultaneous, independent discoveries. Ogburn and Thomas (1922) list 148 such cases. Well-known examples include the formulations of the calculus by Leibniz and Newton, the theory of evolution by Darwin and Wallace, and the conditioned response by Pavlov and Twitmeyer. These suggest that discovery is not dependent on a particular individual.

A third possible source of evidence comes from anticipations or rediscoveries. Frequently discoveries are made but acceptance is delayed, so it appears, until the time is ripe, when they are rediscovered. Such cases have been discussed by Boring (1927) and Idhe (1948). An example is that of the laws of inheritance, discovered in 1865 by Mendel and rediscovered in 1900 by de Vries. We have already noted similar phenomena in the cases of Pavlov and Freud, whose contributions seem to have lain predominantly in getting ideas accepted, perhaps in these instances by providing a sufficient amount of convincing evidence. The same was in fact true for Darwin's theory of evolution.

The contribution of the 'Great Man' has been discussed since James (1880). How far the specific educational experiences discussed above should be taken as indicative of psychological rather than social factors is arguable. They are certainly events in personal biographies though symptomatic of social influences. Specifically personal factors have been argued for in the case of Freud (see Jones, 1955; Galdston, 1956).

Considering the relevance of the topic it is astonishing that more work has not been done on the psychology of psychologists. Discussions are to be found in James (1907) and Boring (1942) and, more recently, in Mahoney (1976b). Taylor and Barron (1963) summarise the personality characteristics of productive scientists. Lehman and Witty (1931) provide an interesting comparison of attitudes in contemporary physicists and psychologists: the former were more likely to accept mystery and show religious affiliation. Roe (1953) compared physical scientists, biologists, psychologists and anthropologists on biographical, psychometric and projective test data. Coan's (1979) factor analysis of psychological theories provided support for William James's dimension of tough–tendermindedness. Stolorow and Atwood (1979) suggest that knowledge of a theorist's background and personality enables corrections to be made for the subjective factors which necessarily limit theories and applied this psychobiographical method to Freud, Reich, Jung and Rank. Caine, Wijesinghe and Winter (1981) have demonstrated the role of personal styles in clinical psychology: these determine symptoms, treatment expectations, allocation to treatment and treatment outcome.

CONCEPTS AND TECHNIQUES

The dual importance of an adequate conceptual framework and technology can be illustrated by reference to the history of work on cortical localisation of function. It was necessary both to have formulated appropriate questions and to have available appropriate techniques.

Theories of the soul had to give way to theories of the mind, and these in turn to be made more precise in terms of faculties. Aristotle thought that the mind resided in the heart. The error of this was less serious than the correct assumption that mental qualities have a physical basis. The late-eighteenth-century revolution in the treatment of the insane was consistent with such an assumption. It acknowledged that the mind might be subject to disease (rather than infiltration by demons) and hence possibly dependent on the body, the usual seat of disease. Similar remarks may be made about the phrenologists, who were wrong in detail – development of faculties is not mapped by corresponding development of part of the brain, nor do bumps on the skull reflect bumps on the cortex – but right in general principle: the brain is the organ of the mind and localisation of function is true to a large extent (see McFie, 1972). The phrenologists borrowed the faculty theory of the Scottish philosophers, Reid and Stewart. Later attempts leaned on psychometric analyses and more recently modularity (Fodor, 1983). Progress is dependent on the belief that different functions are differentially localised in the brain. Currently this approach flourishes as cognitive neuropsychology (see, for example, Shallice, 1988).

However, just as important was the development of techniques. These include: ablation, electrical stimulation of animals and of conscious humans, improvements in the sophistication of behavioural measurements, single cell recording, and brain imaging techniques (computed tomography, positron emission tomography and nuclear magnetic resonance).

In some cases the theory appears to dictate the method. An example from the history of psychology is structuralism which, taking the subject matter of psychology to be conscious experience, employed the introspective method. Conversely, functionalism, considering the behaviour of all animals to be the prime subject matter of psychology, preferred observations of performance responses to introspective reports. These effects are more obvious in the systems of classical psychology, which made methodological recommendations in addition to attempting to provide general theories of behaviour, but to some extent all theories delimit the methods used in their investigation.

Flourens (1842) claimed it was the other way about: that 'it is the method which gives the results'. Examples from the history of psychology where this seems to have been the case are the phenomenological study of what is immediately given in perception leading to the theoretical concept of form qualities, and the lack of methods for investigating heredity leading to an emphasis on the environmental determination of behaviour in behaviourism. Common jibes, which illustrate the point, are that intelligence is what the tests measure, that factor analysis gets out what it puts in, and that Skinner's results are specific to his experimental procedure (which depends on food deprivation).

The contribution of the various factors discussed in this chapter are complementary rather than opposed. The true process is likely to be one of reciprocal interaction (see Carr, 1961). Focusing attention on one or two merely represents selection for the purpose of discussion.

FACTS AND THEORIES

As we pointed out at the beginning of this chapter, there are different stages of scientific enquiry to be considered: problem-finding and problem-solving, hypothesis formation and hypothesis testing, the processes of discovery and justification. Both logical and psychological issues are involved. The logical issues are concerned with the validity of inferences that can be made between observation statements and theoretical statements. The psychological issues are concerned with the way in which scientists actually behave.

The traditional view in the philosophy of science of the way in which science proceeded was empiricist. According to this, experience is the source of knowledge. Facts are prior to, and distinct from, theories. Science proceeds by accumulating observations which are generalised to form laws by the process of induction. Such a method was thought to be objective and reliable. A major exponent was Francis Bacon (1620), who proclaimed that 'the understanding must not ... be supplied with wings, but rather hung with weights, to keep it from leaping and flying', on the grounds that nature is an open book. Whoever reads it with a pure mind cannot misread it. Only if the mind is poisoned by prejudice can one fall into error. More recently, logical positivists and logical empiricists believed that such methods guaranteed truth.

However, a number of inadequacies in this view have become apparent. It has been generally acknowledged that fact and interpretation are not distinct: observations are dependent on theories and are therefore not infallible. According to the Quine-Duhem thesis (named after the two philosophers who formulated it), hypotheses are embedded in a whole network of theoretical assumptions and therefore cannot be tested in isolation. Evidence by itself does not make feasible evaluation of a hypothesis (facts do not speak for themselves; theories are underdetermined by evidence). Some theoretical assumptions may be protected and hence the observation base be revisable.

Evidence for the role of theoretical presuppositions in observation comes from the history of science. As Pasteur put it, 'Chance favours the prepared mind.' Popper has used the example of the discovery of penicillin, a chance observation that could not have been interpreted but for prior expectations.

Brush (1974) reports that many eminent scientists are known to have put forward theories which were not supported by facts, among them Galileo, Copernicus, Newton and Einstein, who held that 'theory cannot be fabricated out of the results of observation, it can only be invented'. Mathematicians frequently grasp a conclusion intuitively before they can demonstrate its truth. Gauss remarked, 'I have had my solutions for a long time but I do not yet know how I am to arrive at them', and Polya, 'when you have satisfied yourself that the theory is true you start proving it'. Certain traditions such as phenomenology and ethology have attempted preconception-free observation, but it is almost certainly impossible and leads to problems of interpretation (see Chapter 13). Psychologists have demonstrated the effect of expectation on perception and stressed the role of top-down processes in cognition. Its application to scientific methodology is illustrated by the work on experimenter bias discussed in Chapter 6.

Justification by induction has also come under attack. Hume pointed out that such a procedure is a matter of psychological practice rather than logical necessity. Scientific hypotheses are unrestricted in space and time; it is their essence to go beyond the information given, to extend from the known to the unknown, from past observed cases to future unobserved cases. Induction – that is inferring a general conclusion on the basis of particular observations – can never meet the standards of deduction, where the conclusion is entailed by the premisses.

We turn now to the consideration of two influential philosophers of science who have stressed rationalist rather than empiricist aspects of science.

POPPER

A fundamental claim of Popper's has been the provisional nature of knowledge. All that can be attained are approximations to doubtful truth. The truth may be attained but one can never know that it has been attained. Logical propositions are always dependent on premisses: assumptions must be made before any programme can begin. Empirical propositions are always subject to falsification.

One of the problems with which Popper was concerned was the delineation of scientific from non-scientific statements. Testability was proposed as the *demarcation principle*: what distinguished scientific from non-scientific statements was the fact that their truth could be checked by reference to empirical evidence. The logical positivists adopted the verification principle as the criterion of meaningfulness. Thus in order for a statement to be meaningful it must be verifiable: there must be some way of deciding whether it is true or false. The universe of propositions was divided into logical propositions which were tautologous – that is, true by definition according to the rules of the system (for example, 'two plus two equals four' is true by virtue of the rules of mathematics) – and empirical propositions which were verifiable – namely, for which a decision procedure to determine their truth or falsity existed. Everything else, which included metaphysical, aesthetic and religious statements, was mere nonsense. However, interpreting testability in terms of verifiability would rule out scientific hypotheses as meaningless. They refer to an open class of events (namely, all future cases) rather than a closed class (namely, all past observed cases) and hence are not conclusively verifiable. There is always the possibility that a negative instance will turn up.

The question of whether or not a statement is treated as a testable scientific hypothesis can be illustrated by reference to the example of the statement 'All swans are white'. In the event of a black swan being observed, two choices are open. One can either admit that one was wrong: that indeed it is not the case that all swans are white, in which case the statement is regarded as having the status of a scientific hypothesis, that is, it is falsifiable; or one can conclude that this black creature is not a swan – in this case the statement is regarded as having the status of a tautology, true by definition, the assumption being that whiteness is an inherent quality of being a swan. It is therapeutic to apply this test to psychological theories, or perhaps, better, theorists, in the event of a negative instance: is it accepted as such and the hypothesis rejected or at least modified, or is the instance deemed not to disconfirm, in some way not to count, or be irrelevant? Popper was quick to point out that such theories, which are impervious to disconfirming evidence, are not scientific.

Noting the asymmetry between verification and falsification, that logically a scientific hypothesis cannot be verified by any number of confirming instances but can be refuted by only one disconfirming instance, Popper was led to an interpretation of testability in terms of *falsifiability* and proposed this as the demarcation principle. He defined the logical content of a scientific hypothesis as the class of non-tautological, derivable statements and the empirical content as the class of potential falsifiers. In his view the empirical content of a scientific hypothesis is directly proportional to its falsifiability, and inversely related to its probability. Scientific hypotheses can be arranged on a continuum of falsifiability ranging from zero to one, bounded at one end by tautologies, which have a falsifiability equal to zero (they make no predictions about the empirical world and hence cannot be falsified), and at the other end by contradictions, which have a falsifiablility of one (they say everything about the world and hence are certain to be falsified). (As an example of a contradiction consider the hypothesis 'It will rain and it will not rain tomorrow'. If it does rain tomorrow the second part of the statement will be falsified; if it does not rain the first part will be.) The more chances there are of a hypothesis being falsified the more information it contains. This may sound paradoxical, but some intuitive insight can be gained by thinking of it in terms of surprise value. It is not very informative to discover that something very likely to happen has occurred; by contrast, it is informative to discover that something unlikely to happen has occurred.

Popper's recommendation then is that scientific hypotheses should be sought which are maximally falsifiable (bold, risky conjectures) and that persistent efforts should be made to seek falsification of existing hypotheses. In short, science should proceed by way of conjecture and refutation.

Popper was partly led to this conclusion as a result of examining Marxist theory and the psychoanalytic theories of Freud and Adler. What struck him about these was their imperviousness to falsification: no matter what happened, these theories seemed able to explain the results.

> I could not think of any human behaviour that could not be interpreted in terms of either theory. It was precisely this fact – that they always fitted, that they were always confirmed – which in the eyes of their admirers constituted the strongest argument in favour of these theories. It began to dawn on me that this apparent strength was in fact their weakness.
>
> (Popper, 1963: 35)

Although the emphasis on testability and falsifiability in science is sound (intellectual honesty consists in specifying precisely the conditions under which one is willing to give up one's position), there are a number of modifications or qualifications that might be made to Popper's theory.

Some have argued that there is a place in science for untestable theories, either those that may become testable at a later stage, perhaps with the development of improved techniques, or those that, though not strictly testable, nevertheless aid understanding in some way, perhaps by unifying diverse material. Evolutionary theory is often cited in this context. Although not totally unfalsifiable, it does not rate high on falsifiability, and much of the relevant evidence is now inaccessible. Similarly, geological (and psychological) theories are often *post hoc* in form, seeking to explain, and testable primarily by reference to, events that have already occurred.

The absolute superiority of falsification over verification may also be questioned. Positive outcomes can be informative as well as negative. Since, as was argued above, all facts are theory-laden and hypotheses are embedded in a theoretical network and cannot be tested in isolation, it follows that complete refutation is no more possible than complete proof (Braithwaite, 1953) and that refutation may be no more definitive than verification: it depends on the stability of theories (Nagel, 1967). More recent formulations (for example, Lakatos and Laudan, see below) have recognised the importance of historical context in the appraisal of a theory. There may be cases where refutation does not (and should not) lead to rejection of a theory. The novice experimenter failing to confirm a well-established scientific law concludes that the experiment rather than the law was at fault. Popper in fact allows for this. His recommended methodology is what he terms 'critical falsification'. Falsifications may be rejected in certain circumstances but systematic rejection of them is to be avoided. Lakatos (1970), in an important and extensive examination of falsification as a research methodology, concludes that falsification is neither a necessary nor a sufficient condition for the elimination of a theory.

Popper's stress on logical factors in the development of science ignores non-logical factors, some of which are discussed in the final section of this chapter.

Empirical work in psychology throws considerable doubt on Popper's account as a psychological theory of the way in which scientists actually behave. Experiments simulating scientific reasoning have demonstrated *confirmation bias* (a tendency to seek confirming rather than disconfirming evidence). Wason (1960) found that very few intelligent young adults spontaneously tested their beliefs adequately. They adhered tenaciously to their own hypotheses when confirming evidence for them could be produced and seemed unable or unwilling to attempt falsification. Mahoney and DeMonbreun (1978) found that scientists (physicists and psychologists) were no more successful than ministers of religion (in fact, the two subjects who succeeded on the task were ministers) and did not show any greater tendency to rely on disconfirmatory rather than confirmatory evidence. Indeed, there were some indications that they were less cautious (that is, tested fewer hypotheses) and more tenacious (that is, more inclined to repeat hypotheses). Tukey (1968) found evidence to support a variety of philosophies of science other than Popper's in the performance of this task; his subjects acknowledged using seven different strategies. Mynatt, Doherty and Tweney (1977; 1978) in another simulated research environment also found reluctance on the part of subjects actively to seek falsification, although they generally made appropriate use of disconfirming data if they were encountered. Gorman *et al.* (1984) found that training on a disconfirmatory strategy improved performance. Studies of real-life hypothesis testing in science have led to similar conclusions. Mitroff (1974) took the opportunity to interview NASA geoscientists during the period when lunar soil samples were being returned by Apollo space missions. Scientists characterised as hard-nosed were relatively responsive to the new data, whereas theoretical scientists were much more committed to their hypotheses and often refused to change their views, the only candidates for falsification being the hypotheses of rival scientists! The psychological reasons for the existence of confirmation bias are presumably both motivational and cognitive: the need for commitment and the requirement to reduce cognitive load.

KUHN

Kuhn's (1962) ideas have been almost as influential as Popper's. His basic notion is that of a *paradigm,* which has been variously defined as a 'strong network of commitments, conceptual, theoretical, instrumental and methodological', 'the source of the methods, problem-field, and standards of solution accepted by any mature scientific community at any given time', and 'universally recognizable scientific achievements that for a time provide model problems and solutions to a community of practitioners'. In its broadest sense, it is essentially a sociological concept and refers to agreements amongst a group of scientific practitioners which range from metaphysical (basic assumptions on which the practice of science depends, such as the belief in determinism), through theoretical (agreements about theoretical frameworks and what questions can reasonably be asked – for example, the belief that all behaviour is explicable in terms of conditioning), to methodological (closer to paradigm in the narrower more conventional sense of well-tried procedures, what Kuhn describes as 'concrete exemplary solutions', such as paired-associate learning).

Kuhn has attempted to describe the pattern of scientific progress. He suggests that initially there is a period of pre-paradigmatic science typified by multiple schools: there is no agreement as to what theoretical framework or approach should be adopted. Once a paradigm is agreed upon, a stage of normal science can begin. Possession of a paradigm is a necessary condition for the conduct of normal science. This is typified by what Kuhn calls 'puzzle solving' – that is, the major issues as to what questions should be asked have already been resolved and relatively minor problems are tackled. An example is filling in the values of the atomic table. Possession of a paradigm has advantages and disadvantages. The advantage is that of precision: it permits the asking of precisely formulated questions; the disadvantage is one of limitation: only certain questions can be posed within a given paradigm.

Science proceeds in this way, Kuhn supposes, until a period of extraordinary science is entered. The point will come when anomalies within the existing system can no longer be tolerated and ultimately a paradigm shift occurs. An alternative conceptual framework is proposed. Examples are the Copernican, Newtonian and Einsteinian revolutions. Such revolutions involve a major reorientation and, according to the original formulation (Kuhn, 1962), paradigms are non-comparable. There will be some questions which can be asked under one paradigm but not under another. This non-comparability or incommensurability of paradigms led Kuhn to query the supposed cumulative progression in science and to propose instead that it was characterised by non-cumulative *Gestalt* switches. Indeed, his writing is of additional interest to the psychologist on account of its use of psychological illustrations. Paradigm revolutions are likened to *Gestalt* switches such as occur in the perception of reversible figures in that the same material is seen from an entirely different perspective. The way in which observations are never theory-free is illustrated by reference to Bruner and Postman's (1949) experiment which demonstrated the influence of expectations or set on perception.

Both Popper and Kuhn agree on the contribution of theoretical preconceptions to observations and on the role of criticism in science. Popper sees the latter as ever present; Kuhn sees it as the exception rather than the rule.

Kuhn's theory has not escaped criticism. It has been pointed out that the concept of a paradigm is extremely vague. Masterman (1970) claimed that Kuhn used it in twenty-one different senses, which she classified as metaphysical, social and artefactual. Kuhn (1970) himself later acknowledged two basic senses: (1) sociological – 'the entire constellation of beliefs, values, techniques, and so on shared by a given community', and (2) exemplary past achievements – 'the concrete puzzle-solutions which, employed as models or examples, can replace explicit rules as a basis for the solution of the remaining puzzles of normal science'.

The fact that paradigms may be implicit rather than explicit, and that they may be relatively immune from empirical testing, suggests that important changes can take place in science independently of the observational base. Their non-comparability implies that science is not cumulative. Such a relativistic view has not proved popular: most scientists would resist the notion that their efforts are not progressive in any real sense. Overall, the Kuhnian view raises doubts about whether science is a rational process.

THE APPLICABILITY OF PARADIGMS TO PSYCHOLOGY

There has been considerable debate about whether Kuhn's proposals, based largely on a consideration of the history of the physical sciences, are applicable to psychology, and whether or not psychology has acquired a paradigm. Warren (1971) argued that psychology is in a preparadigmatic state typified by multiple schools and uncertainty as to the best method of proceeding.

Others (for instance, Palermo, 1971; Reese and Overton, 1970; Weimer and Palermo, 1973) on the other hand have argued that psychology has gone through several successive paradigms. The first paradigm was structuralism, whose task was the analysis of the structure and contents of the mind by means of introspection. This was succeeded by behaviourism, which attempted to provide a functional analysis of behaviour in terms of stimuli and responses based on the 'objective' observation of behaviour. The focus was on learning, for which it attempted to provide general laws, with conditioning as the pretheoretic model. This in turn was superseded by the cognitive paradigm which aims to provide an information-processing analysis of the cognitive system interpreted as a symbol manipulator, based on a computer analogy. Inferences about stages of processing are made on the basis of the results of behavioural experiments, supplemented by computer simulation. A detailed account of information processing as the dominant paradigm in cognitive psychology is provided by Lachman, Lachman and Butterfield (1979). They trace its intellectual antecedents – for example, neobehaviourism, communications engineering, computer science and linguistics – showing in each case which pretheoretical assumptions were retained and which rejected. For alternatives to this paradigm, see Costall and Still (1987) and Chapter 13.

Gholson and Barker (1985) argue that, although heuristically compelling, Kuhn's views may be inaccurate when applied to psychology. The history of learning theory provides ample evidence of the simultaneous existence of more than one paradigm – namely, the conditioning and cognitive paradigms – and of their experimental commensurability. Critical experiments were performed – for example, on transposition and all-or-none learning – and rational progress made. In their view, Lakatos and Laudan provide much better accounts of scientific progress in both physics and psychology. To these accounts we now turn.

LAKATOS AND LAUDAN

As Medawar (1969) observed: 'Theories are not so much affirmed and denied as modified and repaired. They fade or are assimilated.' Lakatos's (1970) sophisticated falsificationism takes into account the fact that science is a historically evolving body of knowledge and recognises the existence of thematic lines of enquiry. A *research programme* is a succession of theories linked by a common hard core of shared commitments. Unlike Kuhn's paradigms they are explicit and subjected to successively more detailed articulation as the programme progresses. This hard core of assumptions is protected from immediate empirical refutation by a belt of dispensable features. A research programme is considered to be theoretically progressive if it leads to new predictions, and empirically progressive if the predictions are empirically supported. Thus progress appears to be a rational process. A new theory must have verified excess content compared with the theory it is superseding; it should accommodate the successes of its predecessors, explain data that brought them into question and lead to new experimentally verified predictions. A research programme is considered to be degenerating if it fails to show theoretical or empirical progress and anomalies can only be met by *ad hoc* manoeuvres. According to Lakatos, several competing research programmes can coexist, and progression and degeneration are both reversible.

Thus Lakatos's theory can be seen to avoid the problems of incommensurability and irrationalism that faced Kuhn's. Empirical evidence is the final arbiter between competing research programmes. Gholson and Barker (1985) illustrate these ideas by reference to the psychology of learning. The conditioning and cognitive paradigms coexisted for about fifty years during the first half of this century. Core commitments of the conditioning paradigm were that learning consisted of associations being formed between specific stimulus–response pairs and that the behaviour of the organism was reactive and determined by the external environment. The cognitive paradigm, on the other hand, was committed to the view that learning consisted of the testing of hypotheses by an active organism and that behaviour was internally determined. These paradigms were experimentally commensurable, as attested by experiments conducted during the period between 1930 and 1960. Each successive theory solved the problems of its predecessors and made experimentally confirmed predictions which its rival could not (see, for example, Spence, 1937). The cognitive paradigm declined from about 1930 but then revived about 1960. Another example is connectionism, which has now revived in the form of neural nets. Gholson and Barker argue that there was constant evolution of core commitments, elements of the conditioning paradigm being incorporated into the cognitive paradigm. The fact that core commitments can change is dealt with by Laudan.

Laudan's (1977) concept of a *research tradition* is a family or cluster of theories sharing a common ontology and methodology. It consists of, first, malleable core assumptions, which can be changed. They provide continuity but can be modifed by empirical testing and so are not functionally metaphysical. Secondly, it consists of a set of metaphysical principles which dictate a particular ontology but need not be explicit. Theories may coexist simultaneously which are contradictory but based on the same fundamental commitments. Examples in the history of psychology are provided by contiguity theory, Hull-Spence theory and Skinnerian theory, which differed with respect to the roles of unobservables and reinforcement; or the different versions of mediation theory. Laudan has also drawn attention to the existence of conceptual factors as additional appraisal criteria. Gholson and Barker (1985) cite as examples in the history of psychology the rejection of mathematical learning theory on grounds of complexity, reinforcement on grounds of circularity, and Piagetian theory on grounds of imprecision.

NON-RATIONAL FACTORS

So far we have been predominantly considering views that emphasise logical factors in the development of science. What of non-logical factors? Although the role of imagination and intuitive processes in science has always been acknowledged, more recently a number of writers have given explicit recognition to non-rational elements. In so far as advances in science are novel, they involve creative problem-solving and are inherently non-predictable. (This may be one reason why the scientific study of creativity has been limited in its progress.) Polanyi in a number of works (for example, Polanyi, 1966) has developed the theme of tacit knowing. He was convinced of the impossibility of the existence of strict rules for establishing knowledge, and the indeterminacy of science with respect to content, coherence and data. Using a perceptual analogy, he suggested that an integration of what he called 'unconscious subsidiaries' (background knowledge or preconceptions) and focal awareness is always involved.

In similar vein Feyerabend (1975) has espoused what he refers to as an 'anarchist epistemology' in which 'anything goes'. In his view there are no absolute judgements, and no fixed method or theory of rationality. His argument is based on a consideration of the history of science which shows it to be complex and unpredictable, and the necessity of anarchy for the growth of knowledge. There is a need for revolutions in which the rules are broken. The importance of play in scientific creativity is stressed. He made three recommendations:

1 A counter-inductive procedure: evidence that is relevant for the test of a theory can often be unearthed only with the help of an incompatible theory.
2 The principle of proliferation: the invention and elaboration of theories which are inconsistent with the accepted point of view is an essential part of critical empiricism.
3 A pluralistic methodology: a variety of approaches should be tried rather than the exclusive adoption of one. Fixed rules are unrealistic and vicious.

Feyerabend's views can be seen as an extension of Popper's taken to their logical conclusion, and in opposition to Kuhn's. In a subject as complex and varied as psychology, Feyerabend's approach has its merits. For a statement and critique of irrationalism, and a warning against the danger of taking *this* approach to its extreme, see Frankel (1973).

Finally, perhaps the role of accidental factors in scientific discovery should be noted. Frequently cited examples in the history of science are the thunderstorm which led to Galvani's discovery of the electrical nature of neural transmission in a frog's leg, and Becquerel fortuitously leaving a uranium compound on a covered photographic plate, leading to the discovery of radioactivity. An example in psychology is Skinner's discovery of the partial reinforcement effect as a result of finding himself short of food pellets one Friday evening.

SUMMARY

The chapter began with a discussion of the relative influence of cultural and personal factors, and of conceptual and technical advances on the development of science. Logical and psychological issues concerning the relations between facts and theories were considered. It was seen that traditional empiricist theories of scientific progress which give priority to observations have been superseded by rationalist theories which give priority to theoretical interpretation. The views of Popper, Kuhn, Lakatos and Laudan, and their applicability to psychology were discussed. Finally, consideration was given to the role of non-rational factors in scientific progress.

Chapter 8

Theories and explanations

The next five chapters will be devoted to an evaluation of different types of theoretical explanation in psychology. In this chapter we shall first define certain theoretical terms and then consider what functions theories serve. This will be followed by a discussion of the dimensions on which theories may differ and criteria for choosing between rival theories. Finally, we shall discuss the nature of explanation and review different types used in psychology.

WHAT ARE THEORIES?

It is first necessary to distinguish systems, theories and models.

A *system* is a general theory plus methodological recommendations. McGeoch (1933) defines a system as 'a coherent and inclusive, yet flexible, organization and interpretation of the facts and special theories of the subject', and mentions six features by which they may be evaluated (definition of the field, explicit postulates, nature of data, mind–body position, organisation of data, principles of selection). Examples are the early schools of psychology (for example, behaviourism) which not only attempted to provide a general theory of behaviour – as indicated by some of the titles of the period, such as Hull's (1943) *Principles of Behavior* or Skinner's (1938) *The Behavior of Organisms* – but also made metatheoretical recommendations about the subject matter, methods and theoretical explanations to be employed. Systems bear some similarities to paradigms, discussed in Chapter 7.

A *theory* has a narrower scope than a system. Bergmann (1957) defines a theory in the traditional way as 'a group of laws deductively connected' and Marx (1976) as 'a provisional explanatory proposition, or set of propositions, concerning some natural phenomena and consisting of symbolic representations of (1) the observed relationships among (measured) events, (2) the mechanisms or structures presumed to underlie such relationships, or (3) inferred relationships and underlying mechanisms'. A theory is essentially an abstraction and distinct from the data.

The term '*model*' has been variously used. In some cases it appears to be synonymous with 'theory', although generally a model is narrower in scope (thus: a theory of perception but a model of pattern recognition). Chapanis (1961) defines models as 'representations or likenesses of certain aspects of complex events, structures or systems, made by using symbols or objects which in some way resemble the thing being modelled'. Essentially models are analogies and typically involve the application of a better developed, better understood system to a less developed, less well-understood one. Thus, although it is true that all theories are models in the sense that they are representations, their mutual identification hardly seems a usage to be recommended. Simon and Newell (1956) suggest that models may be distinguished from theories in the following ways. First, they are useful rather than true. Models are intended as heuristic aids rather than as complete descriptions. Second, they are less data-sensitive: disconfirming evidence is damaging to a theory but not necessarily so to a model. Third, they are more susceptible to type II errors; that is, they are more liable to make false claims.

In psychology, models have come to be used to refer to a particular sub-group of theories, those which employ mechanistic explanations (see p. 112–14). These aim at describing the processes involved, though usually only in an abstract form (see Chapter 10 for a fuller discussion of models).

A *law* refers to a relatively well-established statement of regular predictable relations among empirical variables. They are noteworthy for their scarcity in psychology.

A *hypothesis* is a tentative law.

A *postulate* is an assumption of a theory not intended to be subjected to empirical test; for example, that all behaviour is determined.

A *primitive term* is a basic term not defined within a theory but external to it, if at all; for instance, stimulus, response, reinforcement.

A *protocol statement* is a description of an observation, sometimes referred to as 'data language'.

A *construct* is a concept referring to relations between events or properties, such as anxiety (see Chapter 9 for fuller discussion).

THE FUNCTION OF THEORIES

Are theories necessary at all?

The case against

In a classic paper Skinner (1950) put forward the view that theories, whether of a conceptual, neural or mental type, were not necessary in psychology. His arguments were that: (1) They create new problems of explanation which get covered up (it is true that having a theory may lead to a false sense of security and tend to preclude further investigations). (2) They may generate wasteful research (an examination of some of the research on learning in the 1940s and

1950s tends to confirm this view). (3) More direct approaches exist (Skinner's own approach favours the pursuit of functional laws based directly on empirical research, whose merits and demerits are considered in Chapter 9).

However, many psychologists are not so pure-minded. For most of them theories are a psychological if not a logical necessity. What functions do they serve?

The case for

First, a good case can be made for the view that there are no such things as pure facts. In Chapter 7 we considered arguments and evidence which suggest that data are not theory-free and that all observation involves selection and interpretation. Facts do not speak for themselves. This is particularly true in psychology where much of the subject matter is not directly observable and involves a good deal of inference.

Broadbent (1961) has argued that even Skinner's approach, which seeks only to predict and not to explain behaviour, cannot be theory-free, on the grounds that, because no two events are identical, theoretical assumptions must be invoked to enable selection of the relevant dimensions on which generalisation is to be based. So it appears that even for the limited goal of prediction a theory is necessary.

Theories normally have both backward-looking (retrospective) and forward-looking (prospective) functions. They serve to summarise and organise data that have already been collected, which would otherwise be unmanageable and unassimilable. They bring order and coherence to material. For most people facts are useless unless one takes the intellectual risk of thinking about them. Most theories are attempts at explanation. 'Theories are nets cast to catch the "world": to rationalize, to explain and to master it' (Popper, 1959).

Theories also serve a heuristic function of guiding research. 'Theory is the stage upon which experiments are conducted' (Allport, 1955). They provide a means of selecting from the infinitude of possible experiments. It may be concluded that theories are both a logical and a psychological necessity.

DIMENSIONS OF THEORISING

In this section we shall consider broad dimensions on which theories may vary.

First, not all theories have the same *aim*. The primary aim of a theory is explanation, the main function of which is to increase understanding. The conventionally accepted form of this for scientific theories is deductive prediction (see pp. 109–10). However, there may be other possible avenues to understanding. Some psychological (and other scientific) theories are essentially post-dictive; for example, psychoanalysis. Rycroft (1966) has gone so far as to claim that psychoanalysis is not intended as a scientific theory whose purpose is to elucidate causes, but rather as a semantic theory whose purpose is to make symptoms intelligible; it provides a language for talking about them. Other theories seem to aim more at an empathic type of understanding. These occur primarily in literature (it is frequently claimed that more is learned about people from reading novels than by studying experimental psychology) but also in some phenomenologically and socially based approaches, a particular case in point being hermeneutics (see p. 115).

Secondly, theories may vary in their *mode of formulation*. Simon and Newell (1956) distinguish verbal, mathematical and analogical formulations. They give an example of the same information expressed in three different ways: (1) verbal – 'consumption increases linearly with income, but less than proportionately'; (2) mathematical – $C = a + bY; a > 0; 0 < b < 1$; (3) analogical – the flow of goods and money might be likened to that of a liquid. Psychological examples of verbal theories are Guthrie's theory of learning and Homans's theory of group behaviour, which have been given corresponding mathematical formulations by Estes (1950) and Simon (1952) respectively. Psychological examples of analogical theories are well reviewed in Miller, Galanter and Pribram (1960, chap. 3) and range from Ashby's homeostat to Lorenz's hydraulics (see Chapter 10 for further discussion). It is important to distinguish the logical content of a theory (what it is possible to infer from it in principle) from the psychological content (what is actually inferred from it). Thus, theories may contain the same logical content but differ in psychological content. Simon and Newell (1956) claim that verbal formulations tend to have logical rather than psychological advantages, and mathematical formulations psychological rather than logical advantages. The logical advantages are a function of the theory, the psychological advantages more dependent on the theorist. The latter lies in the realm of differential psychology, which should be able to explain why different theorists prefer different modes of formulation.

In Chapter 7 we considered the roles of data and theory. It is clear that the *relation between data and theory* is a variable on which theories differ. Some are predominantly data-determined, others predominantly conceptually determined. Various relations that may obtain between data and theory have been represented diagrammatically by Marx (1976) (see Figure 8.1). He has considered the direction of inference between theory and data (indicated by arrows); whether the relation is static or dynamic (represented by vertical and slanted lines respectively); and the scope – that is, the extent of inference beyond the data (represented by the length of line). Time is represented on the horizontal dimension. Models and deductive theories tend to be theory-orientated, functional and inductive theories to be data-orientated. We shall consider the four types in turn. A *model* is a conceptual analogue, whose value is predominantly heuristic. According to Marx, inferences exist

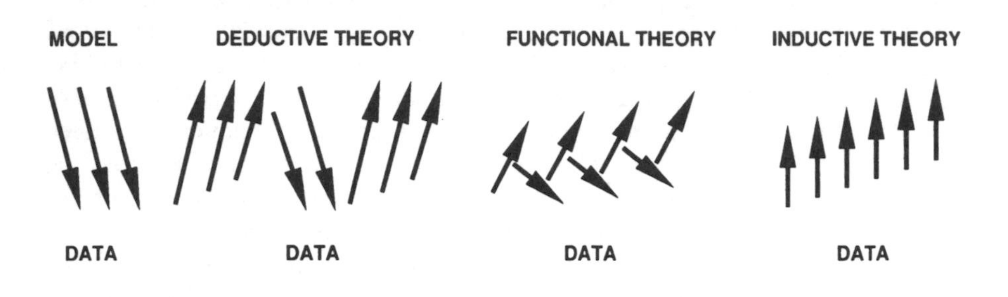

Figure 8.1 Relations between theory and data in four modes of theory construction
(*Source:* Marx, 1976)

in one direction only: from theory to data. It is not data-sensitive; no feedback is planned from data to theory, so there is no interaction. However, this depends on a particular interpretation of the term 'model' (see pp. 100–1) and may not always be true. There are many examples of models in psychology (see Chapter 10), a simple one being Broadbent's filter theory of attention.

A *deductive theory* involves two-way interaction: theoretical generalisations are induced from observations, and predictions of future observations are deduced from theoretical hypotheses. An example in psychology is Hull's theory of learning. Such theories are prototypical in science but have been criticised as being premature in psychology. There is a danger of over-formalisation, which may make the theory difficult to modify. An example of a theory which is predominantly conceptually rather than data driven is Piaget's. Some work in mathematical psychology also gives the impression of the theorist having become obsessed with the mathematics and having lost touch with the data. In a *functional theory* (that is, 'functional' in the sense of a functional law relating stimuli and responses) interaction is two-way but the scope is much narrower. The theory is merely a restatement of the data, theory and data being given equal weight. Examples in psychology are the Weber-Fechner law and Ebbinghaus's empirical law of forgetting. Being closer to the data they are more data-sensitive and easily modifiable but because the theory does not go beyond the data they lack virility and seldom lead to new predictions. In an *inductive theory*, inference is claimed to be only in one direction, from data to theory. The facts are supposed to speak for themselves, the theoretical statements being mere summaries of empirical findings. An example is Skinnerian theory. Such theories, like functional theories, are insufficiently complex and lacking in predictions, and it is doubtful whether any exist in a pure form, without tacit deduction.

Another choice that faces the theorist is *level of analysis*. In psychology there is a wide range of choice, from social to physiological. George (1953) has suggested that the psychologist is faced with speculating about the organism that intervenes between stimulus and response. The issue then becomes one of how detailed an analysis of the organism is undertaken. The molar theorist accounts for discrepancies between stimuli and responses by postulating constructs which represent organismic factors without analysing these in detail or observing the internal state of the organism. The molecular theorist attempts to reduce the vagueness and possible surplus meaning of these constructs by making them more explicit and suggesting possible mechanisms. They can then be tested not only as part of a molar theory but are also open to test by physiological evidence (these issues are more fully discussed in Chapters 9 and 11).

Finally, Brunswik (1939) has raised the interesting notion of what he calls *conceptual focus*. If psychological theories are taken to be concerned with predicting responses as a function of stimuli, there is a choice as to what is selected as stimulus and response. This involves not only what might crudely be described as a spatial dimension (the level or size of unit of analysis just discussed) but also a temporal dimension, in terms of how far back in the history of the individual the cause is sought, and how far into the future effects are predicted. Brunswik confounds these two dimensions in suggesting the following range: the remote past of the organism; manipulable bodies, distal stimuli; proximal stimuli; intra-organismic events and dispositions; proximal reactions, molecular behaviour; distal effects of reactions, molar behavioural achievements; far-reaching successes, products of life activities. He illustrates these by reference to a comparison of classical schools in psychology, different schools selecting different items as stimuli and responses.

CRITERIA FOR CHOOSING BETWEEN THEORIES

Given the necessity of theories and the existence of several rival theories, what criteria may be used for choosing between them? This question has been considered by Goodson and Morgan (1976) and by Paxton (1976).

One relevant consideration is the *scope* of a theory, the range of data covered. Both breadth and completeness of coverage may be considered advantageous.

Parsimony is another requirement of a theory. Although nature may not be simple, the goal of a theory should be to account for the maximum amount of data with the minimum number of theoretical hypotheses. The simplest account compatible with the data should always be preferred. The principle of parsimony was formulated in mediaeval times by William of Occam, after whom it came to be known as Occam's razor. In the early days of comparative psychology, Lloyd Morgan urged his canon in opposition to the anthropomorphism that had characterised eighteenth-century studies of animals, although justifying it with reference to evolution: 'In no case may we interpret an action as the outcome of the exercise of a higher psychical faculty, if it can be interpreted as the outcome of the exercise of one which stands lower in the psychological scale' (Morgan, 1894: 53). More recently, theories such as psychoanalysis have been criticised for their lack of parsimony.

The *clarity* with which a theory is formulated contains a number of aspects. The ease with which predictions can be derived has both logical and psychological implications, as we saw earlier in discussing modes of formulation, and will be inversely related to both complexity and ambiguity. Logical *consistency* is a necessity and maximum *precision* a desirability.

Both the scope and the clarity of a theory will have implications for its *testability*. The greater the empirical content and the more clearly specified the theory, the greater will be its potential for falsification. Sensitivity to data is partly a function of theories but also partly a function of theorists, as was indicated in Chapter 7.

The extent of *empirical support* for a theory is obviously another criterion by which theories may be evaluated. Popper has stressed the importance of variety as well as quantity of corroboration.

As was pointed out in the previous section, a theory has both retrospective and prospective functions. As important as accounting for past observations may be the ability to lead to novel predictions (theoretical progressiveness in Lakatos's sense). A theory may be in error but nevertheless of heuristic value in leading to new discoveries. In the long term then the *fruitfulness* of a theory may be an important criterion.

WHAT ARE EXPLANATIONS?

> There are as many causes of x as there are explanations of x. Consider how the cause of death might have been set out by a physician as 'multiple haemorrhage', by the barrister as 'negligence on the part of the driver', by a carriage-builder as 'a defect in brakeblock construction', by a civic planner as 'the presence of tall shrubbery at that turning'.
>
> (Hanson, 1958: 54)

Each of these suggests a different alternative or contrast class. This has led many (for example, Van Fraassen, 1977; 1980) to conclude that explanation is pragmatic. The stance taken is relative to the strategies of the person trying to explain and predict behaviour (Dennett, 1971).

Explanations may be seen as answers to 'why?' questions (Scriven, 1962; Bromberger, 1966; 1968). They are requests for information. 'It is convenient to regard an explanation as any answer to a why question that is accepted by the questioner as making the event in question somehow more intelligible' (Boden, 1972). She goes on to define a scientific explanation as 'an explanation that is justified by reference to publicly observable facts, and which is rationally linked to other, similar explanations in a reasonably systematic manner'. Some scientific questions might better be regarded as answers to 'how?' questions. Given that explanations are answers to questions of some sort, it seems reasonable to suggest that there may be as many different types of answers as there are types of question, and that the type of explanation adopted will depend on the following three factors:

1 *Who asked the question* An answer will be related to the present state of knowledge of the questioner. For example, an explanation of the motion of the planets given to a child will be different from that given to an atomic physicist.
2 *What the question was aimed at* For what purpose is the knowledge required? Are there practical implications? For example, one suspects that Skinner's option for explanations of behaviour in terms of environmental rather than genetic factors may be motivated by possibilities of modification. Similarly, which explanation of pathological behaviour is preferred may depend on available treatments.
3 *Who gave the answer* What are the personal biases of the theorist? The existence of psychological factors in theorising is beyond doubt (see Coan, 1979; Caine, Wijesinghe and Winter, 1981).

Explanations must supply new information. Ultimately what is accepted is a matter of subjective satisfaction, as William James pointed out clearly in *Pragmatism*:

> Our commerce with the systems reverts to the informal, to the instinctive human reaction of satisfaction or dislike. . . . We philosophers have to reckon with such feelings on your part. In the last resort, I repeat, it will be by them that all our philosophies shall ultimately be judged. The finally victorious way of looking at things will be the most completely impressive to the normal run of minds.
>
> (James, 1907: 38)

In theory there is a wide choice; in practice there is less. In science, as we have seen, certain kinds are preferred to others. The prototype has been a causal explanation embedded in a hypothetico-deductive theory (see below). Whether different types of explanation are possible or whether, for example, only causal ones are acceptable is a much debated issue. Foss (1974) has put the case for multiple explanations in psychology. One thing to be avoided is evaluating one type of explanation from the viewpoint of another. Thus, it is inappropriate to reject evolutionary functional explanations on the grounds that they are not causal: they are not intended to be.

Deutsch (1960) has claimed that psychologists are confused about explanation:

> There is no concord among psychologists about what the facts they have accumulated are evidence for. This does not mean that they are merely in disagreement about the edifice they wish to erect; they have not even decided what constitutes a building. That is, not only do they disagree about the explanation of their findings, but they are not clear what it would be to explain them.
>
> (Deutsch, 1960: 1)

Below we shall distinguish and discuss the relative merits of seven different focal types. For a somewhat different set, see Russell (1984, chap. 1).

TYPES OF EXPLANATION

Description and classification

Preliminary to explanation is description and classification. Phenomena to be explained must be identified and labelled. Whether clasification as such can ever count as explanatory is a controversial issue. In certain cases it is not. The nominalist fallacy exposes the false belief that in naming something it has been explained, instanced in the statement 'Pigs are so called because they are such dirty animals' or the peasants mentioned by Vygotsky who, it is claimed, could understand the discovery of the stars but expressed puzzled amazement at the discovery of their names. An example from literature is Molière's *La Malade Imaginaire*, where he mocks the doctors who suggested that what makes opium have its soporific effect is its *virtus dormitiva*; that is, its soporific power. In psychology a similar case is the use of the concept of instinct, criticised, for example, by Field (1921). Nor is it clear that its successor, drive, has escaped the same fate. In these cases the description may be tautologous. A classification becomes explanatory if it conveys additional independent information. Consider the example, 'Jane goes to parties because she is an extravert'. This is not explanatory if party-going behaviour is the only way of identifying an extravert, if going to parties is what it means to be an extravert. If, however, extraversion has additional implications, either behavioural, such as taking relatively more involuntary rest pauses in tapping tasks, or physiological, such as greater cortical inhibition, then the circularity is avoided and it is explanatory.

Ethologists stressed the importance of describing the behavioural repertoire of an animal before proceeding to more theoretical accounts of the determinants of behaviour. Examples of classificatory explanations in psychology, where events are explained by reference to a class of events of which they are members, include neobehaviourist accounts in terms of drive reduction, and rule-following in social psychology (for example, Goffman, 1959; Harré and Secord, 1972) or language. This last provides an example of another type of description common in psychology, where an attempt is made to characterise the competence underlying behaviour (for example, Chomsky, 1980). These accounts draw attention to important aspects of behaviour, and classification is probably a necessary prerequisite for explanation. However, they need to be supplemented by other types of information, which explain, for example, how the behaviour developed and how it works in detail.

Correlational

A next step might be to establish associations between events – some form of correlation; for example, between smoking and cancer, or weight and mental age in the first few years of life.

The motivations for asserting a relation of contingency rather than causation may be various. In philosophy Hume argued that there was no logical necessity involved in cause, which could be reduced to contiguity.

> We have no other notion of cause and effect but that of certain objects, which have been always conjoined together, and which in all past instances have been found inseparable. We cannot penetrate into the reason of the conjunction. We only observe the thing in itself, and always find that from the constant conjunction, the objects acquire a union in the imagination.
>
> (Hume 1739: Book 1, Part III, Section VI)

In physics, Heisenberg's uncertainty principle has suggested limits to determinacy. In neurophysiology, Burns (1968) has claimed that there are stochastic processes at the cellular level. In psychology, probability statements are the order of the day. Probability implies determinism but one that is imperfectly known. Whether the limits to knowledge are a function of the knower or of the known is an interesting question for speculation.

One of the main proponents of this approach in psychology is Skinner, who deems functional relations between stimuli and responses to be sufficient for prediction and control. 'I do not know why [food is reinforcing to a hungry animal] . . . and I do not care' (Skinner, 1964).

Inductive generalisations which are merely empirical summaries of the evidence can be distinguished from natural laws by their failure to accommodate counterfactual conditions. Inductive generalisations are limited to the cases observed; natural laws, however, apply to cases that have not been observed. As we saw on p. 104, the former have the advantages of being closely related to the data, but more powerful explanations are required for most purposes.

Causal

The standard model of explanation in science is the *deductive-nomological* (Hempel and Oppenheim, 1948), where an event is explained by being deduced as an instance of a general law, for example:

> *General law*: Copper expands when heated.
> *Antecedent conditions*: This bar is copper and it was heated.
> *Conclusion*: This bar expanded.

The description of the phenomenon to be explained is given in the conclusion; the explanation is contained in the general law together with the antecedent conditions. However, there are a number of inadequacies in this as a general model of explanation. For one thing, many laws are probabilistic rather than universally true, and some events occur with low probability. There are a number of different types of law – for example, functional dependence and property attribution (see Nagel, 1961; Cummins, 1983) – but causal laws are an important subset. Functional laws – for instance, Bloch's and the Weber-Fechner laws in psychophysics – are cases of natural laws but lack the temporal feature of causal laws. Whereas causal statements are generally asymmetrical (the cause determines or explains the effect but not vice versa), statements of functional dependence are often reversible.

Causal explanations explain a given event by reference to a past event. The occurrence of an event B is explained as being the result of an antecedent event A having occurred, A being a condition of B. They are equivalent to Aristotle's efficient causes; for example, 'the billiard ball moved because it was hit by the cue'. The implication is that variation in A will produce variation in B. Given the antecedent, it should be possible in principle to predict the consequent.

Although they are considered by many to be the preferred type of explanation in science, there are a number of problems associated with them. Since they are based on the deterministic assumption, there are doubts about their applicability to some areas of science, such as quantum mechanics (see Chapter 2). There are many other types of explanation in psychology; for example, evolutionary theory and psychoanalysis are postdictive rather than predictive. Philosophers have found great difficulty in giving them precise specification (Russell, 1913; Van Fraassen, 1980). Essential ingredients appear to be conditionality and relevance. However, it has not proved possible to give an account of causation in terms of necessary and sufficient conditions. Moreover, an account which is sufficiently precise to enable accurate prediction is likely to be so complex as to be unique and probably useless in practice. It is also difficult to explicate relevance. On the assumption that the world is a net of interconnected events related to one another in a complex but systematic way, Salmon (1978) suggests that causal explanation exhibits the salient features in the causal network. Causal chains may be identified by a process of 'screening off', that is, by interrupting their effects (Salmon, 1984). However, what factors are considered salient is dependent on the context (Van Fraassen, 1980).

Hume suggested three conditions for inferring causality: contiguity, temporal precedence and constant conjunction. He made the important observation that it is a psychological rather than a logical inference. Cause cannot be observed directly but organisms have a predisposition to seek contingencies, which presumably serves an adaptive function. J.S. Mill also suggested three factors: temporal precedence, relatedness and the elimination of alternative explanations. He proposed three methods to help in establishing the last of these: the methods of agreement (presence of the effect if the cause is present), difference (absence of the effect in the absence of the cause) and concomitant variation.

It may be debated whether events are uniquely caused, or whether the same effect can have different causes on different occasions. A case in the literature that might be interpreted as a mistaken conclusion of unique causation is that of Watson (1907), who successively eliminated sight, hearing and touch in rats. On finding that learning was unimpaired for trained and untrained rats, he concluded that it must be mediated kinaesthetically. However, in 1929 Lashley managed to eliminate kinaesthesis surgically and, although their gait was awkward, his rats still managed to learn mazes. The conclusion must be that rats will use any sense the experimenter is generous enough to leave them with and/or that the critical factor lies elsewhere, as Tolman and his followers argued.

A related question is that of multiple causation: can a particular effect have more than one cause? A common occurrence in psychology is that of predisposing factors and precipitating events. This has been documented for psychiatric disorders – for example, with respect to inherited and congenital factors in the aetiology of schizophrenia (Mednick, 1970) and social factors in the development of depression (Brown and Harris, 1978). Freud certainly considered the possibility of overdetermination: the co-occurrence of two events each of which alone would have been sufficient to cause the effect – for example, an instruction given in hypnosis to open a window after returning to the normal waking state together with a stuffy atmosphere.

There are also problems in specifying the temporal relations between cause and effect. (Indeed, this was one of the reasons which led Russell, 1913, to reject the notion of cause.) Although common-sense notions and the testing of causal hypotheses require the temporal precedence of cause in relation to effect, a logically precise formulation requires their simultaneity: otherwise some other factor could intervene to alter the course of events. In practice, psychologists vary considerably in the length of delay tolerated between cause and effect (see Brunswik's notion of conceptual focus discussed on p. 105). Causes for behaviour may be sought in the phylogenetic history of the species or the ontogenetic development of the organism. Psychoanalysts seek causes for adult psychopathology in the early years of life, in contrast to behaviour therapists who focus on current problems; learning theorists may seek the causes of behaviour in past reinforcement contingencies, whereas Gestaltists and field theorists concentrated on current factors. It is sometimes thought that more detailed accounts can be obtained at lower levels of explanation. This may be part of the reason why psychological explanations are often considered softer than physiological, since they appear to tolerate more unknown mediating factors between cause and effect.

Although causal explanations are commonly employed in science, in the mature sciences they are often superseded by statements of functional relations, as Russell (1913) noted. Thus, contrary to what might at first be supposed, that statements of association are crude and possibly inaccurate formulations which later give way to more powerful causal statements, rather, the opposite is the case: causal statements are essentially loose formulations of sequential regularities which precede more precise mathematical statements of functional dependence.

Functional

A number of authors have drawn a major distinction between two different types of explanation (those considered so far and the two that follow). Marx (1963) contrasts 'constructive' explanations, by means of which phenomena are described in terms of more abstract, higher order constructs and hypotheses on the same descriptive level, with 'reductive', by means of which phenomena are functionally related to other phenomena at a different and, in a hierarchical sense, more basic level of description (see Figure 8.2). Cummins (1983) contrasts subsumption under a causal law with functional analysis, claiming that psychological phenomena are typically not explained by subsuming them under causal laws, but by treating them as manifestations of capacities that are explained by analysis: 'Most psychological explanation makes no sense when construed as causal subsumption but a great deal of sense construed as analysis.' Deutsch (1960) distinguishes what he calls descriptive, generalisatory approaches with structural, neurophysiological or mechanical. In the latter type:

> An event is explained by being deduced as the property of a structure, system or mechanism and not as an instance of events in its own class. . . . The precise properties of the parts do not matter; it is only their general relationships to each other which give the machine as a whole its behavioural properties. . . . This highly abstract system . . . can be embodied in a theoretically infinite variety of physical counterparts. . . . Given the system or abstract structure alone of the machine, we can deduce its properties and predict its behaviour.
>
> (Deutsch 1960: 1)

Deutsch recommends this approach as a middle road between what he calls 'positivism run wild' and 'neurophysiologising'. Its power is that it is sufficient for the prediction of behaviour and its advantage that it provides a link to physiology, which ultimately may provide an additional testing ground.

These mechanistic approaches focus on the processes or operations involved in a sequence of behaviour. At this level an attempt is made to provide a functional characterisation of these, independent of their physical realisation; namely, in terms of the software rather than the hardware. Thus the theory may take the form of a flow chart or, if formally developed, a computer program. The approach owes much to cybernetics, information theory and computer science. Examples are Deutsch's (1960) model of need,

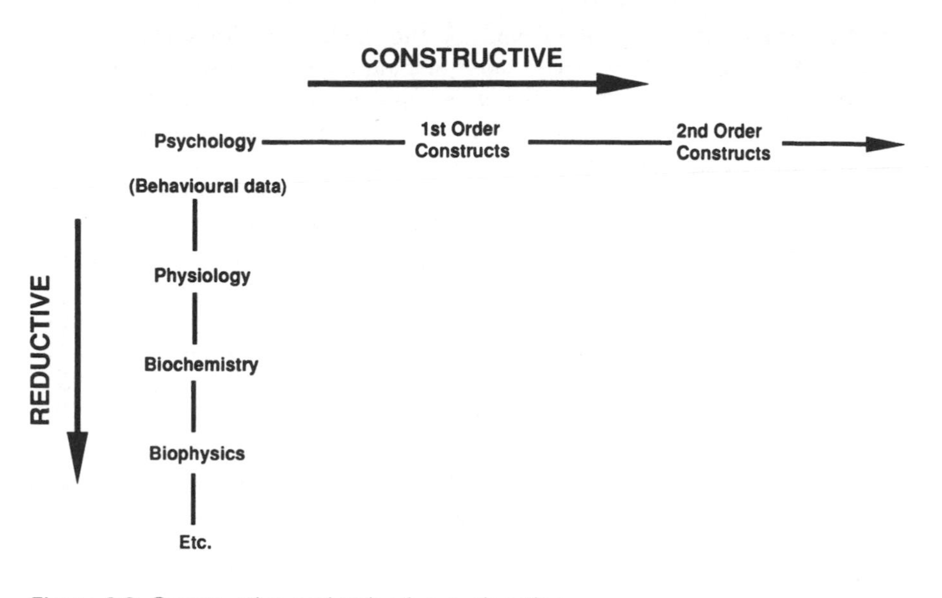

Figure 8.2 Constructive and reductive explanation
(*Source:* Marx, 1963)

Newell and Simon's (1972) theory of problem-solving, Gray's (1975) behavioural inhibition system and models of reading (Coltheart, Patterson and Marshall, 1986). Many theories in cognitive psychology take the form of flow charts; rather fewer are formulated in precise computational terms.

Certain concepts from cybernetics, such as feedback, are crucial to the understanding of behaviour, and the advent of computer simulation has led to a demystification and making precise of many previously mentalistic concepts. Currently the dominant paradigm in cognitive psychology, functionalism offers an autonomous level of description for psychology, which can take advantage of developments in artificial intelligence and be related to work in neuroscience. However, again it is only one approach among many and in particular lacks the historical dimension that a causal account might provide. Models and computer simulation are fully discussed in Chapter 10.

Neurophysiological

Mechanistic approaches can be adopted at two distinct levels. Marr (1982) distinguishes the level of representation and algorithm (just described) from that of the hardware implementation. Dennett (1971) contrasts the design stance with the physical stance. Marr used Hubel and Wiesel's work to support his theory of vision; Gray has looked to neurophysiological experiments to support his model of anxiety. In these explanations the nature of the actual physical embodiment of the process is investigated. It is equivalent to Aristotle's material cause, explaining something in terms of its composition. Some have held that this type of explanation is particularly useful for cases of malfunction. For example, neuropsychologists explain behavioural dysfunction by reference to brain damage; psychopathological disorders, such as schizophrenia, depression and Alzheimer's disease, may be explained in terms of brain chemistry. However, ultimately the distinction between function and structure is relative, as P.S. Churchland (1986) points out. There are many 'levels'; each one could be considered functional with respect to the one below and structural with respect to the one above. Neurophysiological explanations are considered in detail in Chapter 11.

Teleological

In contrast to causal explanations, teleological or purposive explanations explain a given event by reference to a future event. They are equivalent to Aristotle's final cause. Behaviour is explained as occurring in order that some future event (a goal) may be achieved. For example, 'walking for the sake of one's health' (Aristotle's example) or 'Jones crossed the road in order to buy tobacco' (Peters's, 1958, example). In contrast to causal explanations which can be pursued indefinitely, teleological explanations may be considered ultimate if they refer to natural goals. It is often advanced that evolutionary accounts are of this nature (functional explanations in yet another sense of 'functional'); for example, 'hair stands on end in order to frighten the enemy'. This is misleading if it is thought to preclude a causal account. The piece of behaviour evolved because members of the species who possessed it survived to procreate. The analogous case in ontogeny is the law of effect, which was criticised on the grounds of retroaction: how can a satisfying state of affairs strengthen a connection that has already occurred? But of course reinforcement affects the probability of the connection reoccurring in the future. Many psychologists in the past have stressed the purposive aspect of behaviour (notably McDougall, Tolman, Lashley and, in more recent times, Miller, Galanter and Pribram, 1960, who suggest a feedback loop as the basic unit of behaviour). It is particularly appropriate where a variety of means may lead to a particular end, the behaviour thus being classifiable by reference to the end rather than the means. Flexibility and adaptiveness are distinctive if not defining features of behaviour. Peters (1958), for example, has argued that purposive explanations are normally appropriate for behaviour, causal explanations only being resorted to when behaviour is abnormal in some way, such as under the influence of drugs or an obsessional compulsion. Similarly, Taylor (1964) has argued that causal explanations provide necessary but not sufficient conditions for behaviour, on the grounds that a goal may be achieved in a variety of ways. The purposiveness of human behaviour has led some to postulate that the appropriate explanation for human behaviour is to be given in terms of reasons rather than causes (see below). It is clear, however, that purposive explanations are not incompatible with causal explanations. These issues are discussed in detail in Chapter 12.

Mentalistic

A number of traditions have claimed that a radically different type of explanation is appropriate in the social sciences from that which is applicable in the physical sciences. Thus, according to the tradition of *Verstehen* in nineteenth-century Germany, psychology should pursue empathic understanding rather than causal predictive explanation. Using intuition, it aimed to explain the link between events whose correlation would otherwise be puzzling. An example is Weber's classic analysis of the link between the Protestant ethic and economic enterprise. The approach, although useful at the stage of formulating hypotheses, cannot substitute for subsequent testing.

The method of hermeneutics, first applied to the interpretation of texts, was later applied to the analysis of social behaviour. It aimed to make the meaning of an action intelligible by reference to the role played in the social context. Harré and Secord's (1972) approach in terms of rules and roles owes much to this, as does Gauld and Shotter's (1977), based on shared meanings.

In the philosophical analysis of action it has often been maintained that actions should be explained in terms of reasons, in contrast to movements which are causally explained (for example, Melden, 1961). Thus Davidson (1963) (who allows that reasons can be causes but thinks they cannot be generalised), in particular, has urged that behaviour be explained, or better 'justified', by reference to desires and beliefs in the light of which the behaviour is reasonable – a strategy known as 'rationalisation'. This intentional stance (Dennett, 1971) is based on the assumption of rationality. It depends heavily on ordinary language and conceptual analysis, the assumption being that the social sciences have merely to systematise and extend common sense. This mentalistic 'folk psychology' concentrates on semantic content. Russell (1984) makes the important point that rationalisation mistakenly takes the explanation of individual behavioural episodes as the paradigm of psychological explanation, whereas the proper concern of scientific psychology is with the determinants of competence in the species.

These idiographic approaches are considered further in Chapter 14.

SUMMARY

We have contrasted explanations, which explain events by relating them to increasingly higher order generalisations of classes of events of which they are members, with those that seek explanation by analysing the processes involved or their physical embodiment. Some explanations seek to establish associative relations between events and may explain a given event either by referring it to an antecedent (causal) or subsequent (teleological) event, or by attempting to specify relations of functional dependence in mathematically precise terms. Yet other approaches seek an understanding which is not aimed at prediction but is based on empathic intuition. These types of explanation and their associated issues are considered in more detail in the chapters which follow.

Chapter 9

The problem of the organism

THE PROBLEM

The aim of psychology might be thought to be the prediction of responses as a function of stimuli. The problem with which we are concerned in this chapter is how to conceptualise the relations between stimuli and responses. If a hierarchy of sciences is accepted, then each level may be conceived of as making assumptions about the subject matter of the science at the next level down. Thus sociology makes assumptions about psychology and psychology make assumptions about physiology. In Osgood's (1956) words, 'Behavior theory is made up of hunches about how the nervous system operates to generate the lawful relations we observe among stimuli and responses.'

A strict S–R approach, which deals only with observable stimuli and responses, has a very limited range of application. Sooner rather than later, the unpalatable fact becomes apparent that behaviour cannot be predicted on the basis of the stimulus alone. The same stimulus does not give rise to the same response, either across different individuals or on different occasions within the same individual. It becomes necessary to postulate some processes intervening between stimulus and response.

The problem is compounded by the fact that these organismic processes are not directly observable and hence must be inferred. Early behaviourists, influenced by the empiricist view that knowledge is dependent on sensory experience and the positivist requirement that science be based on observation, were concerned that any concepts postulated should be tied to observations. According to the logical positivists' verification principle, the meaningfulness of a proposition depends on being able to specify conditions for determining its truth value. Hence operational definitions, which specified such conditions for theoretical terms, were adopted in physics (Bridgman, 1927) and extended to psychology by Stevens (1939). On the strict version theoretical terms are completely reducible, and identical in meaning, to observations; according to a weaker version they must be related to observations but these do not necessarily exhaust their meaning. For example, hunger drive might be defined purely in terms of hours of food deprivation, or might be taken to refer to some internal processes not directly observed.

Wertheimer (1972) labels these positions 'prescriptive' and 'descriptive' operationism respectively. In a classic paper, MacCorquodale and Meehl (1948) distinguished two types of constructs which they termed *intervening variables* and *hypothetical constructs*. As examples of intervening variables they gave: Hull's concept of habit strength, Tolman's concept of demand, and Skinner's concepts of drive and reflex reserve (the number of responses to extinction); and as examples of hypothetical constructs: Hull's r_g and s_g, Mowrer's movement-produced stimuli, anxiety and ego. They stated that intervening variables do not go beyond what is observed, whereas hypothetical constructs postulate events, entities or processes which are not observed. Thus an intervening variable does not have, but a hypothetical construct does have, surplus meaning over and above empirical content. From this it follows that the truth of an empirical statement (namely, getting the facts right) is a necessary and sufficient condition for the truth of a statement involving an intervening variable, but a necessary but not sufficient condition for the truth of a statement containing a hypothetical construct. An intervening variable is a summary function strictly derivable from stimulus–response laws, whereas a quantifiable form of a hypothetical construct cannot be so derived. (Deutsch, 1960, objects to the distinction on the grounds that it confounds unobservability in practice with unobservability in principle, and prefers a distinction between concepts which form part of 'generalisatory' theories and those which form part of 'structural' theories, see p. 112.)

The problem of the organism – namely, how to deal with the organism conceptually – has been well described by Joynson (1970; see also Kelvin, 1956). Joynson points out that psychologists in the past have tended to evade the issue by concentrating on the stimulus. The formula R = f (S) was superseded by the formula R = f (S, O) but only lip service was paid to the organism. He discusses what he describes as two 'direct' and three 'indirect' methods for investigating the organism. The two methods perhaps somewhat misleadingly called 'direct', following Woodworth and Schlosberg (1954), are introspection and physiology. *Introspection* was the subject of Chapter 5, where we saw there were two main problems: (1) most psychological data are not accessible to conscious introspection, and (2) introspection is by no means an infallible method, being no less and in some cases more susceptible to error than other methods. *Physiology* is at worst a form of intellectual displacement activity (Bannister, 1968) and at best does not generally increase the explanatory power of a psychological theory (Deutsch, 1960) (see Chapter 11).

The three 'indirect' methods are the use of *antecedent variables*, individual differences and cybernetic models. The first of these has been favoured by behaviourists who have attempted to index hunger drive, for example, by reference to antecedent conditions of hours of food deprivation. The essential difficulty with this is that it cannot be done (see below). Koch (1959) doubts the possibility of 'unambiguous linkage' to observable variables. If explanatory power sufficient for the prediction of behaviour is to be achieved, what is postulated must go beyond a specification of externally observable antecedent conditions. The internal representation of the stimulus does not correspond to the external stimulus. The way in which a stimulus is represented by an organism depends increasingly on its past history (and the past history of two organisms is never identical). Organisms interact with and adapt to constantly changing environments. Antecedent conditions interact with one another and with organismic conditions. Attempts to pursue this approach have shown the necessity for multiple indexing of internal processes but these indices have usually been found not to agree. The non-unitary nature of the concept of hunger drive was demonstrated by N.E. Miller (1956) who showed that, as hours of food deprivation increased, tolerance to quinine in food and rate of bar-pressing continued to increase while stomach contractions and water consumption did not. Another classic case of inconsistency between indices is that of arousal.

This suggests that Joynson's second indirect method, approaching the problem through *individual differences*, may hold more promise. Eysenck (1966), for example, has attempted to reduce the error variance in conventionally designed experiments by taking into account such factors as extraversion and neuroticism. (Indeed, he has pointed out that, should these interact with the main variables under investigation, ignoring personality variables may lead to the total obscuration of the effect of experimental variables; see Chapter 14.) However, these approaches, although an improvement, have not been without their weaknesses too. Agreement about the main variables to be considered is not universal, though there is a measure of consistency between, for example, Eysenck's and Cattell's conceptualisations. It is to be doubted, in view of what was said above, whether the number of variables to be considered is finite and hence whether the programme could in fact be carried out adequately. This is an empirical matter; however, the proportion of variance accounted for in most psychological experiments (see Chapter 6) does not inspire optimism. Joynson objects that this method involves inference. But so do all the other methods and not least those labelled 'direct'. In my view this is inescapable and in the nature of the problem. All that can be sought is strong rather than weak inference.

Joynson's third indirect method is through the use of *cybernetic models*. Here psychological processes are accounted for by reference to an abstract system from whose properties the behaviour is deduced (for example, Deutsch, 1960; Newell and Simon, 1972). This too is inferential but has the advantages of power and precision without involvement in the physiological hardware (this approach was introduced in Chapter 8 and is fully discussed in Chapter 10). The problem is central to cognitive psychology where this approach has been most frequently adopted. Newell (1973), in a trenchant critique of the state of the art, bemoaned the immature, non-cumulative nature of the discipline in which issues are never settled. This he attributed both to narrowness of scope (variously described as 'phenomena driven' (Newell, 1973), 'parochialism' (Allport, 1975) and 'paradigm specificity' (Eysenck, 1977)), the adoption of a piecemeal 'divide and conquer' strategy, but also to looseness of theoretical structure. Central to this is the fact that 'uncertainty over what method the subject is using drives a substantial amount of discussion of experimental results'. 'The same human subject can adopt many (radically different) methods for the same basic task.' This leads to selective and *ad hoc* treatment of results and promotes endless debate over their interpretation.

> Much of the ability of the field continually and forever to dispute and question interpretations arises from the possibility of the subject's having done the task by a not-till-then-thought-of-method or by the set of subjects having adopted a mixture of methods so the regularities produced are not what they seemed.
>
> (Newell, 1973: 295–6)

An experimental example is provided by the work of MacLeod, Hunt and Mathews (1978), who showed that different patterns of performance in a sentence-picture verification task could be accounted for by the use of either an imaginal or a verbal strategy; see also Hunt (1980).

Averaging over methods conceals rather than reveals, providing garbage or spurious regularity. In Newell's view, behaviour is a function of the task structure, the subject's goal and what he calls the 'control structure' – the invariant structure of the processing mechanisms, which determines the possible sequences of operations and hence constrains the methods that can be employed, and without a knowledge of which the method actually used cannot be inferred. To what extent behaviour is a function of a general, invariant structure rather than situation-specific optional strategies is a matter of controversy (see Allport, 1975). Specification of the control structure is necessary in order to provide a theoretical framework with which to limit the number of alternative explanations and hence tighten the inferential web that links experimental studies.

Osgood (1956) has suggested that the evolution of behaviour theory can be seen in terms of what is assumed to happen between stimulus and reponse. Following this suggestion, we shall adopt a historical perspective for the remainder of this chapter, in order to discuss the main solutions to the problem of the organism that have been offered in the development of psychology.

FACULTY PSYCHOLOGY

In the nineteenth century a state existed in psychology which Osgood nicknames '*junk shop psychology*'. He describes the situation that pertained as one in which phenomena were attributed to faculties and motives to instincts.

There were as many explanatory devices as things to explain:

> Whenever something needed explaining, a new explanatory device was stuck inside the black box, and it rapidly became chock-full of ill-assorted, ill-digested demons. . . . And, at least for communicating with his patients, Freud had big, flat-footed super-egos stomping around on red-slippery ids, while cleverly anxious little egos tried to arbitrate.
>
> (Osgood, 1956: 168–9)

This approach had as an advantage the freedom to exercise intuition, and it is worth bearing in mind that each approach probably had a contribution to make at the stage in the history of psychology when it was actively pursued. The disadvantage was a lack of parsimony with consequent loss of explanatory power. The aim of a scientific theory should be to seek the lowest possible ratio of explanatory statements to observations. Many of the concepts were circular, lacking independent operational definitions. A more recent example, for which Skinner takes Blanshard to task (Blanshard and Skinner, 1967), is the statement that Hitler exterminated the Jews because he hated them. Explaining Hitler's behaviour in terms of his hatred is otiose if we have no independent evidence for his hatred of the Jews other than his instigation of their extermination.

SINGLE-STAGE S–R PSYCHOLOGY

As might be predicted, the reaction this provoked was a swing to the opposite extreme in the form of radical behaviourism, what Osgood dubs 'empty organism psychology'. Single-stage S–R theory permitted only functional relations between stimuli and responses. What was inside the black box it was not the business of the psychologist to investigate. This view, prominent in the 1920s and espoused by Weiss, Kantor and Watson, was also held by Skinner. At the time it was proposed, it was a healthy antidote to the loose mentalism which had preceded it. It encouraged accurate measurement of stimuli and responses, promoted attempts to establish functional laws and was fruitful in such areas as psychophysics, reaction time and conditioning.

However, it became increasingly clear that there were severe limitations. A number of objections can be made on purely theoretical grounds. In so far as no two events are identical, some theoretical abstraction is required in order to permit generalisation. Broadbent (1961) has argued that the Skinnerian approach is inadequate even for prediction, let alone explanation:

> So long as this implies that psychologists will confine themselves purely to stating what they observe, it is a genuine improvement on Hull's approach. But unfortunately one cannot confine oneself in this way for ever: all of us want to give a scientific account of behaviour in complex situations where more is involved than the frequency of some action. It is possible to make

> predictions in such situations on the basis of experiments carried out under simpler conditions: but we then often have a choice between various features of the simple one. We must therefore make theoretical assumptions in applying the results of the simple case, and as the followers of Skinner have no rules for doing this with greater caution than the Hullians, there is a danger that they may make just as rash pronouncements.
>
> (Broadbent, 1961: 182–3)

In so far as it eschews any attempt to provide reasons for the occurrence of particular stimulus–response contingencies, it fails to provide an explanation for them. Skinner has said that he does not know why food is reinforcing to a hungry animal and he does not care.

Humphrey (1951) has documented the way in which parallel objections were raised against both philosophical and psychological associationism. These may be roughly classified into those primarily concerned with the adequate treatment of stimulus, response and organismic variables respectively. It is clear on empirical grounds that there are a number of classes of phenomena which a single-stage S–R approach is inadequate to handle.

Stimuli

Stimuli are actively processed such that the internal representation of a stimulus does not correspond to its external representation. Underwood (1963) distinguished the functional from the nominal stimulus. This is illustrated in general by selective attention, and in particular by the phenomenon of blocking, in which prior training on one element of a compound stimulus will prevent subsequent conditioning to other elements (Kamin, 1968).

Any account of stimuli in discrete or absolute terms is doomed to failure, as is demonstrated by the existence of generalisation. The *Gestalt* psychologists' claim, that the critical properties of stimuli are configurational and cannot be predicted on the basis of a consideration of their component parts, has a venerable history of at least eight centuries and a philosophical counterpart in John Stuart Mill's illustration of the spectrum in which seven different colours generate white light. Dewey (1896), anticipating *Gestalt* psychology, criticised the reflex arc model, favouring instead a circuit, on the grounds that stimulus and response were artificial distinctions to be defined relative to actions, which were organised coordinations.

Animals typically respond to relative rather than absolute values of stimuli, as is demonstrated by the phenomenon of transposition (Köhler, 1918; Lashley, 1942), in which animals trained to respond to, say, the larger of two stimuli and then tested on the larger one and one even larger will respond to the larger of these two test stimuli rather than the one which exactly matches the positively rewarded stimulus during the training period. Another phenomenon which requires a similar explanation is the overlearning reversal effect (Reid, 1953), in which increased training on a discrimination facilitates learning of the reverse discrimination. This is contrary to what would be predicted on the basis of S–R theory, which asserts that training increases associative strength. Sutherland and Mackintosh (1971) explain these and other similar effects by invoking the concept of 'analyser' to refer to responding on the basis of a dimension. It is now clear that such behaviour is not the prerogative of animals possessing language.

Osgood (1956) has argued that a single-stage S–R approach is inadequate for handling phenomena which are best conceived in terms of stimulus–stimulus relations or sensory integration of some kind, such as perceptual learning and classical conditioning. Bindra (1976) has argued that all learning is of this nature.

Responses

Responses can no more be treated in absolute and discrete fashion than can stimuli. One of the arguments to which Humphrey drew attention is that reproduction of responses does not occur. Conditioned responses are not exact replicas of unconditioned responses; for example, a conditioned avoidance response will be more restricted than the original response to the shock. This is an example of the more general problem we have met that no two events are identical, with its implication that some theoretical content over and above mere association is required if statements are to be generalised and future events predicted.

In a notorious paper, Chomsky (1959) challenged Skinner's attempt to extend a functional analysis to verbal behaviour on several grounds. He pointed out that there were difficulties in deciding on the functional equivalence of responses, which certainly could not be predicted on the basis of a consideration of their physical properties. Secondly, he argued that indices of response strength such as frequency and recency could not be appropriately applied to all responses, in particular verbal responses. (This point seems arguable.) Thirdly, he drew attention to the fact that it is often difficult, if not impossible, to specify the stimulus for an utterance.

Behaviour is more commonly emitted than elicited. Apter (1973) described it as being synthesised or created. Thus recall is reconstructive (Bartlett, 1932; Bransford and Franks, 1971); speech is generated. Many psychologists have stressed the planned, purposive, rule-following characteristics of behaviour (for example, Miller *et al.*, 1960; Peters, 1958; see Chapter 12).

In Osgood's view a single-stage S–R approach is inadequate for handling behaviour that involves response–response relations or motor integration. Lashley (1951) claimed that skills such as speaking and typing involve the production of responses in such quick succession that there would not be time for stimulus control to intervene. Bindra (1976) argued, however, that these must be under the control of central processes as several lines of evidence militate against the notion of response-chaining. Flexibility and substitutability of linkage are necessary in response to environmental demands. The same act can be carried out by different movements and the same movements may occur in different acts. A simple associative theory cannot explain how the same response may be preceded or succeeded by different responses on different occasions, as in double alternation. Moreover, a number of workers have failed to obtain practice effects for sequences of movements repeatedly stimulated (Pinneo, 1966; Delgado, 1965). Pinneo electrically stimulated sites in the brain stem and cerebellar nuclei responsible for the production of specific movements. Sequences of movements could be activated by successively stimulating the sites responsible for each movement, but this never led to a situation in which stimulation of the site responsible for the first movement would trigger production of the rest of the sequence.

The organism

Woodworth (1918) put back the organism into the stimulus–response formula and Hebb (1949) postulated a central autononomous process. It is now generally accepted that stimuli modulate continuous activity in the nervous system. Thus the appropriate formula is R = f (S x O).

The mediating internal structure is inherited in so far as all learning is superimposed on an existing inherited structure and modifies an existing organisation (Lorenz, 1966), and to the extent that there are built-in behavioural processes: reflexes, instinctive behaviour patterns, imprinting, maturation and species-specific predispositions; for example, for language (Lenneberg, 1967), or differential preparedness to learn contingencies (Thorndike, 1935; Seligman, 1970).

To a greater extent the internal structure is the result of learning. Organisms are continually adapting to changing environments. How an organism responds to a stimulus depends on its past experience. This has two important implications. First, it means that the relationship between stimuli and responses is dynamic rather than static, changing over time. Secondly, since no two organisms have the same past experience, these relations will differ between individuals. These two facts pose the most fundamental challenges to psychology.

Shorter-term changes are usually described as motivational. Humphrey (1951) pointed out that some account must be taken of 'direction' in addition to associative strength. This became apparent to the Würzburg psychologists, who proposed that thinking was a function of determining tendencies as well as association. For example, whether 'six' or 'eight' is given in response to the stimulus 'two and four' depends on whether an instruction was given to add or to multiply. The fact that a rat's hunger as well as its knowledge of the maze is relevant to predicting its performance in it was acknowledged by Hull in his neo-behaviouristic theory of learning which included drive and habit strength as intervening variables. De Bono (1967) remarks that the salesman may modify the probabilities of responses not by altering habit hierarchies but by manipulating motivation.

The most obvious class of phenomena that an S–R approach is unable to handle is symbolic processes. The problem of describing unobservables is one of the greatest weaknesses of behaviour theory. Broadbent, who considers himself a behaviourist, writes (1961): 'It is almost universally admitted now that even the behaviour of rats requires us to think of mechanisms operating purely inside their brains, and revealing themselves only indirectly in action.'

Neo-behaviourists admitted that even a phenomenon as simple as avoidance conditioning required the postulation of mediating processes. In a typical experiment, the first stage involves the conditioning of an escape response to shock. In the second stage, a neutral stimulus such as a buzzer is associated with the shock but no escape is possible. In the third stage, presentation of the buzzer alone is tested and an escape response occurs. The problem for the S–R theorist is to explain how the response is produced in stage 3 when it has not previously been elicited by that stimulus. Neo-behaviourists solved the problem by postulating mediating responses and stimuli which they supposed were elicited by the shock in stage 1, became conditioned to the buzzer in stage 2 and served to elicit the escape response in stage 3.

NEO-BEHAVIOURIST MEDIATION THEORY

It seems to be clear then that something must be put back in the black box. The question is what. Parsimony dictates that as little as possible be put back; adequacy demands sufficient explanatory power. The minimum replacement would be intervening variables as employed by Hull and Tolman. But as these are merely summary statements of observed relations between stimuli and responses, and completely reducible to these, they represent in fact no advance. Hypothetical constructs have additional meaning over and above observed relations but they are vague and it is not clear whether they are observable in practice or not, nor what observations could be made to improve them. There are also difficulties in anchoring these reliably (N.E. Miller, 1956) and validly (Joynson, 1970), as was discussed above.

Most neo-behaviourists opted for postulating internal stimuli and responses (represented by lower-case 's's and 'r's) which were unobservable but subject to the same laws as external observable stimuli and responses (indicated by upper-case 'S's and 'R's). Theorists who favoured such an approach were Mowrer (1954) and Osgood (1953). They claimed that external stimuli elicited internal symbolic responses which gave rise to internal stimuli which served to mediate external responses. The application of this scheme to the explanation of conditioning is shown in Figure 9.1. Osgood (1953) explains that the representational mediation process, r_m, is representational

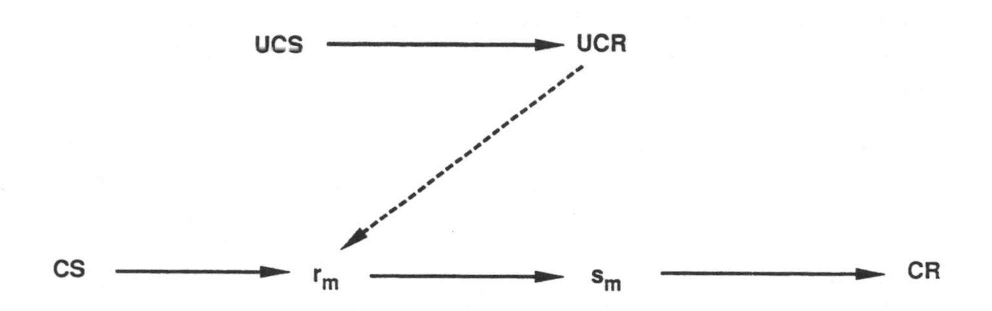

Figure 9.1 Formation of a representational mediation process
(*Source:* Osgood, 1956)

in that it is a fractional component of the unconditioned response, UCR, that would be elicited by the unconditioned stimulus, UCS; it is mediational because it produces self-stimulation, s_m, which is capable of eliciting a variety of instrumental acts, CR. Osgood (1963) and Bindra (1976) postulated three-stage theories (see Figure 9.2).

Such theoretical apparatus could be invoked to explain avoidance conditioning (for example, May, 1948), the combination of paths learned separately when occasion demands (for example, Hull, 1935), reversal shifts (for instance, Kendler and Kendler, 1962) and vocabulary learning (for instance, Mowrer, 1954; Osgood, 1953; 1963).

However, Broadbent (1961) has drawn attention to a number of difficulties with the approach. First, covert responses do not in fact obey the same laws as overt responses. Overt responses can be reinforced by many rewards, but covert responses only by the specific reward to which they correspond. For example, an r_g corresponding to drinking can only be reinforced by water and not by food: a thirsty rat does not go to where it was last fed but to where it found water. Lawrence (1950) found that it was easier to learn to change an overt response to an already learned internal response than to a new internal response. Thus covert responses may be more difficult to learn than overt responses. Secondly, there is a danger of identifying covert responses with too peripheral reactions – Wyckoff's (1952) observing responses or Watson's (1914) laryngeal movements. Thirdly, statements about unobservables can only be made by inference and hence demand caution. As we have seen, this is an inescapable problem. Finally, there is the difficulty of avoiding ambiguity in the description of internal processes. This is the reason why Skinner objects to introspection; namely, there is inadequate knowledge of, and control over, the conditioning history of the use of terms referring to private states.

Fodor (1965) rejects the application of mediation theories to language, denying that meaning could be a mediating response, on account of the

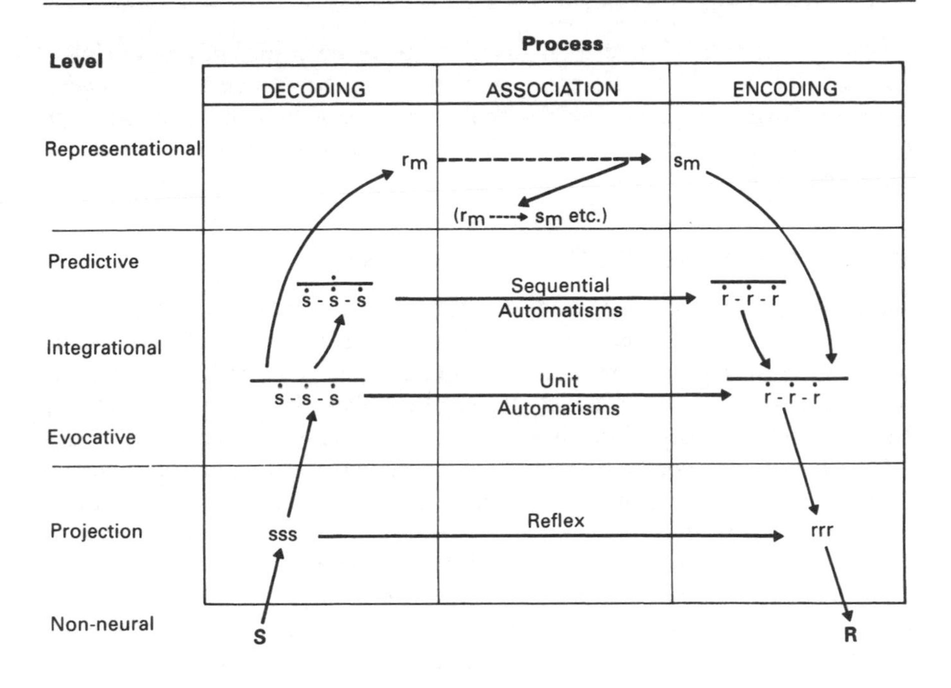

(a)

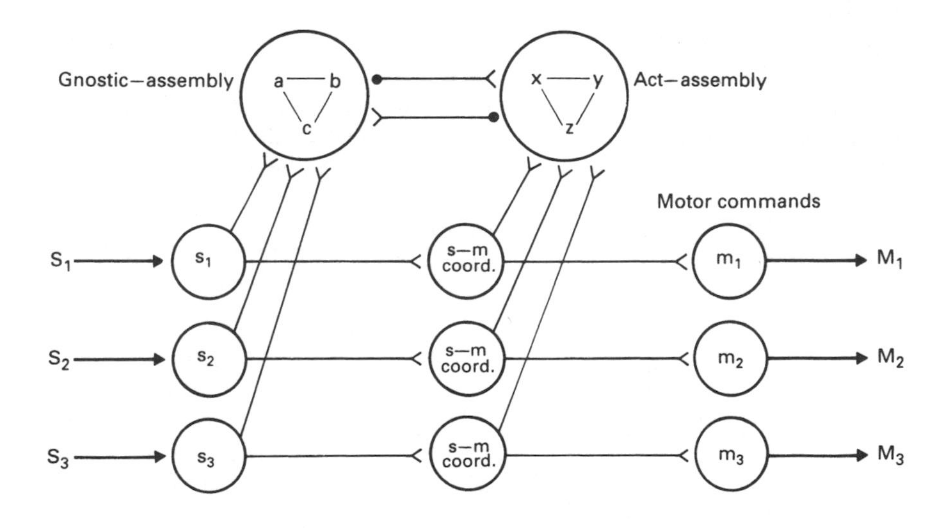

(b)

Figure 9.2 Examples of three-stage theories: (a) Osgood (1963)*; (b) Bindra (1976)

following dilemma. If mediation theories are to be sufficiently powerful to account for linguistic reference, a one-to-one correspondence between mediating response and external stimulus must be assumed; but in this case they are indistinguishable from single-stage models and hence open to the same objections.

INFORMATION-PROCESSING APPROACHES

The main developments since mediation theory have been cognitive approaches based on an information-processing analogy. These have borrowed ideas from information theory, cybernetics and computer science. A problem with early formulations of cognitive concepts such as Piaget's and Bartlett's schemata or Bruner's and Gregory's hypotheses was their ill-defined nature. As Bindra (1976) has shown, cognitive theories are very inadequate when it comes to prediction. Their transformational, mediation processes are not specified; hence they remain descriptive rather than explanatory, *ad hoc* and untestable. They tend to be plausible but imprecise, whereas S–R theories tend to be precise but implausible. A contribution towards greater precision in cognitive theories has been made by the employment of terms and concepts from the disciplines mentioned above. A seminal approach in this direction was the book by Miller, Galanter and Pribram (1960), *Plans and the Structure of Behavior*, in which the reflex model of behaviour was rejected, a single level of analysis was considered inadequate and the feedback loop (which they called the TOTE, an acronym for test–operate–test–exit – see Figure 9.3) was suggested as the basic unit of behaviour. More recently, Allport (1980) has argued that the main contribution of artificial intelligence to psychology has been the provision of a theoretical notation with which to specify possible mechanisms, claiming that 'the advent of artificial intelligence is the single most important development in the history of psychology'.

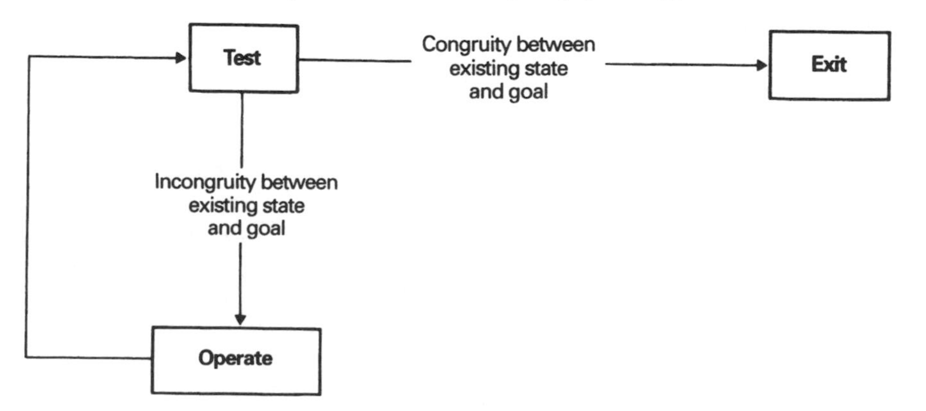

Figure 9.3 The TOTE unit
(*Source:* Miller, Galanter and Pribram, 1960: 26) (Reprinted with permission of the publisher. All rights reserved.)

A number of papers have attempted reconciliations between cognitive and S–R theories. Spence (1950) suggested that the difference was merely one of emphasis. Thus S–R theorists, in contrast to cognitive theorists, concentrated on learning rather than perception and thinking, sought antecedent conditions in the past rather than the present, examined the effect of external rather than internal variables, viewed the organism as passive rather than active, attributed behaviour to nurture rather than to nature, stressed analysis rather than organisation and preferred explanations in terms of S–R rather than S–S relations. Millenson (1967) has gone so far as to claim that the languages of S–R theory and information theory flow charts are in fact isomorphic and intertranslatable. To the extent that any flow chart represents a linear sequence of events this is a reasonable suggestion, and Suppes (1969) has in fact demonstrated it formally. However, there will be some relations in the flow chart that will be obscured in the S–R description, and the flow chart is superficial and needs to become increasingly detailed. Like Spence, Millenson suggests that the differences are more apparent than real and principally reflect differences in emphasis and interest. S–R language is preferable when dealing with simple sequences, response contingencies or the acquisition of units; information theory descriptions are preferable for more complex contingencies. However, the view that S–R and information-processing approaches are not significantly different is one that most psychologists would reject. For the contrary view that they constitute different paradigms see Lachman, Lachman and Butterfield (1979), Gholson and Barker (1985) and the discussion in Chapter 7 (pp. 96–8). In the next chapter we turn to a more detailed consideration of the information-processing approach.

Chapter 10

Models and computer simulation

MODELS

What are models?

In Chapter 8 it was pointed out that the term 'model' has been used in a number of different ways, and three meanings were distinguished: (1) as synonymous with 'theory'; (2) as inferior to a theory on account of reduced scope and associated confidence; (3) as a particular type of theory, which seeks to explain phenomena by reference to an abstract system or mechanism. One of the foremost proponents of such an approach in psychology has been Deutsch (1960) who sees its advantages as compared with those of the descriptive approach as being qualitative rather than quantitative, possessing rigour rather than precision and logical cogency rather than mathematical formulation.

The essential feature of a model is the application of one (better understood and developed) system to another (less well understood and developed) system. Chapanis's (1961) definition of models was 'representations, or likenesses, of certain aspects of complex events, structures or systems, made by using symbols or objects which in some way resemble the thing being modelled'. In some cases a model may be an exemplar of a theory (Apter, 1973), or a representation or embodiment of a theory (Frijda, 1967). A model and a theory are not necessarily identical as is shown by the fact that the former may contain some aspects which are irrelevant to the latter. (For a more technical treatment of the relation between model and theory see Braithwaite, 1953.)

The popularity of physical and mechanical models in science is due to the progress in the understanding of phenomena to which their employment has led. According to Radford and Burton (1974) the first scientific model was Anaximander's map of the world. However, a plan of the town of Çatal Hüyük existed as early as 6200 BC. Later well-known examples of scientific models include Harvey's hydraulic metaphor for the circulation of the blood, Rutherford's planetary metaphor for the atom and Sherrington's telephone exchange metaphor for the central nervous system.

Psychology has been no exception, borrowing models from most other disciplines. Freud and the *Gestalt* psychologists borrowed from physics, the ethologists from biology, Estes from mathematics and Piaget from logic; cognitive psychologists have borrowed successively from cybernetics, communication theory, computer science and linguistics, and social psychologists from drama.

The borrowings have varied in nature from metatheories providing basic frameworks to piecemeal usage of specific concepts. In general terms, different psychological approaches can be characterised by reference to their preferred model. Wiggins *et al.* (1971), for example, classify personality theories according to their model of people as animals (in particular rats; see, for example, Skinner), information processors (in particular scientists; for example, Kelly), machines (in particular computers; for instance, cognitive psychology), or actors (for example, Goffman). A dominant contrast has been between people as active persons (humanistic psychology) or as passive machines (behaviourism) (see Fransella, 1975; Joynson, 1980; and Chapter 13). Examples of borrowings of more specific concepts are hydraulics (Lorenz, 1950), vectors (Lewin, 1951), filters (Broadbent, 1957) and feedback loops (Miller, Galanter and Pribram, 1960). A particularly popular form of modelling in recent years has been computer simulation. Accordingly, we shall devote the first part of this chapter to a consideration of models in general and the remainder to a consideration of computer models in particular.

Types of models

Models can be distinguished both in terms of what is modelled, and of how it is modelled. In illustrating the first of these, Lachman (1960) distinguished models of directly observed events from models of theoretical ideas. An example of the former is the treatment of perception as if it were a conditioned response (Howes and Solomon, 1951), an example of the latter the treatment of r_g (Hull's fractional anticipatory goal response) as if it were a conditioned response (for example, Spence, 1951). It is also pointed out that more checks are provided by the data in the former than the latter case.

The form of a model can also be various. At the most concrete level there are models which are mechanical, what Chapanis (1961) describes as 'replicas'. Examples in psychology are Grey Walter's (1953) 'tortoises' (machines which imitated reflex behaviour and conditioned responses) or Ashby's (1948) homeostat. Mechanical analogies can also be employed at a more abstract level as in the case of flow charts. Some models are predominantly pictorial, such as Broadbent's (1957) filter theory, and possibly Lewin's (1951) topological vector theory of personality, of which it was said that it was a calculus that did not calculate (Braithwaite, 1953). Symbolic models, which allow more powerful inferences to be made, may be verbal in form, as in the neo-behaviourist use of conditioning as a pretheoretic model (see Kendler and Spence, 1971), or mathematical as in Estes's (1959) mathematical learning theory, which treats the stimulus as a population of elements to which statistical sampling theory can be applied, and learning as a stochastic process to which probability theory can be applied. These different types suggest that models may serve a range of functions, to which we now turn.

Evaluation of models

Advantages

At the simplest level a model, by representing the phenomenon to be explained in a new way, may *aid understanding*. This may be the result of the model being better understood and/or more familiar (Young, 1951). A model may reduce complexity by eliminating certain aspects from consideration. The didactic function of models is exemplified in Broadbent's filter theory, which provides a convenient mnemonic for the integration of a body of data and a crutch pending the formulation of a more rigorous theory.

In so far as a model provides a new way of looking at things, it may serve a heuristic function of *generating new hypotheses to test*. For example, viewing people as communication channels suggests the testing of capacity limitations. A more specific example, from a concrete realisation of a model, comes from Grey Walter's (1953) 'tortoises', which produced behaviour that had not been predicted. In this way models may provide a framework for experimentation and here serve a function common to that of theories proper. They have the advantage that they facilitate consideration of the possible as well as the actual.

How explicitly this can be done depends on the nature of the model. Braithwaite (1953) claimed that the essence, and hence power, of a model lies in its inference rules rather than in its symbolism. As Newell (1973) observed, many flow charts in cognitive psychology are insufficient for the performance of tasks. He suggests that a knowledge of the control structure (the invariant structure of the processing mechanism) yields explicit programming problems for the achievement of particular tasks, enabling inferences to be made about the methods used. Other cases where the model is sufficiently formulated to be used to interpret a theory or make specific predictions are mathematical learning theory and the behaviourists' application of the laws of conditioning to the explanation of other behavioural phenomena.

Thus, models may aid in the *evaluation of theories*. They may serve both to examine the logical consistency and completeness of a theory and its practical feasibility. This is particularly so in the case of computer programs, an early example of which was Bush and Mosteller's (1955) 'stat rats', where implications can be worked out quickly and accurately.

If represented in concrete form, models may assist at a practical level in the *learning of skills* (for example, simulated cockpits) and in engineering design.

Finally, models provide *amusement*. 'Scientists often entertain models because their models entertain them', as Chapanis (1961) observed, citing Hull as an example.

Thus models have a number of points of recommendation, whether logical or psychological. Braithwaite (1962), after discussing the issue, concludes that the advantages are all of the latter kind.

Disadvantages

In that a model is necessarily a partial and imperfect representation, the danger of *invalid inference* is ever-present. 'The price of a model is eternal vigilance.' There will always be areas of non-correspondence. There is a temptation to overgeneralise inappropriately from aspects of the model which do not apply to the phenomenon being modelled. The point is brought home by recognition of the fact that there are many possible models of a given phenomenon: the same end may be achieved by a variety of means. A possible explanation is not necessarily either *the*, or the best, explanation. Perhaps because the ultimate test of models is often considered to be usefulness rather than truth, they are insufficiently subjected to test.

There are specific respects in which a model may be *inaccurate*; namely, the *constants* and the *relations between variables*. The latter may be the result of alterations in scale. There is also the problem of the validity of concepts. Examples in psychology are Estes's parameter theta, estimated from the data, and factors extracted in multivariate analysis. The validity of these may be merely mathematical and not psychological.

Finally, if theorising is *wasteful of energy*, as Skinnerians suppose, how much more so must this be true of modelling? The answer to this hinges on whether the psychological advantages of modelling justify their use.

Criteria for evaluation

To some extent, the criteria for evaluating models are similar to those for evaluating theories. However, one criterion of particular relevance to models is that of *deployability*: the extent to which the terms or properties of a model can be applied to the phenomenon modelled. (Thus porridge is not a very good model of the brain. How much better is a computer?)

Secondly, the *scope* or range of data covered will also be a relevant consideration in the evaluation of a model. An increase in deployability will tend to lead to an increase in scope but the reverse is not the case: an increase in scope need not necessarily entail an increase in deployability.

Thirdly, *precision* is a dimension on which models differ greatly. Current psychology notwithstanding, those which enable unequivocal derivation of consequences to be made and hence maximise testability are to be preferred. It is lamentable that, in psychology, 'model' has tended to be used in the sense of approximation or semi-formalised theory rather than in the sense of an interpretation of the theory's calculus. It would be better to call the former 'a *theoruncula* or (affectionately) a *theorita*', as Braithwaite (1962) suggests.

It was suggested in Chapter 8 that the emphasis in the case of models is likely to be on usefulness rather than complete truth. So in the final analysis the question is whether the model serves its heuristic function and is fruitful in leading to new formulations, new predictions and new discoveries. It is not difficult to see the blind alleys that resulted from many of psychology's less appropriate borrowings; for example, from physics (field theory turned out not to apply to the brain), information theory ('information' is used in very different senses in communications engineering and the psychology of communication), and linguistics (there are good reasons for holding that the linguist's constraints and criteria differ from those of the language user). One that looks as though it holds rather more promise is computer science, to which we now turn.

COMPUTER MODELS

Computer simulation, or *artificial intelligence* as it is generally known, has become increasingly popular in psychology over the past thirty years, particularly in cognitive psychology where the computational theory of mind and functionalist philosophy (see p. 32) have become dominant, but also in other areas – for example, personality, psychopathology and social psychology. Although initially a distinction was made between artificial intelligence as the attempt to program machines to behave intelligently no matter how, and computer simulation where the aim is to mimic the methods used by humans, now the distinction has become blurred and the label 'artificial intelligence' more widespread. Apter (1973) suggests that simulations may arise from three sources: (1) psychological theories, such as Colby's (1963) attempt to simulate Freudian theory; (2) behavioural data, either introspections or performance responses – for example, the simulation of problem-solving in symbolic logic and cryptarithmetic by Newell and Simon (1972); or (3) pure artificial intelligence, such as programs to play chess (for instance, Newell and Simon, 1972), draughts (Samuel, 1959), or prove geometry theorems (Gelernter, 1959). Most work has been done on vision, language understanding, knowledge representation and problem-solving. For detailed reviews see Boden (1987), Charniak and McDermott (1985), Waltz (1982) and Winston (1984). The computational analogy is part of the metaview which treats people as information-processing systems. On the *computational theory of mind* (Fodor, 1980; Pylyshyn, 1980; Johnson-Laird, 1983a), mental activity is computation: mental processes consist of operations performed on symbolic representations, the formal manipulation of abstract symbols according to rules. Searle (1980) has distinguished *strong AI*, the realist view that a properly programmed computer is literally a mind (it has mental states and can, for example, think and understand), from *weak AI*, the instrumentalist view that a computer is a powerful and useful tool for psychological theorising.

Certain fears are associated with the employment of mechanistic analogies in the explanation of human behaviour. What is involved in the claim that the mind is a machine? In Chapter 3 two senses of mind were distinguished: (1) conscious experience, and (2) the system that governs behaviour. It is this latter sense that is intended here. To say that the mind is a machine is merely to say that there is a system according to which it works, whose rules can be stated in principle. Turing conjectured that any effective procedure is computable on a universal Turing machine. It may also imply that the principles which govern physical phenomena can be extended to mental phenomena (cf. Gregory, 1961; Sutherland, 1970). Scriven (1960) claims that 'machine' is a term, like 'science' or 'truth', which can be applied correctly in typical cases but not explicitly defined. If the term 'machine' is applied to living systems, it may lose its main classificatory function (Gregory, 1961). There is a danger that explicit definitions will presuppose answers to questions to be asked or be either too imprecise or too restrictive. For example, making predictability of behaviour a defining property of a machine would rule out roulette wheels and radium-driven randomisers (Scriven, 1960). Boden has ably defended the computational metaphor in psychology against the charge of dehumanisation, arguing that the humanist's rejection of mechanism is partly the result of an impoverished image of machine (Boden, 1978), and that

> a psychology that looks to machines for some of its central concepts need not be crudely mechanistic in character, nor inhumanly reductionist in type. On the contrary, the computational approach in psychology stresses (and helps to explain) important features of the mind, such as purpose and subjectivity, which many psychological theories have ignored – or even denied.
>
> (Boden, 1979: 112)

In what sense, then, is the brain a computer? It is important to stress the level at which the analogy is intended, and the distinction between software and hardware. The software is the abstract level, in this case the program governing the system; the hardware is the concrete level, what the system is made of in material terms, in this case perhaps neuroprotein or silicon chips. The level at which the analogy holds is that of the software. The hardware does indeed have aspects in common, but it is not this that is meant but rather that the workings of the mind can be likened to a program. The ultimate aim is to construct programs whose fit is so good that they can be considered theories of behaviour. It may well be that the superiority of this model is due to the level of abstraction at which the analogy is employed.

Comparison of brains and computers

What kind of computer is the brain? What kind of brain is the computer (Radford and Burton, 1974)?

Similarities

First, both consist of networks of connections which operate in *binary* fashion: semi-conductors may conduct or insulate electrical current and neurons fire or do not fire. But Wooldridge (1963) has pointed out that this applies only to the axon: the body of the neuron works according to a summative principle and the threshold for firing may be affected by chemical and electrical changes. So it depends what level is considered: at lower and higher levels than the axon, functioning could be described as summative rather than all-or-none. Moreover, connectionist computers may embody continuously varying levels of activity.

It might be argued that both computers and brains are predominantly *digital* in nature. Representation in digital machines (for example, most computers) is symbolic and discrete, whereas in analogue machines (an example of which is a slide rule) it is direct and continuously variable. However, digital computers can be made to function in an analogue fashion by making steps sufficiently small. Likewise, the nervous system is analogue in some aspects, for instance, endocrine secretion. Wooldridge (1963) suggests that it is unlikely, on the basis of logical considerations and empirical measures (for example, EEG), that there are any purely digital circuits in the brain. Gregory (1961; 1970) has argued that in certain respects the brain (particularly the perceptual system) is analogue, on the grounds of speed of operation and type of errors. Analogue machines have faster transmission rates but limited precision (being subject to random error and dependent on the precision of their construction); digital machines have no limits to their precision in principle but can be wildly wrong. Adaptive behaviour requires fast approximation: it is important to know (and quickly) that an object is, for example, a lion so that effective action can be taken, but its exact proportions are of less importance.

Both are *electrical* in nature though the brain is also chemical. However, these hardware similarities are without significance in the present context. Moreover, the differences between neural networks and electronic circuitry are more obvious (cf. von Neumann, 1958).

More importantly, both are *information processors*, in particular symbol manipulators. Both have input and output mechanisms, storage systems and hierarchies of programs. Both perform complex operations by breaking them down into a series of small steps.

A second broad similarity is *similarity of output* or product. Computers and brains can achieve the same ends (for instance, the solution of problems).

However, this is more pertinent to the goal of pure artificial intelligence; that is, to produce the same results as could be achieved by the human but usually much more quickly and efficiently, not necessarily and probably not by the same means. The goal of computer simulation, in contradistinction, is to mimic the process as well as the product. Not only the end but also the means must be the same. The aim is to represent the operations in a program in such a way that it can be considered a theory of behaviour. It is these software similarities that are of importance. What of the differences?

Differences

How far can the analogy be stretched? In what way is it misleading?

We have already noted the marked differences in *hardware* between brains and computers. These differences in themselves are relatively unimportant but they may be indicative of more significant implications.

Computers are predominantly *digital* in type of processing whereas, as Gregory (1970) and others have argued, brains are *analogue* in important respects. Dreyfus (1979) has attempted to base the claim that strong simulation of brain processes is impossible on such a distinction. Against this, Sutherland (1974) has pointed out that it is not proven, and indeed is in fact false, that analogue processes cannot be represented on digital computers. Furthermore, at the level relevant for understanding the overall working of the brain, digital may be more important than analogue processes. In some cases the processing of analogical information may be rather poor with continuously variable input being coded discretely; for example, short-term memory (G.A. Miller, 1956) and categorical perception of consonant phonemes (Liberman *et al.*, 1957).

In conventional computers knowledge is generally rule-based and *explicit* but it is often *implicit* in humans.

Computers have a high degree of precision and accuracy but are peculiarly (excessively to the novice programmer) sensitive to *error* (a small change in input may have a large effect on output). By contrast, brains approximate but are relatively insensitive to error at least at a fine level.

Computers generally *function sequentially* (though they can be and increasingly are being programmed to function in parallel), whereas brains typically exhibit *parallel processing*. This suggests a reason why humour, insight, creativity and aesthetic appreciation (activities particularly suited to parallel processing in that associations are formed between previously unconnected lines of thought) seem distinctive of the human brain. Parallel processing enables much faster processing but, at the level of individual elements, *speed of processing* in the brain is much slower than in computers.

Some of these differences have important implications for psychological simulation. Mathematical computation is easy to program on a computer but difficult for a human, whereas the reverse is true of pattern perception. This suggests that the processes employed may be essentially different.

Memory is another function where there are obvious apparent differences. In the human, memory is necessarily selective and essentially constructive, whereas in the computer it is typically reproductive. Storage and processing tend to be separated whereas in the brain they are inextricably mixed. Human memory is messier and less reliable but more flexible (Wilding, 1978). The data bases of current computers are severely limited, while even the solution of simple everyday problems requires much knowledge. One problem arises from the fact that there is no definable set of primitive facts from which all knowledge can be deduced, others from the need to organise and retrieve information. Severe problems of programming are raised by internal knowledge, strategies and the whole question of past experience. Forgetting is different too. In the computer, memories can be erased, whereas this is rarely so in the brain; forgetting is more likely to be due to retrieval failure (for example, Bekerian and Bowers, 1983). Neisser (1963) suggests that computers are more docile in that there is greater control over what is learned and what is forgotten. Humans are not so easily able to select or avoid change.

Although an adequate simulation of *learning* poses one of the most serious programming challenges, the objection that computers cannot learn or modify their own programming as a result of past experience cannot be defended. Samuel's (1959) program for draught-playing improves its performance by storing and using information from past games. Sussman's (1975) program HACKER, which writes programs for solving problems, learns to do better by possessing a general knowledge of the kind of mistakes that can occur and how to deal with them. It remembers what went wrong in the past and avoids it in future. Lenat's (1983) EURISKO can learn new heuristics as well as concepts. Computers can learn by optimising probability weights and other internal parameters, but important learning in humans involves changes in the structure of processing itself. It is difficult to simulate Piagetian accommodation adequately, and the cumulative and ordered sequence of cognitive development in which natural learning occurs is lacking in the computer which is not dependent on maturational sequence (Neisser, 1963).

It is often said that computers can only do what they are programmed to do. It is true that computers follow instructions and that all their behaviour is *predictable* in principle, but from this it does not follow that all their behaviour either could be or was predicted in fact. Programs often surprise their programmers, as in man–machine dialogues (for example, Colby *et al.*, 1971). The Logic Theorist of Newell *et al.* (1957) found an original proof for one of the theorems from Russell and Whitehead's *Principia Mathematica*, and Lenat's (1982) AM discovered a minor and previously unknown theorem about the class of maximally divisible numbers. There is no reason why computers cannot produce unpredicted and *novel* results. These are more likely to arise from quantity rather than quality of processing as current computers tend to be poor at complex analogical reasoning. It is more difficult to achieve controlled imprecision than precision in a computer. The reverse might be said to be true of humans.

The limitations in *complexity* of current computers can hardly be held against the analogy, as what is at issue is whether computers can in principle be programmed to carry out tasks in the same way as humans. Already there is an impressive list of achievements that were thought a priori impossible. These include: holistic perception; the creative use of language; musical composition; translation from one language to another by way of language-neutral semantic representation; planning action in broad and sketchy fashion, the details being decided only in execution; and distinguishing between different species of emotional reaction according to the psychological context of the subject. In general, the limits of artificial intelligence and simulation cannot be specified in advance.

Purposiveness is fairly easy to accommodate in machines, from the simple examples of thermostats and guided missiles to programs where goals are pursued by a variety of means, such as GPS (General Problem Solver, Newell and Simon, 1961). Hence purposiveness cannot be a basis for distinguishing brains from computers (see also Chapter 12). Neisser (1963) indeed observes that machines are in general more persistent than humans.

Brains are part of biological organisms, composed of living tissue. They are open systems constantly fighting the second law of thermodynamics. They are motivated by self-preservation and show a certain amount of plasticity in response to damage (as in restitution of function), though ultimately they wear out. Computers might be considered rational and brains selfish. For the latter, the pleasure principle precedes the reality principle (Neisser, 1963). Stimulus information is assimilated largely with reference to needs; human thinking is intimately associated with emotions.

Singlemindedness has been thought a distinctive characteristic of machines, whereas almost all human behaviour simultaneously serves a multiplicity of motives (Neisser, 1963). For example, a chess player's desire to win may be motivated by hope of success or fear of failure (either private or public), intellectual or aesthetic pleasure, aggression or affiliation, or any combination of these. It could never be that of the chess program's: merely to win. Most artificial intelligence programs have a single overall end but a few have been developed with the aim of simulating the multidimensional nature of human motivation. For example, ARGUS (Reitman, 1965) embodies various goals which compete for computational resources available, priority being given to the one which, in the current situation, is most strongly activated. In this case there are conflicting motives but only one functioning system.

It is often advanced that a distinctive feature of the brain which the computer necessarily lacks is *consciousness*. However, as became clear in Chapter 4, the resolution of this depends on an adequate account of the nature of consciousness not yet in existence. Boden (1979) suggests that the charge is misplaced, that no sense can be made of computers seeing, wanting, feeling or knowing (even if true): computer simulations are theories whose aim is to understand and explain rather than to mimic or duplicate experience and behaviour. It is no more to be expected of a psychological theory that it see or feel than 'of a chemical theory that it fizz if put in a test tube'.

Boden (1978) claims that one respect in which computers are lacking is in the possession of intrinsic interests (implied by a strong sense of moral dignity). Intrinsic interests pertain to the individual and cannot be explained further in purposive terms though they could be in evolutionary or physiological terms. The purposes of machines are not intrinsic to them but derive from those of the programmer. But this is due to their artificial rather than their mechanistic nature. Computers are dependent on brains in a way in which the reverse is not true. Computers are made and operated on by people. Who made and operates on people?

Thus certain differences between brains and computers stem from the distinction between natural and artificial machines. In other cases the differences may be more a matter of degree rather than kind. Despite the gaps, the similarities are sufficiently significant for the analogy to be mutually fruitful for artificial intelligence and psychological theory. It is the deficiencies of computers (lack of cognitive development, an emotional base and subtlety of decision-making) rather than their superiorities that are the true cause of humans' fear of them (Neisser, 1963).

Evaluation of computer models

Strengths

The advantages of computer simulation are related to those of functional or mechanistic theories, of which they form a special case. Perhaps the most important of these is the provision of descriptions, and hence understanding and explanation of *processes*, the fundamental aim of psychology. This focus on process provides descriptions at an appropriate level of analysis for psychology. Allport (1980), who regards artificial intelligence as 'the single most important development in the history of psychology', considers its main contribution to be the provision of a theoretical notation with which to specify possible mechanisms. Marr (1982) in fact distinguished two levels of explanation distinct from that of the hardware implementation or physical realisation. The first he confusingly called the computational level. This provides an abstract analysis of the task in information-processing terms – what is computed and why; for example, he (perhaps controversially) described the task of vision as the derivation of properties of the world from images of it. This is similar to Chomsky's concept of competence, which provides an analysis of the capacities of the organism, and Newell and Simon's task analysis. Marr's second level is that of algorithm and process, a description of the actual operations by which the computation is effected, how it is done.

Many theorists have thought that computational psychology offers the promise of theories at a *high level of generality*. Marr stressed the importance of a top-down approach in psychology. Newell (1973) claimed it would result in a disciplined theoretical framework by providing an account of the control structure or invariant structure of the processing mechanism. This is similar to Pylyshyn's concept of the 'functional architecture', the basic, fixed processing operations which are 'cognitively impenetrable' – that is, not subject to influence by knowledge, beliefs, desires and goals but independent of environmental content. To what extent such a psychology is feasible is a matter of controversy. These 'thought experiments prosthetically regulated by computers' (Dennett, 1979) may reveal what is necessary, what is possible and what is impossible; they can provide existence proofs and sufficiency conditions. Others (for example, Fodor, 1981) have considered the utilisation of representations to be particularly suited to modelling the intensionality of behaviour.

Computer simulation demands *precision*, thus enabling processes to be made explicit and theories to be formulated unambiguously. In this respect it has the advantage over verbal theories. Computational psychology in its attention to theoretical detail has provided a lasting contribution to psychological science in the form of a standard of rigour and clarity on which there is no going back (Boden, 1988). It assists in *testing the feasibility of theories* both by examining logical consistency and empirical adequacy. At worst, it highlights theoretical lacunae; at best, it helps fill them (Boden, 1988). On the one hand, it checks the specification of the model: it uncovers implications and derives predictions, revealing whether or not they are as intended. Consequences are often unforeseen. On the other hand, running the program shows whether or not it works and whether it is sufficient to generate the predicted behaviour. For example, the computer simulation by Rochester *et al.* (1956) of Hebb's theory revealed inadequacies which led to Milner's (1957) reformulations incorporating inhibitory (in addition to excitatory) connections. If the program is sufficient to generate the behaviour, it is a candidate for a theory or, more strictly, can be seen as instantiating a theory. By varying the conditions under which it is run, empirical investigation can be extended and the effect of variables examined (for example, Gelernter *et al.*, 1960).

This may result in new insights being gained into the process under study and the *generation of new hypotheses*. For example, artificial intelligence has been particularly fruitful in suggesting possible mechanisms of low level vision (Lettvin *et al.*, 1959; Rolls, 1987; Perrett *et al.*, 1985).

Artificial intelligence has made many *conceptual contributions*. On a general level it has suggested how psychological characteristics can be compatible with mechanisms. It has suggested resolutions of old philosophical problems, in particular the mind–body problem, and hence thrown light on issues such as substance, causation and volition. The proposal is that an intelligible way of formulating the relation between mind (at least in the sense of the program governing behaviour) and body is that between program and hardware. It provides descriptions at an appropriate level for psychology (that is, in terms of software rather than hardware) without the need to specify detail at more molecular levels. It has encouraged a more unified view of cognition (Wilding, 1978), thinking being seen as a series of operations on symbols. Boden (1979) has provided some interesting illustrations of the way in which computer language can be used to aid conceptualisation in specific areas; for instance, dissociated states of consciousness such as cases of so-called 'split-personality' (for example, Thigpen and Cleckley, 1957). The two personalities can be viewed as two sub-routines or modules of the same overall computational system, alternately using the same motor facilities and sensory apparatus but having different degrees of access to each other's information and data store. Artificial intelligence has also contributed a large number of specific concepts, including the following: hierarchical organisation and heterarchical control, linear and parallel processing, plan, compiler and interpreter programs, sub-routine, recursion, mini-maxing, iteration, top-down and bottom-up processing, depth-first and breadth-first search, procedural versus declarative representation of knowledge, content-addressable memory, ring and list structure, and push-down stack.

Weaknesses

On the one hand, it is difficult to build into the computer program *human inferiorities* (for example, being influenced by a multitude of motivational factors), although some beginnings have been made (for example, Reitman, 1965); on the other hand, it is difficult to build in *human superiorities* (for example, not being led into error by small changes, and the ability to make richly subtle comparisons). Most current computers are severely limited and serious problems are posed by the organisation, retrieval and inferential use of information.

Russell (1984) has raised several philosophical objections to the computational theory of mind in its strong form. He argues that it is paradoxically both *behaviouristic* and dualistic. Although acknowledging the need to postulate the internal representations denied by behaviourists, the inability of a functionalist philosophy to deal adequately with consciousness is well known (see pp. 32–3). Russell suggests that it is not without significance that Skinner's approach is termed 'functionalism', and asks rhetorically what could be more behaviouristic than the Turing test (see below), in which the adequacy of a computer program is judged by its output. Although some take the view that psychological theories should not be concerned with consciousness, others believe that 'consciousness is the constitutive problem of psychology' and that a psychology which ignores it would be comparable to a biology that ignored life or a physics that ignored matter and energy (Miller, 1980).

The charge of *dualism* is based on the functionalist claim that mental states are independent of their physical realisation and that the relationship is merely contingent. Brains and computers are said to be functionally isomorphic but materially distinct. The suspicion of dualism is reinforced by the emphasis placed on the distinction betweeen hardware and software, which latter appears as disembodied programs, elusive algorithms which are difficult to pin down on the basis of behavioural evidence and to which neurophysiological evidence is considered irrelevant.

The spectre of dualism is hardly dispelled by a consideration of the computationalists' treatment of mental states as *representational*. What are they representations of? Most psychologists are untroubled by such questions but a major critic of the concept of representation in psychology has been Gibson (1979) in his 'direct theory of perception'. In his view, perception consists of the picking up of invariants in the flux of energy available to the organism's perceptual system rather than the drawing of inferences or the construction of representations.

A final problem for the computational theory of mind is the potential paradox which arises from the claim on the one hand that representations are *intensional* or about something (that is, in Brentano's sense they are directed towards objects or have content), and on the other that they are purely *syntactic*, not semantic (namely, they contain no reference to the world). Searle (1980) has employed the 'Chinese room' thought experiment in an attempt to show that what he calls strong AI is false. He imagines himself in a room with a rule book which enables him to map 'questions' which are sent in onto appropriate 'answers' which he sends out. The questions and answers (but not the rule book) are in Chinese, a language which he does not understand. He draws an analogy between himself and a computer program. Although their performance may appear adequate, neither of them understands; they are merely formally manipulating uninterpreted symbols. Searle argues that understanding cannot consist merely of the instantiation of a computer program but must have the right causal powers. Whether intelligence is intrinsically biological, as he implies, we do not yet know. It may be objected that the analogy is unfair because it depends on Searle himself understanding the rule book. However, the example does seem to demonstrate the inadequacy of strong AI and to favour weak AI. The difficulty is to say what must be added for meaning and understanding to occur. Two quite different possibilities are causal relations with the external environment and conscious experience. It is difficult to see how an adequate psychological theory can avoid reference to the environment, of which organisms are part and with which they interact: Fodor's (1980) 'methodological solipsism' is unacceptable.

Evaluating the adequacy of a simulation

When does a simulation amount to a theory? In the final analysis the problem is the same as that for evaluating a theory. The conclusion rests on whether adequate tests have been made. Some of the criteria used for evaluating a simulation will be the same as those for theories in general, such as scope (its value will depend on the range of problem areas in which it can be applied), fruitfulness in giving rise to new findings, and success in prediction. A central problem is evaluating the fit with behaviour.

A well-known test was suggested by Turing (1950), namely, whether it was possible to discriminate between a machine and a human, both hidden from view, on the basis of their output consisting of answers to any questions put to them. Turing's criterion was that if it was not possible to discriminate between them then the program in the computer was an adequate theory of the performance of the human. It has been pointed out that this is as much a test of the person putting the questions as of the computer program. Fodor (1968) claims (as have others) that this criterion is either insufficient (what needs to be established is that they both do it in the same way), or question-begging (what aspects are theoretically relevant?). Total correspondence is not required (in the limit it would amount to identity) but rather abstraction of relevant features. This raises the important problem of *selection*. There is no algorithm for deciding which are the critical features of the system and the model that are intended to match. As Frijda (1967) points out, there is nothing in the program to indicate which features are relevant and which irrelevant. Fodor (1968) distinguishes two levels of adequacy: (1) *weak equivalence* (namely, similarity of products), and (2) *strong equivalence* (that is, isomorphism or functional equivalence of the underlying processes). The former can be examined by comparing performance (in computers and humans). However, what is required is that any potential products be the same (that is, similarity with respect to competence). Ultimately this amounts to strong equivalence.

Possible quantitative methods for comparing simulations with behavioural data have been discussed by Reitman (1965) and Frijda (1967). Frijda describes three levels of correspondence: with respect to (1) problem solution; (2) quantitative performance measures, such as time, errors, or order of difficulty; and (3) qualitative details of process, as in introspections or intermediate results. He goes on to point out that significance-testing is in general inappropriate on account of the large number of degrees of freedom in a program. It may be necessary instead to rely on the construction of alternative models, or on a common-sense impression of similarity, which is often so striking as to render coincidence unlikely (for example, Newell and Simon, 1961; Simon and Kotovsky, 1963).

Parallel distributed processing

Some of the differences between computers and brains to which we have drawn attention and the relative neglect of neuroscience by orthodox artificial intelligence have motivated the development of an alternative approach, variously called 'neural networks', 'connectionism' or 'parallel distributed processing'. This tradition is by no means new: connectionism is associationism in a new guise and neural nets were being developed in the 1940s. (For accounts of the history of connectionism, see Valentine, 1989b; Walker, 1990.) The two research traditions have been contrasted by Dreyfus and Dreyfus (1988). Orthodox AI is a top-down approach in which intelligent thought is seen as a rational, atomistic, explicit process which can be modelled by the manipulation of symbols according to formal rules (such as the propositional calculus) in digital computers. Parallel distributed processing, on the other hand, is a bottom-up approach, supposedly motivated by a consideration of brain processes, in which neural networks are simulated; perception, memory and learning are seen as holistic processes, and information is analogically and implicitly represented by a pattern of activity, distributed throughout the system rather than being localised. The seeds for both these traditions in artificial intelligence were sown by the 1950s. In the following two decades orthodox AI was in ascendance. Neo-connectionism rose to the fore with the publication of work by Hinton and Anderson (1981) and Rumelhart *et al.* (1986).

A neural network consists of a system of interacting units, which vary in their level of activation, and connections between them which vary in strength (according to weights assigned them). The level of activation of a given unit depends on the activation levels of units with which it is connected and the strengths of those connections. Two main types of modification rules are the Hebbian, where activated connections are strengthened, and error correcting methods requiring a teacher – for instance, the Widrow-Hoff delta rule and back-propagation, where weight change is proportional to the discrepancy between obtained and desired outcome.

Systems exhibiting parallel distributed processing have several significant features. Neural network simulations are more biologically realistic than those of orthodox AI in a number of respects. The fact that processing is parallel – that is, can occur in a number of units independently and simultaneously – leads to increased speed (thus enabling the speed with which complex decisions are made to be accounted for). Distributed representation has several important implications. Information is represented by the overall pattern of activity: each representation involves many elements and each element is involved in many different representations. Patterns of activity can be reconstructed from incomplete or degraded inputs. Thus such systems are content-addressable (for example, memory for an event can be retrieved in response to inputting part of it) and resistant to local damage (they show 'graceful degradation').

They are well suited to giving a realistic account of a number of psychological phenomena, notably pattern recognition, generalisation, learning and memory (for example, cued recall and the blurring of the distinction between veridical recall and confabulation). Storage and processing are not separate. The absence of an executive is also seen as an advantage by some (see Allport, 1980; Valentine, 1989c).

Neo-connectionism has been fruitful in both physiological and psychological research. The hypothesis that the cerebellar cortex functions as an associative net has been explored by Eccles *et al.* (1967), Pellionisz and Llinas (1979) and Marr (1969). Similar ideas have also been applied to the hippocampus (see McNaughton and Morris, 1987). Psychological applications have included programs to learn the past tense (Rumelhart and McClelland, 1986) and pronunciation (Sejnowski and Rosenberg, 1986) in English.

Despite the excitement generated by parallel distributed models, certain criticisms have been voiced. First, on closer inspection, neural realism breaks down in certain respects. Nothing resembling back-propagation (a powerful modification rule used in some of the most successful simulations, in which weights are adjusted so as to reduce error, beginning with the output units and working backwards layer by layer through the intermediate units to the input units) is known in the nervous system and no attempt has yet been made to model neurochemical aspects of nervous function. However, Hebb's rule has been supported by recent studies of long-term potentiation (see McNaughton and Morris, 1987). Secondly, some have maintained that neural nets are inadequate to model thinking and language. Fodor and Pylyshyn (1988) have argued that an account of the 'language of thought' must involve reference to syntactic and semantic structure. In my view this is a matter of level of description. Neural nets exhibit behaviour implicitly which at one level can be characterised in terms of explicit syntactic and semantic rules. Some aspects of psychology are better represented by one level of description, others by another – compare Millenson's (1967) contrast of S–R and information-processing languages, discussed on p. 129.

In this chapter we have been concerned with attempts to explain behaviour by reference to abstract properties of the system governing it at the level of software; that is, with functional descriptions of the processes involved. In the next chapter we turn to a consideration of approaches which have focused attention on the hardware and sought the explanation of behaviour in terms of the physical embodiment of the system – namely, neurophysiology.

Chapter 11

The relation of physiology to psychology

INTRODUCTION

As we saw in Chapter 1, one of the assumptions of science is that different disciplines are related in a hierarchical way varying from high level sciences at one end, such as sociology, which deal with large units of analysis, to low level sciences at the other, such as physics, which deal with small units of analysis. Thus, a possible ordering might be: sociology, psychology, physiology, chemistry, physics. What is relatively molecular for the high level scientist is relatively molar for the low level scientist. At each level the scientist makes assumptions about that which is the business of the scientist at the next level down. For example, the sociologist, when theorising about the economic behaviour of a society or the language of a culture, makes assumptions about individual people's motivations and acquisition of language; the psychologist, when theorising as opposed to merely observing, makes assumptions about what goes on inside the organism. 'Behavior is made up of hunches about how the nervous system operates to generate the lawful relations that the psychologist observes between stimuli and responses' (Osgood, 1956). There are also different levels of description within each discipline: explanations may be relatively molar or molecular. In psychology, a response may be related to the role it plays in a larger unit of behaviour or to the muscular movements of which it is composed.

As we saw in Chapter 9, looking inside is a possible solution to the problem of how to deal with the organism. It is one common type of explanation, Aristotle's 'material' cause, mechanistic explanation where reference is made to the physical embodiment of the system governing behaviour.

THEORETICAL POSITIONS ON THE RELATION OF PHYSIOLOGY TO PSYCHOLOGY

The relation of physiology to psychology is an area of much controversy. We shall consider various views in order of increasing closeness of the posited relation.

No relation

The most extreme position at one end is that there can be no relation. Bannister (1968), who has argued that physiological psychology is impossible, gives the impression of holding such a view. 'In terms of a logic of sciences, there are reasons for believing that no form of physiological psychology can be a science or part of a science', he writes. 'Psychological and physiological concepts stem from such different semantic networks that they cannot be meaningfully related into a subsystem', where a sub-system is a group of constructs which has a great many internal lines of implication and relatively few relations with other systems. He presents four arguments in support of his case:

1 The constructs of physiology and psychology have partially non-overlapping fields of convenience, they deal with different phenomena, or in Kellyan jargon: 'they link down to different subordinate constructions'. Physiology trafficks in sub-skin phenomena whereas psychology trafficks in molar movement phenomena. They have different subject matters. This would meet with widespread agreement but does not rule out the possibility of their being related.
2 Physiology need not be, but psychology needs to be reflexive – that is, self-referring. Doing psychology is part of the subject matter of psychology in a way that doing physiology is not part of the subject matter of physiology. Again, this is true, and suggests that psychology may have some peculiarities, but does not seem sufficient to establish his case.
3 Physiological processes of individuals are largely independent of and unrelated to one another, whereas psychological processes are interactive between individuals. In this case the distinction is probably invalid. Although it is true that no one is an island, it is not the case that all psychology is social psychology. There are large areas of psychology where social factors are unimportant; for example, physiological psychology and some aspects of cognitive psychology. Conversely, in some cases physiological processes are affected by social factors, such as pheromones (see, for example, McClintock, 1971).
4 Physiology uses a mechanistic, deterministic model, whereas this has failed in psychology, Bannister argues, because of the existence of concepts such as consciousness and choice and the paradox that an experimental prediction about a subject's behaviour may be invalidated by its having been made (for example, the publication of opinion poll results may influence the electorate's behaviour in such a way as to invalidate them). On this last point, as indicated previously, I think we are faced with complexity rather than indeterminism. Most psychologists would reject the charge that the deterministic model has failed in their discipline. Consciousness and choice can be given interpretations which are consistent with a deterministic framework (see Chapters 2 and 4 for discussion of these concepts).

In summary, although Bannister's article draws attention to some of the differences between physiology and psychology, it is not sufficient to establish his case that physiological psychology is impossible.

Putnam (1973) and Fodor (1974) have argued for the autonomy of psychology, the latter on the grounds that psychological concepts may not correspond to physiological concepts: classifications in the two disciplines may cut across each other. Bannister (1968) believes that the 'myth' of physiological psychology depends on verbal trickery. The illusion that physiology and psychology can be meaningfully related rests on the false assumption that concepts such as 'arousal', 'stimulus', 'response', 'inhibition' and 'threshold' have the same meaning in the two disciplines whereas in fact they have quite different meanings. Indeed, as Kelvin (1956) points out, certain phenomena such as selective attention and subliminal perception depend on discrepancies of this kind, where a physically or physiologically adequate stimulus may fail to produce a psychological effect.

Irrelevance

A possible position might be to allow that physiology could be related to psychology but to claim that it is irrelevant. An exponent of this is Skinner (1950), who argued that in the case of theories of learning there was no need for those of a mental, conceptual or neural kind, on the grounds that all that is required for the prediction and control of behaviour are functional laws between stimuli and responses. Theories of any kind, he argued, create new problems of explanation which get covered up, generate wasteful research and can be replaced by more direct methods. This approach avoids the pitfalls of extreme physiological theories which may be wrong and generally do not lead to an increase in explanatory power. However, there are cases where physiological findings may have implications for psychology (see pp. 153–5). The inadequacies of strict behaviourism as a general approach were discussed in Chapters 8 and 9.

Hypothetical construct

Another view recognises the existence of the organism but goes no way towards exploring the nature of the processes involved. In this case physiological events are simply treated as hypothetical constructs in psychology. Hull (1943) was a famous representative of such a position, but there has been a long line of concepts postulated as intervening between stimuli and responses: schemata, implicit stimuli and responses, representational mediation processes, insight, images, set, expectations, cognitive maps and so on. Frequently, however, these have served little more than a labelling function. Cognitive concepts have generally had few predictive implications and neo-behaviourist concepts mainly empirically falsified predictions. In favour of the approach is the recognition that the postulation of internal mediating processes is required but it does not go far enough. The suggestion that physiological events intervene between psychological events is misleading if it implies that different types of event occur in an alternating sequence (see Maze, 1954).

Causal interaction

Sometimes it appears as if there were causal interaction between physiological and psychological processes. Examples of apparent behavioural causes having physiological effects are activity and increased heart rate, eating and obesity, stress and ulcers, life style and cardiac disease. Examples of apparent physiological causes of behavioural effects are Down's syndrome, phenylketonuria, epilepsy and the Pülfrich phenomenon. In these latter cases, explanations in physiological or physical terms seem to be largely satisfactory. Possibly Valins's (1966) demonstration that perceived changes in sounds alleged to be recordings of heart beats resulted in subjects rating slides of semi-nudes as more attractive, or simply putting on more clothes when cold, are other examples. However, cause is a relatively crude concept and there are conceptual difficulties with statements of causal relations between different realms of discourse. These statements result from selective attention to the physiological aspect and neglect of the psychological or vice versa. We see neither wavelengths nor nerve impulses but colours; we hear not frequencies but tones. Psychology, physiology and physics provide different accounts which may pick out different features of a causal chain.

The claim that physiological events cause psychological ones is particularly common and perhaps due to the belief (probably correct) that physiological statements are better incorporated in a body of knowledge. However, in general it is misleading to speak of physiological events causing psychological events. In principle, a causal account could be given at either level. Physiological events do not universally precede psychological ones, which would be required if it were to be said that the former cause the latter (Kelvin, 1956).

Correlation

Many experiments in physiological psychology seem to have as their aim the discovery of correlations between behaviour and physiology. Examples range from early attempts at cortical localisation of function and Funkenstein's (1955) work relating aggression and fear to the secretion of noradrenalin and adrenalin respectively, to more recent attempts to trace concomitant physiological and behavioural changes in the orienting response and the work of Lassen *et al.* (1978) relating sensory and motor functions to increased cerebral blood flow. Clark (1980) claims that the only kind of statement which currently relates psychological terms to physiological terms is a statement of localisation of function, citing examples such as the reticular formation as the neural basis of arousal, the ventromedial nucleus of the hypothalamus as a satiety centre and the hippocampus as underlying habituation.

Double aspect

If correlations can be established, the issue then becomes one of the nature of such correlations. One view is that psychology and physiology provide different descriptions of the same events (a 'double aspect' view). Kelvin (1956) suggests that psychology and physiology provide descriptions of the same events from different points of view, and gives the example of a movement of the hand, which may be described in terms of a series of muscle contractions, some kind of response or as an expression of sadness. An event is in this sense like a cube seen from different angles, or a playing card whose significance changes with the rules of different games. Some of Bannister's (1968) article can be interpreted in this way. He writes, 'In line with Kelly (1955) it is assumed that it is not useful to talk of physiological *events* or psychological *events* but only of physiological and psychological modes of construing events', and gives the following illustration:

> Thus if we contemplate a young lady crossing a bridge (a lay construction) then we may equally well construe her as 'a series of movements of force about a point' (engineer's construing), as 'a poor credit risk' (banker's construing), as 'a mass of whirling electrons about nuclei' (physicist's construing), as 'a soul in peril of mortal sin' (theological construing) or as 'a likely dish' (young man's construing). We do not have to assume that she is *really* any of these. We can accept that they are all constructions which have some explanatory value and predictive utility, depending on the networks of constructs from which they stem.
>
> (Bannister, 1968: 229)

On this view, experiments in physiological psychology are cues to translation (Kelvin, 1956). They tell us where to look in the other discipline's language for the alternative description of the event; for example, mass action experiments tell one that the physiologist's account of learning will be concerned with the total cortex, not just one part of it.

Function and structure

A currently popular way of conceiving of the relation between physiology and psychology is to use a computer analogy and to suggest that psychology's concern is with the software that governs behaviour whereas physiology is concerned with the hardware. On this view, the relation of psychology to physiology is one of function to structure: psychology specifies what the system does and physiology specifies how it does it. However, as many writers have pointed out, the relation of function to structure is context-relative rather than absolute: a given piece of research may be functional in relation to the level below but structural in relation to the level above. This position was recommended for psychology by Deutsch (1960) who labelled it 'structural' but is now generally known as 'functional' following Putnam (1960). It has been developed by Clark (1980). Central to it is the view that behavioural processes should be described in terms of relations between states of a system: the parts of a psychological model are specified in terms of their relation to other parts and thereby to the input–output relations of the system as a whole. This can be done at an abstract level (for instance, in the form of a flow chart, program or Turing machine operations) without specification of the physical embodiment. Indeed, functionalism assumes that the same system can be physically represented in a variety of different ways (which leaves open the possibility of assigning mental states to machines). It is the task of physiology to identify the neural structures which subserve psychological functions: functional isomorphism can be established if a neural structure plays the same causal role as a postulated part in the psychological model – that is, it bears the same relations to input and output variables (Clark, 1980).

Deutsch (1960) saw the approach as a middle road between 'the sterility of positivism run wild' and 'the absurdities of the pseudo-physiologist'. Its advantages are that it is adequate for the prediction of behaviour, it enables use to be made of discoveries in cybernetic theory and computer science, and ultimately is mappable onto physiology which can provide another empirical check. Weiskrantz (1968) raised the following objections to Deutsch's position: (1) although the distinction between abstract structure and physical embodiment may be logically valid, it may not be important in practice, where a pragmatic approach is to be recommended; and (2) a postulated structure may be logically capable of producing certain behaviour but empirically incorrect.

Neurophysiologising

'The problem of understanding behaviour is the problem of understanding the total action of the nervous system and vice versa', wrote Hebb (1949) who saw his book as a 'sedulous attempt to find some community of neurological and psychological conceptions'. In favour of this approach are the facts that psychological processes are closely related to physiological ones and ultimately some physiological basis must be found for them, and that fruitful cooperation between the disciplines is likely to increase as discoveries continue to be made. Co-evolution between psychology and neuroscience is recommended as a research strategy by P.S. Churchland (1986), amongst others, who cites tensor network theory (see P.M. Churchland, 1986), neural nets and Crick's (1984) neurobiological model of visual attention as evidence of its success. However, it depends on the possibility of establishing good correlations between psychological and physiological descriptions which may be easier to achieve in some areas than others. Against it, it may be argued that psychology exists in its own right, that specifying the physical embodiment does not generally lead to an increase in explanatory power and that 'neurologising' is merely a form of intellectual displacement activity. Gregory (1961) has drawn attention to some of the difficulties of interpreting experiments in physiological psychology. Ablation may demonstrate the necessity but not the sufficiency of a given brain area for a given psychological function. It would be unwise on finding that a radio squeaked after the removal of a part to conclude that what was removed was the squeak suppressor. Similarly for stimulation experiments, the fact that a bang on the head may give rise to seeing stars and experiencing headaches does not justify the conclusion that what has been hit is the centre for stars and headaches. His general point is that, in an interactive system, knowledge of individual parts is not much use without knowledge about the functioning of the whole system. In attempting to localise psychological functions in neural structures it is always necessary to rule out the possibility that other functions or other structures were responsible, which is difficult to achieve since there are nearly always alternative explanations for a given result (Clark, 1980).

Mehler *et al.* (1984) have argued that there are severe limits to the implications of neuropsychology for the psychology of language and that attempts to draw such inferences may be irrelevant or misleading. In limited cases where constraints do apply (as in the characteristics of the sensory apparatus or the search for modules of an information-processing system) they depend on a one-to-one mapping and prior knowledge of the units of analysis at each level. It is always necessary to consider the implications for psychological functioning, and psychological evidence is best for this.

MUTUAL CONTRIBUTIONS OF PHYSIOLOGY AND PSYCHOLOGY

Psychological and physiological descriptions must be compatible and hence impose mutual *constraints*: neither discipline can put forward a theory which has implications which conflict with what is known or possible in the other discipline. Pavlov's theory of generalisation as irradiation of excitation in the cortex, the *Gestalt* electrical field theory of perception and Hebb's original formulation were all physiologically flawed (Bass and Hull, 1934; Lashley, Chow and Semmes, 1951; Milner, 1957, respectively) and could only be salvaged by a reformulation compatible with known physiology.

Physiological findings may be able to contribute to the *development* and *evaluation* of psychological theories. It could be argued that brains are more appropriate than computers as models for psychology. Weiskrantz (1968) suggests that physiological studies may enable inferences to be made about: the sequencing of behaviour, the independence of known categories, fractionation, the capacity of sub-parts, or normal function on the basis of exaggerated dysfunction.

Neuropsychological evidence, in particular *double dissociation of function* (that is, impairment of one function but intact performance on another in some patients and the reverse pattern in other patients, intact performance on the first function but impairment on the second), has frequently been invoked to help determine the existence of separate information-processing modules. Double dissociations of function have been established; for example, between visual object processing and word reading, and a number of language sub-systems (see Shallice, 1988). Baddeley (1982) has argued that neuropsychology has helped in the differentiation not only of short-term and long-term memory but also episodic and semantic, and declarative and procedural memory sub-systems, as well as in the fractionation of working memory. Shallice (1988), in a careful analysis, argues that double dissociation of function may justify a conclusion of functional specialisation but that this need not necessarily take the form of isolable sub-systems (there is a variety of possible alternatives). Neuropsychology has also provided useful evidence in the study of dyslexia and theories of reading (for example, Coltheart, 1981). However, note that in most of these cases neurophysiology is secondary: the investigator is merely taking advantage of the results of neurological damage; the tasks performed by the subject are psychological and provide behavioural evidence.

McFie (1972) suggests two other ways besides *differentiation* in which physiological findings may contribute to the analysis of psychological abilities. First, it may elucidate their *nature*. For example, the discovery that impairment of the ability to calculate is sometimes associated with right hemisphere lesions might lead to the conclusion that calculation involves spatial ability; conversely, the discovery of an association between an impairment in reading and left hemispheric lesions would lead to the conclusion that there was little spatial involvement in such performance. However, note that this depends on a previously established correlation between spatial ability and right hemisphere function. Secondly, it may lead to the *discovery* of new psychological functions – for example, an aspect of performance on picture arrangement tasks sensitive to right fronto-temporal lesions – not previously revealed.

Farah (1988) has argued that neuropsychology can provide *less equivocal data* than those provided by the methods of experimental cognitive psychology, in relation to the debate over the nature of imaginal representation. Techniques such as electrophysiology and cerebral blood flow show that the cortical areas involved in imagery are the same as those involved in perception. These methods have the advantage that they are not open to alternative interpretations in terms of tacit knowledge and expectations.

Neuropsychological evidence may also be used to *refute* psychological theories. The existence of patients with impaired short-term memory but intact long-term memory has been used to discredit the 'modal' model, according to which information must pass through a short-term store before reaching long-term memory. The implication is that either material does not have to pass through short-term memory in order to reach long-term, or that there are other types of short-term memory than those considered.

Ideally, physiological theories should suggest *mechanisms* capable of accounting for psychological phenomena: for example, a three-colour receptor theory is faced with the problem of accounting for the perception of yellow (in the periphery beyond the areas for the perception of red and green). Likewise, physiological theories of learning and memory should be capable of accounting for the known psychological facts in these areas.

In addition to providing evidence which may have implications for theories of the other discipline, each may be able to supply *methods* to the other. Thus the psychologist may use drugs to study personality differences (for example, individual differences reflected in reaction to alcohol) or clinical disorders; conversely, the pharmacologist may use behavioural measures in the analysis of drugs.

REDUCTION

Reduction is a relation of logical derivation between statements or theories. What is at issue in the case of psychology and physiology is not the reducibility of mental states to brain states but whether a theory of mental states can be explained in terms of a theory of neural mechanisms. 'What gets reduced are theories . . . the stuff in the universe keeps doing whatever it is doing while we theorize and theories come and go' (P.S. Churchland, 1986). Thus the result of a reduction will not be, for example, that headaches become illusory but that their occurrence will have been explained. Phenomena are explained rather than explained away. Nagel (1961) gives the following definitions of reduction: 'the deduction of one set of empirically confirmable statements from another set' and 'the explanation of a theory or set of experimental laws established in one area of enquiry, by a theory usually though not invariably formulated for some other domain'.

Hooker (1981) provides examples illustrating the logical diversity and 'bewildering variety and complexity' of reductions. They may involve derivation of laws, aimed at explanatory unification and perhaps increased systematicity, and/or identification of terms, aimed at ontological simplification (a reduction in the number of entities postulated). They may be strict or weak (the claims ranging from logical equivalence of statements at one extreme to mere empirical correlations at the other). They can be total or partial (depending on their scope); in some cases they take the form of 'micro-reductions', where the relation between units of analysis at different levels is that of whole to part.

Conditions for reduction

A prerequisite for reduction is the ordering of sciences from higher to lower levels; for example, sociology, psychology, physiology, chemistry, physics. There are other possibilities and there are levels within conventional disciplines. Oppenheim and Putnam (1958) proposed six levels in their suggested framework for micro-reduction: (1) social groups, (2) multicellular living things, (3) cells, (4) molecules, (5) atoms and (6) elementary particles. In this case the units of analysis at each level have as parts the units of analysis at the next level down. P.S. Churchland (1986) offers a set biased towards neuroscience (behaviour, circuit, cell assembly, synapse, cell, membrane) as well as discussing levels of organisation in terms of research methods applied to the study of learning and memory, ranging from studies of neurotransmitters at the cellular level to neuropsychological, ethological and psychological studies at higher levels.

The essential requirement of reduction is *derivability*; that is, the possibility of deducing the laws of one science from those of another. In practice, laws of higher level sciences can only be deduced from laws of lower level sciences with the addition of statements specifying boundary conditions and other limiting assumptions (see below). All interesting cases of reduction also require a further condition, that of *definability* – that is, a mapping of the terms in the two theories – by biconditionals or some kind of bridging laws. The status of these (whether, for instance, logical identities, deliberately created conventions, contingent identities or empirically established correlations) is controversial and may be difficult to decide.

Further, there must be some advantage to be gained, either theoretical (such as explanatory unification and ontological simplification) or heuristic (like the development of fruitful research strategies). Finally, the reduction must be empirically supported.

There has been a historical shift, in the conditions considered necessary for reduction, away from positivism. Schaffner (1967), in a useful paper, describes four versions of reduction, two positivist models and two weaker modifications:

1 The 'direct' model, adopted by Nagel, Woodger and Quine, which specifies two main conditions: (1) definability – that is, a biconditional relation between the terms of the two theories; and (2) derivability of the laws of one theory from the laws of the other theory. This is a positivist model, in which explanation is seen as a matter of logical deduction (see pp. 109–10).
2 The 'indirect' model, espoused by Kemeny and Oppenheim (1956), which requires merely that the data explicable by one theory can be explained more systematically and/or simply by another theory. Even in this model, described by Hooker (1981) as 'austerely positivist', it is admitted that the translation from one theory to another does not follow precisely by means of biconditionals: the reduced theory holds only approximately and within

certain limits. Kemeny and Oppenheim (1956) acknowledge, on the one hand, that these points are of fundamental importance but, on the other, that if they are taken into account 'the problem of reduction becomes hopelessly complex'. 'Any actual example has to be stretched considerably if it is to exemplify connections by means of biconditionals, and most examples will under no circumstances fall under this pattern.'

3 The 'approximate' model, supported by Popper, Feyerabend and Kuhn. An examination of the history of science has led to the rejection of the positivist model. Feyerabend (1962) claims that no intuitively plausible example of reduction in the history of science actually fits empiricist theory. In general, it has been argued that derivability neither implies reducibility nor guarantees explanatory or ontological unification, on the grounds that the criteria for reduction are not purely logical but involve semantic assumptions about the meaning of terms, as well as pragmatic and normative considerations. Hence they depend on the state of technological development and practice, and are relative to a specific point in time. In particular, it is argued that theories need varying amounts of revision before they can be reduced: they are likely to become corrected in the process. What needs to be explained is reconfigured. A later reducing theory may explain where and why a previous reduced theory did not work. Thus reductions are typically approximate, being only indirectly related to the original theory and directly related only to a revised version.
4 The 'isomorphic' model developed by Suppes (1967), in which all that is required is an isomorphism between models of the two theories concerned, probably a one-to-one correspondence between values of the variables in the two domains.

Hooker (1981) postulates a *retention–replacement continuum*, which determines whether a reduction is smooth or bumpy (P. S. Churchland, 1986). At the retention end, ontological commitments are retained (that is, entities do not cease to exist) as are laws or close approximations to them. Examples are the identification of light with electromagnetic waves, and mind–brain identity theory where mental states are contingently identified with brain states. At the replacement end, entities may be eliminated. Some fairly neutral observation statements may be retained but the ontologies and accounts are substantially different; the old theory is explained away. Examples are the replacement of phlogiston by oxygen, demons by dopamine, the caloric theory by the kinetic theory of heat, and eliminative materialism in which mentalistic language or 'folk psychology' is replaced by more scientific physicalistic descriptions. Intermediate cases, as examples of which Hooker (1981) gives the reductions of thermodynamics to statistical mechanics and psychology to neurobiology, may be characterised by any of the following features. First, the reduction is partial or holds only within certain limits; for instance, the relation of Einstein's special theory of relativity in relation to Newtonian mechanics, where the reduction only applies in the limit; or the applicability of concepts such as consciousness, intentionality and rationality which may depend on certain limiting conditions. Secondly, a single concept in one theory may map onto a multiplicity of concepts in the other theory; for example, the reduction of temperature is said to be domain-specific – that is, different for gases, plasmas and solids (but see Hatfield, 1988); similarly mental functions may be realised by a variety of physical embodiments; for example, binocular stereopsis is carried out by anatomically and evolutionarily distinct systems in the owl and the cat (Pettigrew and Konishi, 1976). Thirdly, there may be co-evolution and mutual feedback between the two theories; for example, as in the interaction between psychology and physiology in the study of vision or neural networks.

Arguments in favour of reduction

The main arguments in favour of reduction are theoretical unification and increased explanatory power, as well as mutual benefit resulting from research cooperation between disciplines. The unity of science has been explored in depth as a hypothesis by Neurath (1938) in the context of logical positivism, by Oppenheim and Putnam (1958) as a fruitful working hypothesis which stimulates research, and by Causey (1977), who has attempted to specify technical conditions for micro-reduction. The ideal of positivism was to provide a unified body of knowledge based on observation and logic, whose truth could be guaranteed. Oppenheim and Putnam (1958) consider indirect and direct evidence for reduction in relation to their six levels described above. The indirect evidence is from evolution, ontogenesis and synthesis (that is, higher levels evolve, develop ontogenetically, and can be synthesised, from entities at lower levels). As an example of direct evidence for reducing the social level to the multicellular, they cite the explanation of economic phenomena in terms of the psychology of individual choice behaviour, and as examples of the reduction of the multicellular level to the cellular, Hebb's (1949) theory of cell assemblies and (foresightfully) neural networks.

Arguments against reduction

Definability

We have already noted that there is controversy about the status of the bridging laws which connect terms in one discipline with those in another. It is generally agreed that they cannot be analytic or logically necessary. Concepts from different disciplines have different meanings: they are drawn from different contexts, belong to different conceptual frameworks, have different observational criteria and different implications. Experience is different from behaviour (for instance, a headache is not a disposition to take aspirins) and actions are different from muscular movements (the same action may be carried out by a number of different movements). Responses are normally defined in terms of consequences rather than constituent movements (Bindra, 1976). Claims of identity are therefore generally for contingent identity: identity of reference rather than identity of properties. Jessor (1958) argued against reduction on the grounds that lower level sciences lack some of the concepts of higher level sciences, in the case of psychology, concepts dealing with the functional environment and the context of behaviour. Bannister (1968) suggested that psychology and physiology have different semantic networks. Putnam (1973) has argued against the identification of psychological states, such as jealousy, love and competitiveness, with Turing machine states, on the grounds that the former are continuous and dependent on learning, whereas the latter are discrete, instantaneous and independent of learning and memory. However, the question is whether a mapping can be achieved. Fodor (1974) suggests that the terms in psychological laws may not correspond with, but may 'cross-classify', the terms in neurophysiological laws. There is no a priori reason why the two descriptions should map onto each other, since to some extent there are arbitrary and pragmatic factors involved. What is salient at one level of description may not correspond with what is important or useful at another level (Wimsatt, 1976).

It is clear that many problems confront the mapping of psychological and neurophysiological states. Absence of an area may not be accompanied by a corresponding lack of function (as in some cases of hydrocephaly and callosal agenesis). The relationship may be one-to-many in either direction: the same function may be carried out by different structures (equipotentiality) or the same structure may have different functions. Functionalists stress token rather than type identity on the grounds of multiple instantiability, claiming that mental states may be realised in neurobiological or computer hardware. The same psychological function or mental state may not correspond to the same neural mechanism in different species (such as the mediation of pattern perception by different parts of the brain in rats, monkeys and humans), in different individuals (for example, the localisation of speech with respect to hemisphere) or at different times in the same individual (functional reorganisation may occur as a result of maturation or damage, according to the degree of plasticity available). Thus, the bridging laws linking psychological descriptions to neurophysiological descriptions may be disjunctive and/or incomplete – which makes Fodor (1974) doubt whether they could be laws. For an example of multiple socio-psychological interpretations of the same physical event, see Figure 11.1.

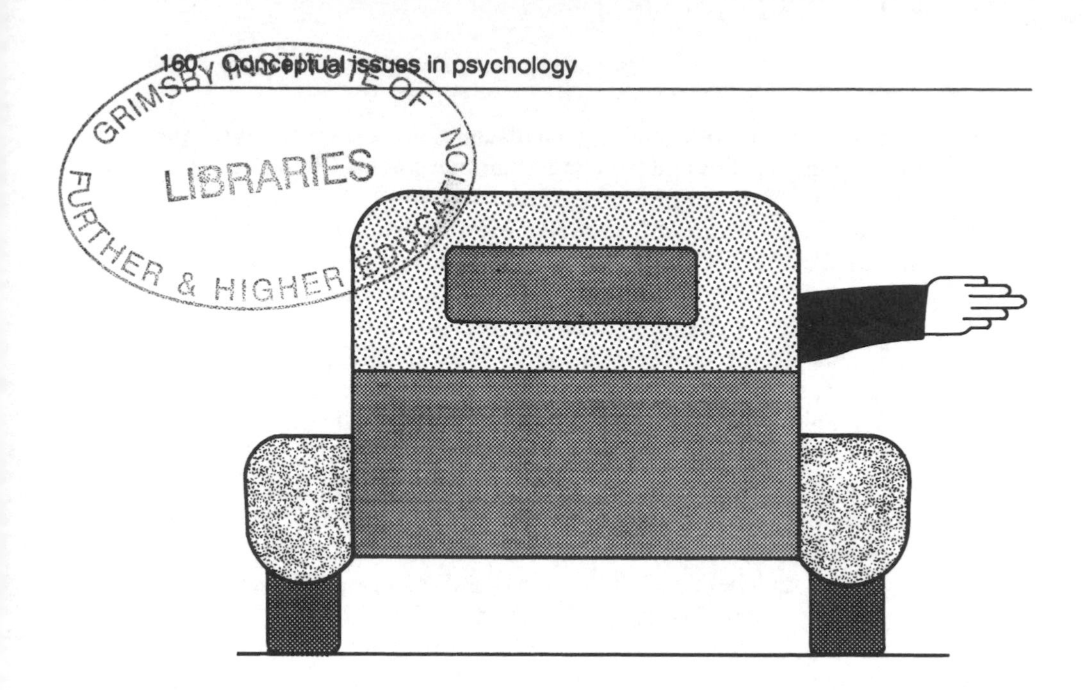

'I am going to TURN to my RIGHT'.

'I am going to TURN to my RIGHT,
and when I discover that it's the wrong turning,
I am going to TURN BACK again just in time
to give you the FRIGHT of your LIFE'.

'The rain is OFF, I think'.

'The house over there with the GREEN door
is where our cook's MOTHER lives'.

'LOOK, I can drive with one HAND off the WHEEL'.

Figure 11.1 Interpretations of a physical event
(*Source:* after Fougasse and McCullough, 1935)

Derivability

We have already seen that laws of higher level sciences cannot be deduced directly from laws of lower level sciences but need not only bridging laws but also additional statements specifying boundary conditions, indicating domain-specific or other limiting conditions. Putnam (1973), who has done a complete volte-face since 1958, argues for the autonomy of psychological laws on the grounds that they can only be derived from lower level laws with the addition of auxiliary hypotheses. Higher level laws depend on boundary conditions which are crucial to them but accidental to the lower level laws. For example, laws governing the flight of an organism or machine cannot be derived simply from a knowledge of its structure without also knowing about atmospheric conditions.

Secondly, derivability is to be distinguished from explanation. An explanation should make the relevant features explicit. Lower level explanations are likely to contain additional, irrelevant details which obscure rather than reveal. Important higher level generalisations are likely to be lost. The reason why a square peg does not fit in a round hole is best given in terms of the rigidity and relative sizes of the peg and the hole rather than in terms of the micro-structure; for example, positions and velocities of elementary particles (Putnam, 1973). Even if it were possible, for example, to give a biochemical account of wine-tasting it might not always be very useful. This is partly because it may not refer to relevant aspects or accessible variables, and partly because it may be too detailed or clumsy. Similarly, even if it did turn out to be possible to provide a biochemical account of memory, this might not be useful in helping to decide to which school to send a child. Another example comes from psychotherapy: which explanation is useful may depend on the practical possibilities of treatment (for instance, drugs versus group psychotherapy). Some reductions may neither lead to an increase in simplicity nor be very useful.

Putnam (1973) remarks that the reducibility of psychology to physiology depends on what is meant by psychology. It could equally well be argued that it depends on what is meant by reduction. The concept of reduction has itself been reduced almost out of existence. Bechtel (1988b) discusses some more liberal schemes for relating disciplines, such as Darden and Maull's (1977) concept of interfield theories and his own of cross-disciplinary research clusters (Bechtel, 1986a). These can apply within as well as between disciplines, allowing cooperation between disciplines with different objectives and the pursuit of relations other than derivability – for example, whole to part, function to structure, physical embodiment, or cause; appeal for further explanation may be made to higher as well as lower levels.

SUMMARY

A variety of positions on the relation of physiology to psychology has been discussed. There has been a shift away from attempts to establish logical relations between psychological and physiological descriptions, and a recognition that they belong to different conceptual frameworks. This does not preclude the possibility of their being related. A currently popular view of the relation is that of function to structure. Thus, psychology describes processes in terms of a functional model, whereas physiology describes the physical embodiment in terms of neural structures. Correlations are easier to establish in some areas than others. In many cases they are not straightforward and involve one-to-many relationships; for instance, the same function may be physically realised in a variety of different structures. Although there has been a weakening in the claims for the reduction of psychology to physiology, this has been accompanied by increased optimism about cross-disciplinary research as a fruitful strategy likely to lead to theoretical integration.

Chapter 12

Teleological explanation

INTRODUCTION

In this chapter we shall be concerned with the nature and function of teleological explanations and in particular with the problem of whether laws of the physical sciences that govern inorganic matter are adequate to account for the behaviour of living organisms, the subject matter of the biological sciences, or whether laws of a fundamentally different kind are required. It has frequently been argued that human behaviour has certain essential characteristics such as that it is purposive, goal-directed or self-determined, which render a mechanistic account inappropriate. This has sometimes been the motivation for the postulation of teleological explanations of behaviour, explanations which make reference to an end or goal (from Greek *telos* meaning 'end') but there has been a good deal of controversy about the status of teleological explanations and about their relation to mechanistic ones. In addition, some of these apologias have not been very clearly expressed.

Perhaps one of the most obvious characteristics of the behaviour of living organisms and one which increases as the phylogenetic scale is ascended is *plasticity*. Key biological concepts involve the notion of change over time; for example, adaptation, modifiability, growth, maturation, development and learning. Indeed, such phenomena are the basis of survival. Most of the behaviour of living organisms is *sensitive to consequences*. Phylogenetic adaptation in evolution by means of natural selection is paralleled in ontogenetic development by reinforcement in learning, which may be interpreted in terms of the law of effect (Thorndike, 1911) or, in the case of human learning, as extrinsic feedback in the form of knowledge of results (Annett, 1969). More particularly, much of behaviour is goal-directed. Ends may be valued independently of the means whereby they are achieved. Such phenomena range from homeostasis, where a fixed state is continuously maintained within certain limits, possibly by comparatively simple and rigid operations, to the active seeking of goals which can be realised in a variety of different ways. 'So long as people are behaving, *some* Plan or other must be executed' (Miller, Galanter and Pribram, 1960).

THE CONCEPT OF PURPOSE

Purposive behaviour may be defined as behaviour *directed towards a goal*, whose attainment results in the termination of the behaviour in question. That subsequent quiescence is not a distinguishing feature, however, can be seen by considering cases such as volcanic eruptions which are followed by periods of quiescence but would not be said to be purposive (Braithwaite, 1947).

> Coming to a definite end or terminus is not *per se* distinctive of directive activity, for inorganic processes also move towards a natural terminus. . . . What *is* distinctive is the active persistence of directive activity towards its goal, the use of alternative means towards the same end, the achievement of results in the face of difficulties.
>
> (Russell, 1945: 144)

Nagel defines the characteristic feature of systems which have a goal-directed organisation as that

> they continue to manifest a certain state or property G, or to develop 'in the direction' of attaining G, in the face of a relatively extensive class of changes in their external environments or in some of their internal parts.
>
> (Nagel, 1953: 205)

The essential ingredient is thus the attainment of a goal despite variations in initial conditions which are likely to necessitate the employment of different means. Behaviour is modified as a result of its consequences with reference to a goal.

The attribution to behaviour of purposive characteristics requires a *molar* analysis. As early as 1896 Dewey, in a famous paper which antedated much later *Gestalt* criticisms of behaviourism, recognised the need for a more holistic description of behaviour in which stimulus and response are seen as integrated into one act: 'The fact is that stimulus and response are not distinctions of existence, but teleological distinctions, that is, distinctions of function, or part played, with reference to reaching or maintaining an end.'

Some of the difficulties which a purposive analysis poses for behaviourism were pointed out by Perry:

> In the case of hunting for a pin, the organism is not, strictly speaking, responding to an object or fact of its environment. The organism is not hunting for any particular pin; and is quite capable of carrrying on the hunt, even though there be as a matter of fact no pin in its environment.
>
> (Perry, 1918: 7)

The fact that the goal does not exist objectively, and indeed may never materialise, indicates that an *intensional* analysis is required (see Boden, 1972). A crucial feature of purposive behaviour is an internal representation of the goal which guides behaviour. Whether or not such an intention need be conscious is a matter of controversy. Nagel (1953), Miller *et al.* (1960) and Dennett (1978) argue that it need not be, and I would agree with them; Boden (1972) and common sense, on the other hand, argue that intentions are necessarily conscious. According to Dennett (1978) the explanation of behaviour may require the assumption of rationality and the ascription of information and goals, but this 'intentional stance' is a purely pragmatic strategy which leaves open the question of whether the system really has beliefs and desires. The attribution of consciousness may be objectionable on several grounds: (1) if it is implausible (did the chicken have a conscious intention to cross the road?); (2) if there is no means of identifying it independently of the ensuing behaviour, in which case it is circular: cf. Skinner's objection to Blanshard's statement that Hitler ordered the extermination of the Jews because he hated them, if we have no evidence of his hatred other than his having given the order (Blanshard and Skinner, 1967); or (3) if metaphysical properties are implied, as in the case of McDougall's (1932) *hormē* (a kind of psychic energy) or other vitalistic notions invoking mysterious, non-physical forces.

Ethologists have long recognised that there are a number of different mechanisms by which apparently goal-directed behaviour may be brought about (McFarland, 1981). Behaviour which has an obvious function may appear goal-directed without the mechanisms responsible for the behaviour having any obvious goal-directed feature. Woodlice appear to be actively seeking out damp places, but in fact their behaviour can be simply explained as the result of their moving about more rapidly in a dry atmosphere and hence by default spending more time in areas of high humidity. The food-begging response in herring-gull chicks is elicited by sign stimuli (the red spot on the parent's bill), which induces the parent to regurgitate food. The obtaining of food may appear as the goal of the behaviour but is merely its function. Similarly, a lapwing disturbed by a ground predator typically leaves the nest and feigns injury. This behaviour distracts the predator, hence serving the function of protecting the nestlings. We do not have to suppose that the lapwing engages in the following soliloquy: 'Here comes a predator; all of a sudden I feel a tremendous urge to do that silly broken-wing dance' (Dennett, 1983). McFarland (1985) reserves the term 'intentional' for behaviour which involves some representation of a goal which is instrumental in guiding behaviour, and gives the example of song-learning in small birds, which appears to take the form of progressive improvements towards a template formed earlier in the bird's life on the basis of exposure to a model song. The postulation of such internal representations makes it possible to explain how animals distinguish the consequences of their own behaviour from events of environmental origin (as in reafference), their regulation of various aspects of their internal environment (as in the case of homeostatic mechanisms), and the making of relative judgements about features in the external world.

HISTORY

In Greek science the categories of explanation for inorganic phenomena were derived from those for organic phenomena, the difference between the two realms being one of degree rather than kind. Functional explanations have been popular in accounts influenced by evolutionary theory, where attention has been focused on the survival value of behaviour patterns; for example, the ethologists' concepts of appetitive behaviour and consummatory acts. Some of these behaviours, however, may be insufficiently flexible to merit the predicate 'purposive'. Biologically orientated theorists have generally recognised the need to take account of the modifiability of behaviour; for instance, Piaget based his theory of cognitive development on the adaptive mechanisms of accommodation and assimilation.

McDougall (1912), in whose theory the concept of purpose was a cornerstone, claimed that 'the manifestation of purpose or the striving to achieve an end, is, then, the mark of behaviour'. He listed seven objective marks of purpose: spontaneity; persistence; variation of means; cessation of movements when, and not until, they result in the attainment of the goal; anticipation; improvement in efficiency; molarity: 'that is to say, it is an activity in which the whole organism takes part so far as necessary' (McDougall, 1925).

Lashley (1930) concluded that 'the facts of both psychology and neurology show a degree of plasticity, or organisation and of adaptation in behaviour which is far beyond any present possibilities of explanation'. His physiological work and analysis of skilled movements such as language convinced him that the units of cerebral function were 'modes of organization' rather than conditioned reflexes.

Tolman's 'purposive behaviourism' attempted to take account of the purposive aspect of behaviour while yet subscribing to the behaviourist programme.

> Wherever the purely objective description of either a simple or complex behavior discovers a *persistence until* character there we have what behaviorism defines as purpose. And upon further analysis, we discover that such a description appears whenever in order merely to *identify* the given behavior a reference to some 'end object' or 'situation' is found necessary.
> (Tolman, 1925: 33)

Later, the status of purposive concepts took on an explanatory role in the form of intervening variables which, together with independent variables, determined behaviour. These former consisted of demands such as food and sex, and cognitions such as intentions and expectations, and were operationally defined in terms of behavioural dispositions. Tolman admitted that they were drawn from everyday common-sense terms, and they have been much criticised for their failure to lead to precise, quantitative predictions.

Perhaps the most important development in the history of the purposive analysis of behaviour has been cybernetics, which restored respectability to teleology. It demonstrated that machines can possess teleological characteristics and that it is possible to give a mechanistic account of goal-directed systems, which may show considerable flexibility of behaviour before the target is reached; for example, guided missiles. The notion of a servo-mechanism was foreshadowed in Dewey's (1896) analysis of James's (1890) example of the child learning to avoid fire. The concept of the feedback mechanism was introduced by Ashby (1940). Rosenblueth *et al.* (1943) argued for a uniform functional analysis applicable to machines and living organisms. They defined teleological behaviour as behaviour controlled by negative feedback.

> All purposeful behavior may be considered to require negative feedback. If a goal is to be attained, some signals from the goal are necessary at some time to direct the behavior. . . . The behavior of an object is controlled by the margin of error at which the object stands at a given time with reference to a relatively specific goal.
>
> (Rosenblueth *et al.*, 1943: 19)

Wiener (1948) developed the analogy, demonstrating the relevance of cybernetics to biology, and to neurophysiology and psychology in particular. One of the most influential theoretical applications of the concept of the feedback loop to psychology was that of Miller, Galanter and Pribram (1960), who defended what they called the 'cybernetic hypothesis', that the fundamental building block of the nervous system is the feedback loop, or TOTE (an acronym for test–operate–test–exit) as they called it, which is an incongruity-sensitive mechanism.

> The TOTE represents the basic pattern in which our Plans are cast, the test phase of the TOTE involves the specification of whatever knowledge is necessary for the comparison that is to be made, and the operational phase represents what the organism does about it.
>
> (Miller, Galanter and Pribram, 1960: 31)

Their suggestion was that behaviour as a whole is capable of description in terms of hierarchies of feedback loops.

The application of the concept of the feedback loop to behaviour ranges from relatively simple cases such as homeostatic mechanisms (for example, temperature regulation) and sensorimotor coordinations (cf. von Holst's 1954 theory, according to which any discrepancy between reafference and the 'efference copy' produces a perceptual or motor effect on the system), to more complex cognitive skills. Rosenblueth *et al.* (1943) describe predictive behaviour which requires the discrimination of at least two coordinates, a temporal and at least one spatial axis – for example, the pursuit of a moving object; and higher order cases, such as throwing a stone at a moving target. Goals may be fixed or flexible, and set externally or internally to the system. MacKay (1981) distinguishes a simple level of evaluation where the standard is externally specified and fixed (involving an open loop at the normative level but a closed loop at the executive level) – for example, a thermostat – from more complex cases where goals are flexible and set internally by the system (involving closed loops at both the normative and executive levels), the analogue for self-determination. See also Johnson-Laird's (1983a) distinction between Cartesian, Craikian and self-reflective automata, discussed in Chapter 2 (p. 11). One part of a system may transfer information to another part (transfer of control). More powerfully, one process within a system may modify the operation of another process (adaptive control). Broadbent (1977) presents evidence on decision-making in complex environments which requires the postulation of the operation of a closed loop on an open chain.

THE NATURE OF TELEOLOGICAL EXPLANATIONS

Mechanistic explanations explain events by reference to past events, in terms of efficient causation. They state the conditions for their occurrence. Given the antecedent condition, it should be possible in principle to predict the consequent. In addition, there is an assumption that the laws will be of the kind that have so far worked in the physical sciences. An example of a mechanistic explanation is 'the billiard ball moved because it was hit by the cue'. *Teleological explanations*, on the other hand, explain events by reference to future events, ends or goals. An example of a teleological explanation is 'the chicken crossed the road in order to get to the other side'. They represent Aristotle's 'final' cause, the end for the sake of which an event occurs; for instance, walking for the sake of health. Causal explanations can be pursued indefinitely, whereas teleological explanations provide natural stopping-places (they are in a sense ultimate), particularly if they refer to biological needs.

The notion that a future event is somehow involved in current behaviour has appeared problematical to some, because it seems to imply that time goes backwards; similar difficulties arose over the supposed retroflex action of the law of effect – see Postman (1947). However, this would only be so if it is held that the future event has a causal effect on current behaviour, in the generally accepted sense of cause (namely, Aristotle's 'efficient' cause). 'Final' causation, if it involved the influence of later events on earlier events, would be an absurd notion. Rather, it is some representation of a future event or the result of past contingencies that is effective. In an evolutionary context, Wimsatt (1972) and Wright (1976) have attempted to redeem teleology and make it compatible with mechanism, by suggesting that natural selection is the efficient cause. Whether or not conscious intentions can be said to play a causal role is a controversial issue. As we have noted before, there are a number of difficulties with such a view (see Chapters 3 and 4). Some contemporary philosophers have preferred to consider the relation between intention and action as conceptual rather than contingent (see below).

Braithwaite (1947) maintains that teleological explanations are distinguishable from mechanistic ones on epistemological as well as logical grounds. They tend to be discovered inductively by inference from past experience of similar behaviour patterns, rather than being deduced from causal laws. Skinner (1953) points out that we cannot attribute the purpose of posting a letter to someone walking down the street unless either we see the letter being posted or we have observed similar behaviour and consequences before.

THE RELATION BETWEEN TELEOLOGICAL AND MECHANISTIC EXPLANATIONS

Opinion has varied both on the relation of teleological (or purposive) to mechanistic (or causal) accounts and on which is or are appropriate for the explanation of behaviour. It has been debated whether they are logically equivalent (one being reducible to the other) or whether different logics are involved. Two issues have often been confounded: (1) the temporal direction of explanation – that is, whether by reference to past events or antecedent conditions (as in causal explanation) or by reference to future events or consequences (as in teleological explanation); and (2) the level of explanation – namely, the unit of analysis – for example, whether explanation is in terms of the functioning of a system as a whole or in terms of its constituent parts. The term 'mechanistic' is somewhat ambiguous, implying not only explanation in terms of efficient causation but sometimes also carrying reductionist overtones. Those who consider teleological and mechanistic accounts to be non-equivalent are faced with the choice of which to adopt in the explanation of behaviour. Three views may be distinguished: namely, that such explanations should be (1) exclusively causal, (2) exclusively teleological, or (3) that both are required.

Most psychologists, particularly behaviourists, would probably take the view that *mechanistic explanations of behaviour are sufficient* and that teleological ones are unscientific. For example, Skinner writes:

> Statements which use such words as 'incentive' or 'purpose' are usually reducible to statements about operant conditioning, and only a slight change is required to bring them within the framework of a natural science. Instead of saying that a man behaves because of the consequences which *are* to follow his behavior, we simply say that he behaves because of the consequences which *have* followed similar behavior in the past. Purpose is not a property of behavior itself; it is a way of referring to controlling variables. On this view purposive accounts of behavior are lay shorthands to be replaced by mechanistic accounts in a scientific description.
>
> (Skinner, 1953: 87)

Thus, Skinner holds the slightly paradoxical position that teleological and causal explanations are equivalent (purposive accounts can be reduced to mechanistic ones) but that causal explanations are to be preferred in the scientific explanation of behaviour (purposive accounts should be replaced by mechanistic ones).

The opposite extreme view, espoused more by philosophers than psychologists, is that the two types of explanation are incompatible and that *teleological explanations are to be preferred in the explanation of behaviour*. This is the common-sense view. If people are asked what they are doing they will nearly always answer in terms of goals or purposes, which itself requires explanation. Presumably one reason is that the consequences of behaviour are often consciously anticipated whereas the causes of behaviour are often unconscious. Amongst early psychologists, Tolman and McDougall defended the primacy of purposive over mechanistic descriptions.

> Behavior as behavior, that is, as molar, *is* purposive and *is* cognitive. These purposes and cognitions are of its immediate warp and woof. It, no doubt, is strictly dependent upon an underlying manifold of physics and chemistry, but as a matter of first identification behavior reeks of purpose and cognition.
>
> (Tolman, 1932: 12)

A compromise position between these two extremes is the claim that teleological and mechanistic explanations are different but compatible. An early expression of this view appears in Conklin:

> the relation of mechanism to finalism is not unlike that of structure to function – they are two aspects of organization. The mechanistic conception of life is in the main a structural aspect, the teleological view looks chiefly to ultimate function. These two aspects of life are not antagonistic, but complementary.
>
> (Conklin, 1943: 117)

Perhaps one of the clearest, most thorough exponents of such a view is Boden (1972). Her thesis is that *teleological amd mechanistic accounts are compatible but complementary*. Their compatibility implies that empirical reduction is true: teleological phenomena are dependent on causal mechan- isms. Causal mechanisms provide necessary, but are unlikely to provide sufficient, conditions for teleological phenomena. The complementarity between teleological and mechanistic accounts implies that strict reduction is false. Different languages are involved: the two accounts are not intertranslatable.

Teleological and mechanistic explanations as equivalent

Nagel (1953) has argued that teleological (or functional) explanations are equivalent to non-teleological ones. They contain the same factual content, the difference being merely 'one of emphasis and perspective in formulation'.

Teleological explanations focus on consequences and whole systems, whereas causal explanations focus on conditions and constituents:

> Teleological explanations focus attention on the culminations and products of specific processes. . . . They view the operations of things from the perspective of certain selected wholes to which the things belong. . . . Non-teleological explanations, on the other hand, place chief emphasis on certain conditions under which specified processes are initiated and persist. . . . They represent the inclusive behaviour of a thing as the operation of certain selected constituents into which a thing is analysed.
>
> (Nagel, 1953: 215)

Nagel claims that teleological explanations are of the form 'B is an effect of A' (an atypical interpretation), whereas non-teleological explanations are of the form 'A is a cause or condition of B'. He provides a biological and a physical example. The biological one is as follows:

Teleological version

The function of chlorophyll in plants is to enable them to perform photosynthesis.

Non-teleological versions

Plants perform photosynthesis only if they contain chlorophyll.

A necessary condition for the occurrence of photosynthesis in plants is the presence of chlorophyll.

However, these versions are not equivalent (Valentine, 1988). In the teleological case, chlorophyll may be a sufficient condition for the occurrence of photosynthesis but there is no implication that it is a necessary condition (the possibility that there are other means of carrying it out is allowed), whereas in the non-teleological case it is stated to be a necessary condition. This is particularly serious since teleological explanations are typically invoked where a variety of causes produce, or means serve, an end. A teleological generalisation is appropriate if it 'captures a class of events that is not covered by any *one* generalisation of a mechanistic sort' (Bennett, 1983). Thus they cannot be considered equivalent to the non-teleological formulations, where this is contraindicated.

The physical example is as follows:

Non-teleological version

The volume of a gas at constant temperature varies inversely with its pressure.

Teleological versions

The function of a varying pressure in a gas at constant temperature is to produce an inversely varying volume.

Gases at constant temperature under variable pressure alter their volumes in order to keep the product of pressure and volume constant.

These teleological versions are distinctly odd. This may be due to the absence of any biological need or adaptive function, the lack of variation of end, or the belief that inanimate things cannot have purposes. The example given is a functional law which is neither properly teleological nor properly causal for two reasons. First, there is no temporal sequence involved. Causal and teleological explanations are inherently temporal, referring to antecedent and consequent conditions respectively. Secondly, functional laws are symmetrical, whereas teleological explanations are typically involved where a variety of initial conditions may result in the same end. Therefore, Nagel's conclusion depends on an inappropriate example (Valentine, 1988).

Teleological and mechanistic explanations as non-equivalent

McDougall (1936) baldly states the case: 'Active striving towards a goal is a fundamental category of psychology, and is a process or type that cannot be mechanistically explained or resolved into mechanistic sequences.' There have been two main arguments for the non-equivalence of teleological and mechanistic explanations. The first depends on the *impossibility of specifying initial conditions* in the case of teleological explanations. It is usually argued that purposive explanations provide sufficient conditions whereas causal accounts only provide necessary ones in this case. Sufficient causal conditions cannot be provided because it is impossible to specify the initial conditions exhaustively since, quintessentially, the same end can be achieved by a variety of means. Gauld and Shotter (1977) give an equivalent form of the argument when they claim to demonstrate that concept- and rule-governed behaviour cannot be accounted for in terms of a generalised finite-state machine (giving input–output relations) because the input cannot be physically delimited.

Peters (1958) has expressed the view that the appropriate type of explanation for most human behaviour is the 'rule-following, purposive model'. He describes the paradigm case of human action as when something is done in order to bring about an end. For example, the answer to the question 'Why did Jones cross the road?' might be 'to buy tobacco'. Such a model is normative; for example, in this case it assumes that crossing the road is a reasonable way of achieving this aim, and logically distinct from causal explanations. In the case of actions which can be described in terms of the rule-following model, causal explanations (which imply the statement of sufficient conditions) are said to be not only otiose but also inappropriate. In support of the claim that an exhaustive account of the necessary and sufficient conditions for an action cannot be given, Peters cites the fact that a given action (say, signing a contract) may be carried out by a variety of movements (for instance, the legal implication would be the same even if you signed with your foot). However, as Locke (1974) has pointed out, this example confuses the issue of teleological versus causal explanation with that of level of analysis.

According to Peters, causal explanations are not irrelevant but their contribution is strictly limited. They may be able to state the necessary conditions for the occurrence of human actions, to show that some individual differences in performance are dependent on slight differences in these necessary conditions, or to give sufficient conditions for breakdowns in behaviour. The causal model, he argues, is only appropriate when behaviour has deviated from the normative, purposive model and can be viewed as having broken down in some way, as in an obsessional state, where we would be more likely to characterise the person as suffering or as something having happened to them. Thus the possibility of an all-embracing theory of human behaviour, particularly of the mechanical kind espoused by Hobbes and Hull, is rejected.

A similar position has been developed by Taylor (1964; 1970) who likewise argues that mechanistic accounts state sufficient conditions for abnormal behaviour but that in the case of normal behaviour they state necessary but not sufficient conditions, on the grounds that there is an infinite set of sufficient conditions. (There may not be an infinite set but it may be impossible to specify them.) He claims that a teleological account can provide sufficient conditions for normal behaviour by referring the response to a goal state (the one that is required by the goal state given the current situation). A behavioural event is explained, in his view, by the fact that the state of affairs obtaining prior to it was such that it (the behavioural event) was required for the goal to come about: 'In a system S which tends to a goal G, when the state of the system S and the environment E is such that the event B is required for the attainment of G, B will occur' (Taylor, 1964). He assumes that the system has a natural tendency towards the goal. However, as Sutherland (1970) has pointed out, there is no known system of which it is true to say that an event's being required for a goal is a sufficient condition of its occurrence. The occurrence of the behaviour cannot be inferred from the existence of the goal.

A related point of view has been put forward by Harré and Secord (1972), who reject the claim that the mechanistic model is the only scientific one and argue that rule-following can be scientific. They deny that the most scientific conception of cause is one which focuses on external stimulation and urge a shift from explanations in terms of substances and qualities to those in terms of powers and potentialities. They recommend a 'dramaturgical' model, as employed by Goffman (1959), in which behaviour is treated as a performance whose meaning is interpretable in terms of rule-following and role-playing. Other defenders of this general line of argument are Gauld and Shotter (1977), who support an hermeneutical approach to the study of human behaviour, which involves the interpretation of actions in terms of goals, purpose and intentions; and those who claim that behaviour can be explained and predicted on the basis of the common-sense concepts of 'folk psychology' (see Searle, 1983; Fodor, 1987; Dennett, 1988). The case against folk psychology has been presented by Stich (1983). (For further discussion, see Chapter 14.)

Contrary to the view that teleological explanations provide sufficient conditions whereas causal explanations provide only necessary conditions, I have argued that the opposite is much closer to the truth (Valentine, 1988). Causal explanations typically provide sufficient conditions but are unable to provide necessary ones, whereas teleological explanations often point to necessary features. Sufficient causal conditions can often be given for the achievement of a goal. Generally, we can predict that the performance of a particular piece of behaviour is likely to result in the attainment of a certain goal. It is not necessary to supply all the possible sufficient conditions. Indeed, what teleological phenomena imply is that the sufficient causal conditions are not necessary, since there are a variety of ways of achieving a goal. The conditions specified are typically sufficient but not necessary. The achievement of a goal can be inferred from the occurrence of a piece of behaviour, bar some extenuating circumstances, but the occurrence of the behaviour cannot be inferred from the existence of the goal. In that the relation of the goal to behaviour is one to many and the achievement of some goals are necessary for biological survival, it would be closer to the truth to say that the teleological account draws attention to necessary rather than sufficient features.

The other argument for non-equivalence claims that *teleological explanations are subject to intensional logic whereas mechanistic explanations are subject to extensional logic* (Boden, 1972; Gauld and Shotter, 1977). Certain conditions, which apply to extensional statements, may fail to hold in the case of intensional statements which involve propositional attitudes such as intending, hoping, desiring, believing or imagining. These include, first, existential generalisation – that is, that anything referred to actually exists objectively. One can imagine and hope for things that may never exist. Secondly, substitutivity of co-designative terms; that is, the replacement of a term in a sentence by another which has the same reference does not alter its truth value. Although the statement 'Oedipus believed he was married to Jocasta' is true, the statement 'Oedipus believed he was married to his mother' is not true if he does not know that they are one and the same person. Hamlet intended to kill the man behind the arras but he did not intend to kill Polonius. Thirdly, the truth value of a compound sentence is derivable from the truth value of its constituents. Again this can fail in the case of intensional statements; for instance, it is possible to believe a proposition that is false, such as that unicorns exist. (See Chisholm, 1967, for a technical exposition of the criteria for intensionality.)

The relation between an intention and an action is held to be conceptual; in other words, the meaning of one is part of the meaning of the other; the intention to perform an action contains that action as part of its meaning. By contrast, the relation between cause and effect is contingent; that is, the evidence for them must be independent. However, Davidson (1963) has pointed out that the question of whether two events are logically related depends on how they are described. McGinn (1982) argues that it is important to distinguish the content of a mental state from its existence. It is the content of the intention that is logically related to the action; the existence of an intention may be causally related to the action but does not entail its occurrence, since the action may never occur.

EVALUATION OF TELEOLOGICAL EXPLANATION

According to Braithwaite (1947), teleological explanations are only valuable when discovered independently of knowledge of causal laws. Foss (1974), arguing the necessity of different types of explanation for a full understanding of human behaviour, points out that in the case of ends functionally important for survival there is likely to be a variety of means serving them; for example, body temperature is regulated by a number of built-in processes such as sweating and shivering, as well as learned processes such as adjusting the amount of clothing worn. In such cases it may make sense to focus on the common function and search for different means by which it is achieved. Sutherland (1959) suggests that the behaviour of systems, for which we prefer an explanation in terms of ends, changes systematically in such a way as to achieve different ends at different times (we would not use a teleological explanation for water finding its own level because its final state does not vary from one piece of water to another), and the same end under a very wide variety of initial circumstances. Hence, an explanation of the behaviour of a system in terms of ends is useful to the extent to which these two conditions are fulfilled. Teleological explanations are likely to be favoured where we are more interested in the result rather than in the details of the behaviour (which might be too complex or less useful for prediction). Braithwaite (1947) observes that an advantage of teleological explanation is that the exact time taken to attain a goal is not specified.

Because the essence of teleological phenomena is a relation of many causes to one effect, and because even philosophers are agreed that time cannot go backwards and there can be no such thing as a final cause, teleological explanations are generally bound to lack predictive power and can only provide explanatory satisfaction in the sense of increasing the intelligibility of a sequence of behaviour. (However, given sufficient background knowledge about the organism's behavioural repertoire, there may be occasions where they can be predictive.) Hempel (1959) also provides plentiful evidence that, as commonly used, 'functional explanations' are frequently sadly lacking in precise specification of scope and operational testability of their key terms. To quote one of the examples he gives: 'Suicide does not have adaptive (survival) value but it does have adjustive value for the organism. Suicide is functional because it abolishes painful tension.' The main use of teleological explanations must be as a heuristic research strategy: given a biologically important end one may set about looking for ways in which it is realised.

Bechtel (1986b) argues that teleological functional analysis as distinct from teleological explanation has an important role to play in science, since it recognises the interaction between levels and the organisation of parts in relation to the functioning of a system as a whole (in this respect being superior to a reductionist framework); it focuses attention on significant features of behaviour important for adaptation to the environment, thus providing an evolutionary and ecological perspective.

CONCLUSION

In this chapter we have discussed some of the controversial issues concerning teleological explanations and their relation to mechanistic accounts of behaviour. It has been argued that they are best considered as complementary approaches. Teleological accounts are not reducible to mechanistic ones (future and possibly unattainable goals cannot be the causes of behaviour) but neither are they mutually incompatible (mechanistic accounts of goal-directed behaviour can be given in terms of feedback loops). Although teleological accounts are thus not applicable exclusively to organic phenomena, nevertheless their main advantage is to focus attention on the adaptive function of behaviour.

Chapter 13

Alternative perspectives

INTRODUCTION

Many objections have been raised against orthodox psychology, particularly behaviourism and cognitive psychology. These range from radical challenges to the underlying framework (for example, dualism of mind and matter or subject and object, and the causal model) to methodological critiques (such as the role of the individual and subjective experience) and charges of lack of relevance and ecological validity. Behaviourism has been seen as mechanistic, reductionist and pessimistic, and cognitive psychology as ignoring content, context and purpose (Claxton, 1980). Both have been considered dehumanising. In this chapter we shall consider alternative perspectives which go some way towards answering these challenges: phenomenology, existentialism, humanistic psychology and Eastern psychology. (Methodological problems were considered in Chapters 5 and 6, and limitations of the computational model in Chapter 10; the role of the individual is discussed in Chapter 14.)

PHENOMENOLOGY

The term 'phenomenology' was coined in the mid-nineteenth century (from the Greek *phenomenon*, meaning appearance, that which shows itself) to refer to the study of the essential nature of consciousness. It is to be distinguished from 'phenomenalism', the metaphysical theory that only phenomena or appearances need to be postulated as existing, as distinct from some underlying reality, *noumena* or things-in-themselves. According to phenomenology, reality is relative to consciousness but transcends it. It is also to be contrasted with introspection, which studies facts within consciousness. The goal of phenomenology is the systematic description of the invariant structures of consciousness which constitute the necessary preconditions for experience and knowledge. In this sense it is prior to other studies. Its aim is to discover 'what the mind has to be in order for the world of objects to exist for it' (Bolton, 1979) or, in their terminology, how the objective is subjectively constituted. Consciousness is both presupposed by, and reveals, reality.

In order to reach *zu den Sachen selbst* (to the things themselves), it is necessary to pursue the *phenomenological method of reduction*, a graded series of alterations in perspective. The *naturalistic standpoint* is exemplified by the natural sciences which investigate objective reality. In *descriptive phenomenology* consciousness itself becomes the object of study. Spiegelberg (1971) distinguishes three phases: (1) intuiting: intense concentration on, and attentive internal gaze at, phenomena; (2) analysing: finding various constituents of phenomena and their relationship; and (3) describing: providing an account of intuited and analysed phenomena such that they can be understood by others. *Transcendental phenomenology* involves the intuiting of essences by means of eidetic reduction, in which an idea of something can be attained by studying instances of it; the method can be extended by examining imagined variations in order to determine the limits and hence the essential nature of the object (compare what philosophers refer to as 'thought experiments').

The phenomenological method requires the elimination of presuppositions as far as possible. Central to this is the operation of *bracketing* (that is, putting in brackets) or setting aside assumptions characteristic of the naturalistic attitude; for example, belief in the existence of objective reality, space, time and the self. If this suspension of judgement (or *epochē*, after the Greek word meaning abstention) is perfectly achieved, then only the stream of pure consciousness is revealed. Experience is retained but its mode of apprehension is transformed. (There are striking parallels here with the aims and described results of certain meditational practices, see Valentine, 1985.)

A central tenet of phenomenology is the interdependence of knower and known. Science constitutes rather than discovers the world. No view has ontological priority. Essentially a dialectical model is involved. Both a dualism between subjective and objective and the reduction of one to the other is rejected, thus avoiding the extremes of rationalism which overemphasises the contribution of the mind, and empiricism which overemphasises the contribution of the world. For a contrast of phenomenology with Piagetian interactionism, see Bolton (1978). As applied to psychology, it has led to the focusing of attention on the subject's perspective and the meaning of the situation for the participants, which is considered crucial for understanding their behaviour; and to the study of intersubjectivity and shared meanings. Emphasis has been placed on understanding rather than explanation, and an anti-reductionist stance taken.

The origins of phenomenological thought can be traced to Augustine and Aquinas, and to *Kant*, who was concerned with the preconditions of knowledge. He concluded that there were twelve a priori categories of understanding, such as substance and cause, and two fundamental 'forms of intuition'; namely, space and time. These were presupposed by both analytic and synthetic knowledge. The other precursor was Franz *Brentano* (1838–1917), who introduced the notion of *intensionality*, according to which mental acts (such as seeing, thinking or desiring) necessarily intend or imply objects (something seen, thought or desired), though these need not necessarily exist in the external world.

The founder of phenomenology was *Edmund Husserl* (1858–1938), who provided a formal statement of the system in *Logical Investigations* (1901) and *Ideas* (1913). A central concept was the *Lebenswelt*, literally 'life-world' – that is, the world of everyday experience. The idea of the *Lebenswelt* as the world of lived experience and the dynamic relation between consciousness and reality was developed by Merleau-Ponty in the *The Structure of Behaviour* (1942) and *Phenomenology of Perception* (1945).

A number of psychologists became interested in phenomenology, particularly with a view to its methodological implications. Goethe and Purkinje had applied what might be described as phenomenological methods to the study of colour perception; and similarly Stumpf with respect to tone perception. David Katz, whose work together with that of E.R. Jaensch and Edgar Rubin anticipated *Gestalt* psychology, was directly associated with Husserl, as was Karl Buhler, a member of the Würzburg school of psychologists. Both they and the *Gestalt* psychologists favoured a procedure of 'naïve' observation. Wertheimer, Koffka and Köhler worked at Göttingen contemporaneously with Husserl but did not acknowledge him initially, and Köhler later dissociated himself from him philosophically. Others who have employed phenomenological methods include: Buytendijk, E. Strauss and Michotte (see Thinès *et al.*, 1991) on the Continent; Goldstein, Snygg and MacLeod in the USA; and in more recent times Rogers, Goffman and Shotter. A group who share some of their methodological ideals, though forming a distinct tradition, are the ethologists, who take the view that the description of behaviour in its natural environment should take precedence over the explanation of behaviour in artificial laboratory conditions.

Evaluation

Phenomenology studies the nature of consciousness. The issue of conscious experience as subject matter in psychology was discussed in Chapters 4 and 5, where it was concluded that it was legitimate subject matter and, although raising methodological difficulties, these were not insuperable nor radically different from those posed for other subject matters. In so far as phenomenology is concerned with the essential characteristics of consciousness necessary to constitute the world of objects, it is more closely related to epistemology than to psychology, but fundamental to all science.

The concept of intensionality has, in my view, closer affinities with philosophical than psychological frameworks. It has, nevertheless, led to important developments in the notion of representation central to cognitive psychology (see, for example, Fodor, 1981). For a sympathetic treatment of its application to the explanation of behaviour, see McGinn (1979).

The concept of the 'life-world', involving the rejection of both subject–object dualism and the reduction of one to the other, represents a radically different framework which has not been fully acknowledged in psychology, although moves towards consideration of the subject in interaction with the environment may be seen in Piagetian developmental psychology and some models of social psychology (for instance, Mischel, 1973). The dialectical model implied by phenomenology (see Rychlak, 1981) stands in radical opposition to the causal model pursued by psychology.

Philosophical difficulties in giving a coherent account of the notion of causation, current work in social science and particularly developments in modern physics – see Capra (1975) and Zukav (1979) for popular treatments – suggest that the phenomenological perspective may be the more appropriate.

The need to focus on subjective meaning, anathema to the behaviourist and problematic for any scientist, has been increasingly realised in psychology, attempts to take cognisance of it having been made particularly in cognitive, social and dynamic psychology. For the view that ethology constitutes the application of this phenomenological perspective to animal psychology see Thinès (1977).

Phenomenology recommends a method of theoretically neutral observation and description, in common with ethology and to which Skinnerians claim to aspire. Although unattainable in the limit (presuppositions cannot be entirely eliminated nor can non-conceptualised experience be communicated), it is laudable as an aim. It is particularly desirable at an initial stage in a complex discipline and too often bypassed in psychology.

Can phenomenology be reconciled with behaviourism

The answer to this question depends largely on what is meant by 'phenomenology' (Continental or American) and 'behaviourism' (methodological or radical). If the original Continental formulations of phenomenology and existentialism (see below) are taken, then there are serious areas of conflict at the conceptual level with respect to the relation between subject and object, choice and determinism, and dialectical and causal models. In my view these are irreconcilable.

However, much of the literature suggests that a reconciliation between them is possible. For example, of the six contributors to the Rice symposium on behaviourism and phenomenology (Wann, 1964), four were in favour of a reconciliation in some form. Brody and Oppenheim (1966) in considering tensions between the two schools suggest two forms of *rapprochement:* terminological and complementary roles. The latter, they suggest, could consist of the use of either behaviourist methods to construct theoretical systems and phenomenological methods to test them, or vice versa: phenomenological methods to construct theoretical systems and behaviourist methods to test them. The second of these alternatives – namely, the application of behaviourist methods to phenomenological problems – is proposed by Day (1969), who is of the opinion that 'there are numerous ways in which a flourishing phenomenology and radical behaviourism need each other'.

It is clear that many of these reconciliations involve a very much watered-down version of phenomenology. Kvale and Grenness (1967), in an extremely interesting paper, point out that phenomenology in the Rice symposium is taken to mean merely the study of experience and the acceptance of verbal reports. They then go on to develop the thesis that Skinner's radical behaviourism shows some remarkable similarities to Sartre's and Merleau-Ponty's views on psychology. They present evidence to document the claims that both schools reject a dualism between private and public or psychologists and their subjects. 'The "boundary" for public–private is not the skin but the line between the verbal community's being able to reinforce behaviour differentially and its not being able to, or able to only with great difficulty' (Skinner, 1964). Both reject what Kvale and Grenness refer to as the illusion of the double world, the view that the inner world is a copy of the external world (on this see also Still, 1979); the prejudice of the objective world, the view that physics is more 'real' than perception; and the flight to the inner man, the explanation of behaviour based on the assumption that it is an index of and/or caused by an inner process. Both emphasise adequate description, stress behaviour in relation to the environment as the fundamental subject matter of psychology, and conceive of knowledge as action.

In sum, a reconciliation between phenomenology and behaviourism in the form of the application of behaviourist methods, with their advantage of rigour, to phenomenological problems, with their advantages of relevance and significance, is possible and desirable; but at the level of conceptual framework there are fundamental differences between behaviourism and phenomenology. Nevertheless, contrary to expectation, there are some striking parallels between Skinner's radical behaviourism and phenomenology.

EXISTENTIALISM

Existentialism was a movement in philosophy and literature, the seeds of which were sown in the mid-nineteenth century, although the label (from the Latin *ex-sistere* meaning to stand out, emerge, become) did not appear until the 1920s, coming into general use by the 1940s. Those most often designated as existentialists are *Søren Kierkegaard* (1813–55), *Martin Heidegger* (1899–1976), *Jean-Paul Sartre* (1905–80) and the psychiatrist *Karl Jaspers* (1883–1969). Existentialism constitutes a reaction against Hegelian philosophy in particular and Western philosophy in general, with its emphasis on positivism, materialism, pragmatism and a distinction between subject and object.

As their label suggests, the emphasis is on existence (namely, conscious experience) in contradistinction to classical philosophy's preoccupation with essence (that is, the analysis of the nature of things). Interest is centred on the individual and subjective experience, which is accepted as valid and considered a sufficient criterion for truth. Non-rational processes are acknowledged and the supremacy of reason denied. In their view all human characteristics and properties are consequences of existence. The central concern is with the human condition and the meaning of life. The negative aspects of the human condition are mortality and the subjugation of the individual by society. The positive aspect is freedom. It is an essential part of the existentialist credo that choice is real: people are self-determining agents who create their own destiny. In the words of Karl Jaspers: 'What Man is, he ultimately becomes through the cause which he has made his own.' The emphasis is on potential, 'becoming', the possibilities of existence. The goal is to seek authenticity.

Evaluation

Existentialist philosophy has frequently been criticised for being unintelligible, confused or excessively subjective. Its only methodological contribution has been insistence on the validity of subjective experience, a faith which is not always justified (see Chapter 5). The existentialist claim that choice is real is in conflict with a deterministic psychology unless a coherent account of self-determinism can be given. This issue was discussed in Chapter 2, where it was concluded that although there is an interpretation of free will which can be reconciled with determinism it is not the sense usually intended. Moreover, the findings of scientific psychology suggest that there are severe limitations to choice and freedom.

Existentialism's main contribution has been to provide new foci of attention. Its emphasis on the meaning of life and striving for authenticity have made a significant impact, predominantly in clinical psychology and psychotherapy, influencing the work of people such as Binswanger, Frankl, Erikson, Fromm and Laing. The study of positive aspects of the human condition, particularly self-actualisation, has been developed by humanistic psychologists, to whom we now turn.

HUMANISTIC PSYCHOLOGY

The term 'humanistic psychology' was coined by Cantril in 1955 with its aim as the building of 'a science *of* man that is *for* man' (Smith, 1969). Maslow introduced the term 'third force' in 1958, reflecting dissatisfaction with the other two forces, namely, psychoanalysis and behaviourism, which was considered by many to be dehumanising (mechanistic and reductionist), pessimistic and narrowly based ('ratomorphic', to use Koestler's term).

Its themes centre on people and in particular the study of characteristics deemed to be distinctively human, such as experience, uniqueness, meaning, choice and dignity. Human nature is positively evaluated and attention focused on superior qualities and their development; hence the human potential movement and the stress on personal growth and self-actualisation. Concentration is directed towards the present (and the future) rather than the past. Humanistic psychology adopts a phenomenological attitude towards individual experience and emphasises uniqueness within an organismic and holistic theoretical framework. Meaningfulness of problems is valued over rigour and objectivity.

Existentialism was the main historical antecedent of humanistic psychology. The immediate factor leading to its development was the emigration of Continental Europeans to a receptive atmosphere in the United States where there was dissatisfaction with the first and second forces, and disenchantment exacerbated by the world wars. The movement gathered momentum with the translation of Continental books especially into English. It was formally established in the United States in the 1950s, Maslow providing a general sketch in 1954 and a paper specifically on humanistic psychology in 1956. The *Journal of Humanistic Psychology* appeared in 1962 and the Association for Humanistic Psychology was formed the following year.

Humanistic psychologists have much in common with neo-Freudians such as Jung, Adler, Rank, Horney and Fromm and with the defenders of the tradition of *Verstehen* and idiographic psychology (discussed in Chapter 14).

Probably the most central humanistic psychologist has been *A.H. Maslow*, whose major work was *Motivation and Personality* (1954), in which he postulated a hierarchy of needs: physiological, safety, belonging and love, esteem and self-actualisation, claiming that satisfaction of the lower ones was a necessary prerequisite for satisfaction of the higher. He made an exploratory study of self-actualisation, based on an examination of people selected by him as self-actualised, resulting in the description of fifteen characteristics of self-actualised people. He also described peak experiences, moments of the highest happiness and fulfilment.

One other person who perhaps should be singled out for special mention is *Carl Rogers*, the developer of client-centred therapy and an independent originator of encounter groups. His work includes an account of what he calls the 'fully functioning person'. Conditions necesssary for successsful therapy are considered to be positive regard for, empathy with, and unconditional acceptance of the client by the therapist. One of his main contributions has been the conduct of empirical research in support of these claims, although inadequacies still remain (see Shapiro, 1976). Nevertheless his approach calls for optimism with regard to the possibility of combining humanistic ideas with rigorous research.

Evaluation

On the credit side, it may be said that humanistic psychology has focused attention on positive characteristics and been prepared to study aspects ignored by other approaches, thus somewhat redressing the previous imbalance. Humanistic psychologists have had the courage to face the challenge of relevance and to tackle significant and meaningful issues. Its applications have been far-reaching through encounter groups, the Esalen Institute and other developments of the human potential movement.

On the debit side, humanistic psychology may be criticised for inadequate conceptualisation. Geller (1982) exposes the difficulties in giving a coherent account of self-actualisation. Normative theories such as those of Maslow and Rogers presuppose the concept of a self or human nature with intrinsic properties, whereas the self is essentially social, the result of an interaction between organism and environment. It is to be doubted whether the optimism of humanistic psychology is justified. In so far as self-actualisation is an end consciously striven for, it is self-defeating and risks becoming an ideology promoting what it seeks to avoid. Although humanistic psychology has inspired the development of alternative methods (such as experiential and participatory; see Reason and Rowan, 1981), these may fall short of the standards of science. Even Maslow (1969) admits that humanistic psychologists 'hover on the edge of antiscience and even irrational feelings in their enthusiasm for "experiencing"'. Ineffable experience cannot be communicated; rigour and controls are often lacking. In general, there have been deficiencies in evaluative criteria and a lack of empirical support.

EASTERN PSYCHOLOGY

Over the last decade there has been an increase in interest in Eastern psychologies, deriving from ancient spiritual traditions, particularly Buddhism (Claxton, 1986; Crook and Fontana, 1990). In the West, religion and science are seen as opposed; by contrast, in the East they are more frequently seen as mutually enriching (Paranjpe, 1984). Moreover, it is arguable whether Buddhism is so much a religion in the strict sense as a system of ideas and practices aimed at self-development. Its main, though not exclusive, impact has therefore been on psychotherapy.

The metaphysical assumptions underlying Eastern psychologies include: (1) the dynamic interdependence and relativity of the universe; (2) a process view, in which impermanence and change are endemic; (3) an all-embracing determinism: nothing is uncaused and all actions have consequences (strictly the total situation at one moment leads into the total situation at the next in an unbroken, flowing whole); and (4) the rejection of dualism, particularly of subject and object, or self and other.

A central claim in Buddhist theory is that the idea of a personal self as enduring, separate and autonomous, the recipient of perceptions and initiator of actions, is an illusion. Although contrary to common-sense and some current psychology, this is in accord with a long tradition in philosophy (cf. Hume's assertion that the mind is merely a bundle of ideas), much social psychology, behaviourist psychology (which abhors homunculi and espouses epiphenomenalism) and recent work in artificial intelligence and neurophysiology (Valentine, 1989c). A constructivist view of perception is also accepted by most cognitive psychologists. Buddhist theory contains detailed models of consciousness, perception, attention and memory (see Valentine, 1991). Psychological analyses of meditation as a deconstructive process, in which an attempt is made to break the habitual modes of categorisation, have been offered by Deikman (1966) and Brown (1977). However, empirical research on the physiological and psychological effects of meditation has been somewhat disappointing (West, 1987).

Eastern psychology is essentially practical. The purpose of meditation is to eradicate attachment, believed to be the root of all suffering. In addition, the literature is full of techniques for self-management, many of them based on mutual inhibition; for example, the replacement of negative thoughts by positive. Parallels between these and current ideas in cognitive behaviour therapy have been explored by de Silva (1984; 1990).

Evaluation

In its insistence on the artificiality of categorisation, Eastern psychology may appear anti-intellectual. Further, linguistic difficulties result from the fact that most of the original texts are in Pali and exact translation of terms is often not possible. Eastern and Western psychology differ in their aims and methods. Although both may be considered empirical, Eastern psychology is experiential and subjective rather than experimental and objective, the result of systematic self-observation and intuition as opposed to hypothetico-deductive reasoning based on observation of other people. The aim is the practical and personal one of enlightenment, in contrast to the development of general models for explanation and prediction.

Despite these different traditions, the fundamental assumptions of Eastern psychology are consistent with Western science and sufficient common ground can be found, between Buddhist theory and certain areas of cognitive and clinical psychology, to suggest that further exploration would be fruitful. The emphasis on practical applications in the form of techniques for training attention and strategies for living answer the call for relevance.

In this chapter we have considered the possible contributions to psychology of frameworks drawn from traditions far removed from those of orthodox

Western psychology. These challenge conventionally accepted assumptions of causation and duality; offer alternative methods, often focusing on subjective experience; and open up new areas for investigation, frequently addressing the issue of relevance. In the final chapter we turn to a discussion of the role of the individual in psychology.

Chapter 14

Idiographic psychology

INTRODUCTION

The final issue to be considered concerns the appropriate treatment of the individual. The traditions of *Verstehen* and idiographic psychology raise a number of questions about the foundations of experimental psychology, particularly in relation to personality and social psychology. They favour an intuitive, holistic approach aimed at empathic understanding of the quality of a unique pattern, in contrast to the analytic, hypothetico-deductive approach aimed at generalised, quantitative predictions. We shall consider whether a science of the individual is possible and what role can be played by the study of single cases.

A problem arises from the fact that science is concerned with generalities: means and probability statements. According to an old adage: *scientia non est individuorum* – that is, science does not deal with individual cases. The problem with aggregate statements is that they may reflect no single individual case – see the discussion of Baloff and Becker's (1967) work in Chapter 6. This issue has arisen in many areas of psychology. In neuropsychology, for example, Caramazza (1986) has argued that valid inferences about the structure of normal cognitive systems from patterns of impaired performance can only be drawn from single cases, on the grounds that group studies can only be used if homogeneity can be assumed. Averaging is only justified if the patients are equivalent in relevant respects. However, it is generally not possible to determine this independently of the theories which are being evaluated, and hence the procedure is circular. The issue has a long history in the psychology of personality.

> In every concrete individual, there is a uniqueness that defies all formulation. We can feel the touch of it and recognize its taste, so to speak, relishing or disliking, as the case may be, but we can give no ultimate account of it, and have in the end simply to admire the Creator.
>
> (James, 1912: 109)

The scientific study of the individual has been thought problematical on the grounds that the individual constitutes a unique pattern which is more than the sum of component parts and not fully represented by, for example, scores on dimensional tests.

> We spend scarcely one per cent of our research time discovering whether those common dimensions are in reality relevant to Bill's personality, and if so, how they are patterned together to compose the Billian quality of Bill. . . . The organization of Bill's life is first, last, and all the time, the primary fact of his human nature.
>
> (Allport, 1962: 410)

These problems have led to the relative neglect of the study of individual differences and failure to integrate experimental and differential psychology, the consequences of which have been discussed by Eysenck (1966). His own solution to the problem is through the compromise position of studying typologies.

Allport, who rejects the view that assigns the unique to art and the general to science, has called for an *idiographic* psychology of personality (from the Greek *idios*, meaning own or private as distinct from public) whose function is to study the individual, in addition to *nomothetic* psychology (from the Greek *nomos*, meaning law) which is concerned with dimensions, norms and general laws. We shall consider the validity of this distinction. Allport's claim is that idiographic interpretations can be made testable, communicable and predictable but that special morphogenic methods (from the Greek *morphē*, meaning form), suited to studying the pattern of individuals, are required in addition to dimensional ones.

The tradition of *Verstehen* is based on the premiss that different methods are required by the social sciences from those used in the natural sciences, the former demanding empathic, intuitive understanding in contrast to the latter's preoccupation with prediction and explanation based on causal statements. Its supporters are likely to be sympathetic towards the view that more is to be learned about human nature by reading novels than by studying academic psychology.

James (1907) pointed out that much of the variance between thinkers can be accounted for by reference to a dimension he labelled 'tough-tendermindedness', for which experimental support, with respect to psychological theorists, has been provided by Coan (1979). Idiographic psychologists belong to the latter group or, to use Boring's terms, to the 'something more' rather than the 'nothing but' school. In general they are opposed to mechanistic quantification and reductionist analysis of holistic properties.

HISTORY

The origins of these movements lie in nineteenth-century Germany, as part of a general swing away from classicism (represented by objectivity, positivism, materialism and mechanism) towards romanticism (represented by subjectivity, intuitionism and vitalism) (Holt, 1967). A central theme was the claim that the social sciences were distinct from the natural sciences and demanded different methods, notably that of *Verstehen* (understanding). Eighteenth-century precursors can be found in *J.S. Mill*, who distinguished the science of character (ethology) from the science of mind in general (psychology), the task of the former being to study the operation of psychological laws in specifically individual combinations, such as the pattern of a particular person or culture; and *Kant*, who suggested that the study of the mind required the method of intuition of the whole in addition to the analytic and generalising methods of the natural sciences devised for the study of matter.

In 1851 *Cournot* distinguished the exact sciences in which precise laws were possible from history, which he believed to be dominated by chance so that it could only be probabilistic in nature. This distinction between *Naturwissenschaften*, the natural sciences, and *Geisteswissenschaften* which covered the social sciences plus philosophy, history, jurisprudence and the humanities, was developed by several writers:

Windelband introduced the terms 'nomothetic' to refer to the kind of science that dealt with general laws and 'idiographic' to refer to the kind of science that dealt with structured patterns – terms which Holt (1967) dismisses as pretentious jargon, 'mouth-filling polysyllables to awe the uninitiated'. The former was said to give knowledge of being (*Sein*), the latter consciousness of relatedness to norms (*Sollen*). It was claimed that different methods were appropriate in the two cases: analysis, quantification and explanation in the former but understanding in the latter. 'We explain nature but we understand human beings' (Dilthey, 1937).

Rickert distinguished the historical and cultural from the generalising, natural sciences on the grounds that the former was concerned with individuals and values.

Simmel stressed the subjective understanding of meanings by reference to typical cases and the need to acknowledge plurality of interpretations.

Dilthey (1833–1911) thought the difference between the social and the natural sciences lay in their content, the subject matter of the former being characterised by mental activity. In this context he introduced the concept of *Verstehen*, himself beginning with what might be described as psychological understanding but moving towards a more cultural endeavour. In his view *Verstehen* psychology strove for direct insight into the vital nature of things as articulated wholes ('*Strukturzusammenhang*'), involving the systematic description of the nature and development of consciousness and the inner unity of individual life. Experienced relations were stressed over analysis into elements. The most important unifying forces in people were seen as purpose and moral character, and human character as intimately related to, and an outgrowth of, social institutions.

An important follower of Dilthey was *Spranger*, whose *Types of Men* was published in 1922. He distinguished descriptive from explanatory psychology, favouring the former '*Strukturpsychologie*' whose concern was intelligible wholes grasped through the method of *Verstehen*. A person's values were of primary interest, and Spranger is probably best known for his six ideal values – theoretical, economic, aesthetic, social, political and religious – on which Allport, Vernon and Lindzey (1960) based their test of values. *Weber* employed the psychological understanding of motives, as well as the identification of actions through the understanding of meaning by recourse to complex conceptual structures such as 'the spirit of capitalism'. His distinction between direct and explanatory understanding is similar to Jaspers's between static understanding ('the presentation to oneself of psychic states, the objectifying to oneself of psychic qualities') and genetic understanding, of an empathic kind.

In the post-war years the positivists held sway but more recently there has been a resurgence of doubts about the method appropriate for the social sciences (see, for example, Harré and Secord, 1972; Outhwaite, 1975; Gauld and Shotter, 1977; Antaki, 1988).

IS A SCIENCE OF THE INDIVIDUAL POSSIBLE?

There are a number of issues raised under this head. One concerns the questions of whether the individual can be studied in science and, if so, what role case studies play in such a discipline. An individual case can be and often is the subject of scientific investigation. In areas where data from individual subjects are thought to be reliable and representative, single-subject designs are considered acceptable. A noteworthy example is the experimental analysis of behaviour by radical behaviourists (see Sidman, 1960). In these cases, subjects typically serve as their own controls, and special methodology has been developed for the purpose (see Barlow and Hersen, 1984). In other cases, such studies may provide data which are unique, otherwise unobtainable and of great theoretical interest. As Newcombe and Marshall (1988) point out, the dichotomy between single-case versus group studies is misconceived: the importance of an effect is not simply related to the size of the sample but is a function of the theoretical context. In neuropsychology, where single cases may be all that are available, necessity has been made a virtue. However, the results of such studies are scientifically uninterpretable unless an adequate baseline for comparison is provided (either in the form of the patient's performance before the onset of the illness, usually unavailable, or scores from a normal population on standardised tests). In isolation it is difficult to determine whether or not the results from a single case are due to chance and, without replication, whether or not they are generalisable. Such data are insufficient to establish general laws.

> No matter how intensively prolonged, objective and well-controlled the study of a single case, one can never be sure to what extent the lawful regularities found can be generalized to other persons, or in what way the findings will turn out to be contingent on some fortuitously present characteristic of the subject – until the investigation is repeated on an adequate sample of persons. As excellent a way as it is to make discoveries, the study of an individual cannot be used to establish laws.
>
> (Holt, 1967: 397)

The individual is subject to laws, but study of particular cases, like the method of *Verstehen*, is useful for hypothesis formation rather than testing.

The reasons for supposing that a scientific study of the individual is impossible or that some important aspects must necessarily be neglected are various. It may be argued that science deals with general statements whereas the individual is *unique*. However, as Grünbaum (1952) and others have pointed out, all particulars are unique. Scientific laws relate only certain aspects of events which are classified together on the basis of some common feature(s). Total identity is not required. Individuality is a matter of degree. Kluckholn and Murray (1953) observe that each person is in certain respects (1) like all other people, (2) like some other people, and (3) like no other people. The first two are no less significant for predicting behaviour than is the last. If there were no commonalities between individuals then an idiographic discipline must be dumb or incomprehensible (Holt, 1967). Holt has argued that, paradoxically, the greater the degree of abstraction and generality of conceptualisation, the better the fit to the individual case. Moves towards the concrete and particular sacrifice flexibility and hence explanatory power.

It may be objected that *qualitative properties* of individuals cannot be subjected to quantification. For a discussion of the view that psychologists have sacrificed quality for quantity, see Hudson (1972). Meanings and values can be measured and great progress has been made in their objective investigation, as the more inspired work in personality and social psychology testifies. It must be left to the reader to assess its significance.

It is frequently argued that individuality lies in the unique combination of traits and that a whole person cannot be reduced to the sum of scores on a set of dimensions, which ignores their pattern or *structure*. It is ironical that those who called themselves 'structuralists' were some of the worst offenders. However, science can and does study structure, and the problem of different levels of analysis is common to all its departments. The idiographic study of personality has focused attention particularly on individual patterns. The problem becomes serious if there are interactive effects, if the expression of a trait is differentially affected by the combination of other traits with which it occurs, for which there is indeed plenty of evidence. The issue then becomes an empirical one.

Whether there can be a science of individual differences depends on whether these effects are systematic. It seems likely that they are but that their complexity and extent is such that practical investigation of them may be impossible. Eysenck (1966), for example, has suggested that, as a minimum, experiments should have 27 cells: three levels (high, medium and low) of intelligence x three levels of extraversion x three levels of neuroticism.

> Only when we have relatively pure-bred strains of animals representing these three dimensions, and all possible combinations of them, will we be able to devise experiments which come up to the requirements of scientific investigation. Until then we cannot properly specify, identify, or duplicate our experimental subjects, and will for ever be at the mercy of strain differences of an accidental kind yielding results which may not be duplicated when other strains are used.
>
> (Eysenck, 1966: 26)

This is only considering the variables which he thinks are important. Others might want to add more.

> No doubt our designs will be much more complex and difficult, experiments will be more time-consuming and expensive, and background knowledge will have to be more extensive and less idiosyncratic; but all this is inevitable if we are serious in our scientific quest.
>
> (Eysenck, 1966: 26)

TO WHAT EXTENT HAS THE INDIVIDUAL BEEN NEGLECTED IN PSYCHOLOGY?

In Chapter 9 we noted the examination of individual differences as a strategy for dealing with organismic variables. However, in general, experimental and differential psychology have maintained an apartheid and attempts to integrate them have been few (see, for instance, Cronbach, 1957; Eysenck, 1977). Individual differences are customarily excluded from experimental designs. Taken together with the fact that, as we saw in Chapter 6, only a small amount of the variance is accounted for by main experimental variables, Eysenck's (1966) warnings about the *consequences of neglecting individual differences* may be heeded:

1 The failure of experimentalists systematically to investigate individual differences opens the door to non-scientific theory and practice in the field of personality. Although remedying the former may not prevent the latter, it does at least provide a weapon against it.
2 Main effects apply only to means and do not enable predictions about the individual case to be made.
3 Theories and explanations based on one type of subject may not be replicated on another type. This is the problem of atypical sampling and non-replicability.

4 Failure to consider individual differences may lead to main effects being swamped (for example, Hovland, 1939), or obscured (for instance, Eysenck and Slater, 1958, where systematic functional differences accounted for only 1 per cent of the variance).

Obscuration of main effects may be caused by their interaction with personality variables. For example, it has been found that extraverts work to obtain light and noise whereas introverts work for darkness and quiet (Weisen, 1965), and that the effect of performance under frustration is differentially affected by heart rate (Doerr and Hokanson, 1965). Interactive effects with neurosis have been shown for rate of stimulus presentation (Jensen, 1962), and for the effect of drugs such as meprobamate on mood and performance (Munkelt, 1965; Janke, 1964). Similarly, the strain of animal has been shown to interact with the size and duration of the effect of a drug (McClearn, 1962) and with prenatal stress.

According to Jones and Fennell (1965), such differences might have been responsible for the long controversy between Hullians and Tolmanians. They discovered that Spence used animals descended from C.S. Hall's 'non-emotional' strain whereas Tolman's were less selected and probably closer to the 'emotional' strain. In their own studies they found that the latter were much slower in latency and running time than the former. They comment: 'These differences between the two strains of rats are strikingly congruent with the theoretical accounts of the investigators who used them', and go on to suggest that such differences may even have been responsible for differential choices of experimental equipment and design, as in their own work they found that neither strain settled very well in the apparatus used by the opposite camp. They conclude: 'The possibility that there may exist genetic differences between them cannot be dismissed; nor can we be sure that hereditary differences may not have played some role in the great debate between S–R and S–S theorists.'

When linear correlations with single personality dimensions cannot be found, conceptualisations which take account of more than one personality variable may be required. These include zone analysis (Furneaux, 1961), based on the hypothesis that different combinations of traits produce different types of behaviour, so that means on tests will differ according to zone, zones being produced by combining two or more traits; and its mathematical equivalent, moderator variables (Ghiselli, 1963). Kogan and Wallach (1964), for example, used anxiety and defensiveness as personality variables to moderate correlations with risk-taking measures. One of their findings was that low anxious, low defensive subjects showed post-decision satisfaction proportional to their winnings, whereas high anxious, high defensive subjects showed the opposite: the less they won the more satisfied they were. They write:

> It is evident that the consideration of personality dispositions of test anxiety and defensiveness as moderator variables has rendered clear a

> psychological picture that otherwise would have been totally ambiguous. Overall sample correlations that were nonsignificant or, although statistically significant, so low as to be of doubtful psychological value have been found to be substantiated in one moderator subgroup, negligible in another. In some cases, these overall correlations have been found to be significant in a positive direction in one moderator subgroup, significant in a negative direction in another. Such findings require the conclusion that consideration of potential moderator variables is nothing less than essential in psychological research involving the study of correlations.
>
> (Kogan and Wallach, 1964: 188)

Eysenck (1966) sees typology as a compromise between the false extremes of the experimentalist, who seeks to establish general functional relations, and the idiographic personality theorist, who 'embraces the concept of the individual so whole-heartedly that it leaves no room for scientific generalization, laws, or even predictability of conduct'. The experimentalist has the advantage of control and objectivity but runs the risk of sterility and irrelevance. Individual differences are liable to be neglected on the grounds that they are negligible, unsystematic, or systematic but incapable of investigation. The idiographic psychologist has the merits of significance and understanding but runs the risk of making statements that are untested, and so perhaps untrue, or untestable. Eysenck applauds Spence, Cattell and himself for having made efforts in the typological direction.

The questions, as he points out, are (1) whether people can in fact be sorted into groups such that they perform differentially in an experiment of the $a = f(b)$ kind (an empirical issue), and (2) whether the relationship between (a) and (b) can be predicted on the basis of a personality theory (a theoretical issue). He and others have produced a large body of evidence favouring an affirmative answer to the former. By constructing a theoretical superstructure for the dimensions of extraversion and neuroticism and frequently invoking the Yerkes-Dodson law, he has attempted to do the same for the latter. However, any result can be explained *post hoc* by the use of the Yerkes-Dodson law. (For two points on a U-shaped curve, the direction of their difference on the ordinate can be reversed as a function of their position on the abscissa.) It is crucial that the levels of the dimensions are established independently and the theoretical predictions made a priori.

Typologies have also been popular in neuropsychology where patients have been classified on the basis of clusters of symptoms (for example, Coltheart, 1980) but such categorisation has been fraught with difficulties (see, for instance, Wilding, 1989).

MORPHOGENIC METHODS

A prime champion of the idiographic approach has been *Gordon Allport*. Following Meehl (1957), he pointed out some of the limitations of the dimensional approach in personality. First, it is restricted in its application to circumstances where the dimensions can be objectively defined, reliably measured, validly related to the prediction target and normed for the appropriate population. Secondly, there may be a mismatch between the dimension measured and those relevant to the individual, in that some measures may not be particularly relevant, and conversely other important ones may be omitted. Finally, there is the problem of weighting the scores on the dimensions, which is an empirical matter. The crucial question is whether there is something left unaccounted for when the weighting has been achieved.

He went on to suggest a number of so-called *morphogenic methods*. The basic idea underlying these is that they should serve to study the pattern or structure of an individual without reference to nomothetic norms, instead being subjectively validated. Their 'basic emphasis is upon the individual as a unique being-in-the-world whose system of meanings and value orientation are not precisely like anyone else's' (Allport, 1962). The morphogenic methods suggested by Allport were:

1 *Matching* (Allport, 1961), in which correlations between different records of personal expression – such as voice and hand-writing – are examined.
2 *Personal structure analysis* (Baldwin, 1942), in which the letters of one subject were analysed for such things as associative complexes and feeling tone.
3 *Questionnaires* designed after intensive interview specifically for use with one patient (Shapiro, 1961). These can then be used longitudinally during the course of therapy to evaluate progress. Comparisons are made within rather than between subjects.
4 *Structural foci* – that is, major themes and intentions – usually essential motivational or stylistic characteristics. The number and range of these for a given life can be examined.
5 *Self-anchoring scales* (Kilpatrick and Cantril, 1960), in which subjects rate their position on a scale anchored at both ends – for example, 'worst possible' and 'best possible'. These can be used to increase objectivity.

A number of *semi-morphogenic methods*, which involve the adaptation of dimensional methods for the study of the individual, were also suggested. These included:

1 *Rating scales*. Conrad (1932) showed that agreement between observers on traits rated of central importance to the individual was 0.95 compared with 0.45 for traits overall, suggesting the possible irrelevance of non-central traits, the inclusion of which may merely serve to increase error. The simple

adjective checklist, in which only traits that seem appropriate to the primary trends of an individual's life are rated, takes advantage of this.

2 *The repertory grid* (Kelly, 1955), which is nomothetic in its requirement that significant others be specified, in mode of response and in measures obtained, but allows for some morphogenic discovery.
3 *Ipsative scores*, introduced by Broverman (1960) for use in the measurement of cognitive style. Standard tests are given but within-subject comparisons made, in that the performance of a subject on a given test is related to his/her performance on other types of test.
4 The Allport-Vernon-Lindzey *study of values*, which also makes within-subject rather than between-subject comparisons.
5 *The Q-sort* (Stephenson, 1953), in which statements are sorted according to their judged accuracy as self-descriptions. This is dimensional in its use of standard propositions and the injunction usually given to produce a quasi-normal distribution among sorts but might be considered morphogenic in that it makes use of self-report and can be used for measuring changes in the self-concept (Nunnally, 1955).

Evaluation

Holt (1967) argued that the idiographic–nomothetic issue is based on a false dichotomy, and that 'these mischievous and difficult terms ... had best disappear from our scientific vocabularies'. Truly idiographic methods cannot exist in science. A scientific method must be communicable and in principle generalisable. Allport's so-called idiographic methods are merely more or less nomothetic methods applied to individual cases. With reference to one of the semi-morphogenic methods, he says: 'The Q-sort is quite unacceptable in the traditional meaning of the term idiographic, and the use of the term to signify the fact that it is applied to individuals is simply grandiloquent prose' (Holt, 1967). Idiography is merely a label indicating that interest is focused on the individual, but this is a question of subject matter. As different methods are not required and science is defined by its methods rather than by its subject matter, idiography, in Holt's view, does not constitute a distinct science.

CLINICAL VERSUS STATISTICAL PSYCHOLOGY

Similar to the idiographic–nomothetic issue in psychology is that labelled 'clinical versus statistical'. Here it is argued that experimental conclusions apply to means which enable only actuarial predictions to be made and not exact outcomes with respect to the individual case. But as far as the individual is concerned the conclusion is either true or not true. Even though it may be impossible in practice to predict exactly the events of an individual life, this does not mean they are not determined.

Clinical and statistical approaches may be contrasted with respect to methods and aims. The clinical can be distinguished from the statistical *method* at both the stages of data collection and decision procedure (Meehl, 1954). The clinician favours a flexible, unstandardised procedure such as the interview or case study, whereas the statistician favours a rigorous procedure such as the administration of tests with standardised norms. The advantage of the former is that the procedure can be modified to suit the individual case; the advantage of the latter is that individual scores can be compared with generalised norms. At the stage of decision procedure the clinician interprets the data relying on judgement, whereas the statistician employs a mechanical procedure – for example, applying a formula to weighted scores. Meehl (1954) reviewed twenty empirical studies which compared the predictive success (with respect to recidivism, psychiatric prognosis or benefit from training programmes) of statistical and clinical methods of combining data. The results of his survey were that in about half the cases the statistical methods gave superior results to the clinical, in the other half there was no significant difference between them and in only one was the clinical possibly superior to the statistical. Subsequent studies have also favoured the statistical method (Goldberg, 1965; Sawyer, 1966). However, Meehl comments that listening with the 'third ear' may pay off therapeutically while not leading to predictive success of the kind studied; namely, choice among a few predetermined, crudely socially defined outcomes rather than the creation and selection from among an unlimited set of concrete, specific predictions more typical of the therapeutic situation.

In Holt's view, the spheres of activity of the statistician and the clinician overlap very little. Where the same task is performed it could be argued that the clinical method only differs from the statistical in that it is covert rather than overt. The clinician may not be able to formulate the basis of the judgements, but in so far as they are valid there must be a basis and one that is nomothetic – that is, in principle generalisable. This issue is now of current interest in relation to decision-making in general, with increased scientific knowledge of judgemental biases and heuristics (for example, Tversky and Kahneman, 1974; Nisbett and Ross, 1980) and the development of machine intelligence and expert systems. The superiority of combining clinical and statistical methods (subjective judgements mechanically combined) over either alone has been demonstrated in a range of situations (for example, Einhorn, 1972; Blattberg and Hoch, 1990). Kleinmuntz (1990) in a recent review therefore recommends using one's head *and* the formula.

With respect to *aim* it might be argued that the clinician is concerned with empathic understanding and the statistician with explanation and prediction. However, this is to oversimplify. Prediction, control and understanding are inextricably mixed. The experimentalist seeks understanding (though of a different kind) and the clinician may predict and/or control.

THE METHOD OF *VERSTEHEN*

The method of *Verstehen* or interpretative understanding is central to the debate about whether the social sciences are distinctively different from the natural sciences (some of the features claimed as distinguishing the former being subjectivity, value, meaning, purpose, mental activity, agency, actions and intention). *Hermeneutic understanding* (from the Greek *hermeneutikos* meaning interpreter) was first applied in theology to the interpretation and clarification of the meaning of biblical texts, where its aim was to grasp the intentions of the author. It became popular in philology and history, where it was hoped that it would reveal 'cultural objects'. Its application to social phenomena is based on the assumption that they are in some important way analogous to texts. Proponents of the method believe that as humans we have a special ability to understand human behaviour and that appropriate explanation of social phenomena should remain close to everyday concepts and common-sense. Droysen (1858) voiced the opinion of many who followed when he claimed that the data of social science are already partially interpreted and hence the role of the scientist is to systematise, deepen and qualify. A similar view was expressed by Schutz (1932): objective science can have no other basis than 'the already constituted meanings of active participants of the social world'. A community of outlook is presupposed, language being seen as having a particularly important role to play, in that it embeds everyday concepts.

There are two aspects: empathic identification of motives, which may involve either participatory dialogue or solitary imagination, and interpretation of the social significance of actions. Typical is the emphasis on structure and explanation of the parts by reference to the whole. 'Explanation is nothing other than the incorporation of this structure, as a constituent element, in an immediately embracing structure ... in order to render intelligible the genesis of the work' (Goldmann, 1959). The aim is to identify the meaning of an action in terms of the role it plays in the social situation. For example, the writing down of a formula might be explained as being part of the task of balancing a ledger or solving a mathematical problem. People's marching in the street might be explained by the fact that there is a demonstration going on, in terms of the reasons people go on demonstrations or by reference to the private motives of individuals.

Abel (1948) describes the operation of *Verstehen* as involving two stages: (1) the internalisation of factors in a behavioural situation, analysed in such a way (usually in terms of 'feeling states') that they parallel some personal experience of the interpreter, and (2) the hypothetical interpolation of a behaviour maxim (a generalisation based on personal experience – for example, that frustration tends to lead to aggression or aggression to guilt), which makes an otherwise puzzling connection between two observed events relevant or meaningful. He gives several examples. To explain the link between a drop in temperature and someone lighting a fire it might be assumed that the reduction in temperature decreases body temperature, the feeling state imputed being that of feeling cold, and that lighting a fire will produce heat. The behaviour maxim that is applied is that feeling cold leads to seeking warmth. The correlation between a changing and hostile world and belief in eternal truths might be explained by assuming that the former gives rise to feelings of inadequacy and, by applying the behaviour maxim, that these lead to seeking feelings of security which are provided by the belief in eternal truths. Similarly, a correlation between crop failure and a fall in the marriage rate may be made intelligible by assuming that the former results in a reduction of income which gives rise to a feeling of anxiety, and that this leads to fear of new commitments which marriage would bring. Weber's famous application was the explanation of the link between the Protestant ethic and capitalist enterprise by reference to feelings of the sacredness of worldly calling, leading to such virtues as honesty being valued. However, as von Schelting (1934) pointed out, rather more is required in this case, including a consideration of the Calvinist conception of God.

Evaluation

The method of *Verstehen* may satisfy curiosity and relieve apprehension in the case of unfamiliar or unexpected behaviour. In its favour it may be said that it recognises the role of meaning, and the hermeneutic base of, and importance of language in, social behaviour. There is a sense in which interpretation of meaning is prior to any causal analysis. It has an important role to play in hypothesis formation and it is interesting to speculate whether it is indispensable in this respect.

However, there are a number of limitations. Many are agreed that it is inadequate alone. Sympathetic imagination is relevant to the origin but not the validity of explanatory hypotheses. Empathic identification may serve a heuristic function but it does not guarantee knowledge. Conjecture is not fact nor plausibility probability. The logical canons of the social sciences are no different from those of other sciences (Nagel, 1961). Objective evidence is required through the application of experimental and statistical tests. Outhwaite (1975) distinguishes between the psychological understanding of motives 'from below', which he thinks can and should be incorporated within a natural science framework, and the hermeneutic interpretation 'from above', which he is less confident about.

The criteria of *Verstehen* appear rather to be coherence and consistency. There is a problem of circularity, known as the hermeneutic circle.

> We understand the whole from the part and the part from the whole. We derive the 'spirit of the epoch' from its individual documentary manifestations – we interpret the individual documentary manifestations on the basis of what we know about the spirit of the epoch.
>
> (Mannheim, 1952: 74)

Dilthey (1937) describes it as the 'central difficulty of the art of interpretation': 'The totality of a work must be understood through its individual propositions and their relations, and yet the full understanding of an individual component presupposes an understanding of the world.'

There is a difficulty in verification, both with respect to testing the validity of the interpretation of the subjective mental states and the objectivity of the behavioural maxim. Abel (1948) comments that there is no objective method for the internalising of either the stimulus or the response, which is largely a matter of imagination. The motives are inferred from their consequences and constrained by the total situation into which they must fit. Similarly, the behaviour maxims, the generalisations which link the feeling states and imply functional dependence between them are constructed *ad hoc* on the basis of introspection and self-observation rather than being experimentally established. Interpretation is much dependent on the observer. To what extent it is dependent on the observer's own experience and hence how far it is limited in its application to societies with which the observer is familiar is a controversial issue. Parallel problems arise in cultural anthropology and comparative psychology.

Nor does *Verstehen* add to our store of knowledge, as it merely involves the application to observed behaviour of knowledge we already possess from personal experience. In my view its fruitfulness has yet to be demonstrated.

The problem of the relation of understanding by means of *Verstehen* to causal explanation has been the subject of much debate (see Chapter 12). The most extreme view (Peters, 1958; Winch, 1958) is that the method of *Verstehen* is necessary and sufficient for the study of behaviour, and distinct from causal explanation. In contrast, most of the original exponents of *Verstehen* – for example, Dilthey and Rickert – saw it as a complementary method distinct from, but a necessary supplement to, the method of causal explanation traditional to the natural sciences. For Weber *Verstehen*, involving intuition, a wordless act of identification with the object or some attempt to live in it without analysing its *Gestalt*, is merely the first of three stages in the scientific investigation of anything. The positivist view (Abel, 1948; Nagel, 1961; Holt, 1967) is that it is a preliminary method helpful at the stage of formulating hypotheses but inadequate for testing them.

Davidson (1963) and his followers, Pettit (1979) and McGinn (1979), have argued that reasons provide a species of causal explanation. According to them, the primary reason for an action is its cause. A reason is a rationally structured combination of desires (what Davidson calls 'pro-attitudes') and beliefs. 'Rationalisation' is the explanation or justification of an action in terms of reasons: it shows why it was rational for an agent to perform the action given certain beliefs and desires. For example, the desire might be 'I want to have a cup of tea', and the belief, 'boiling a kettle of water is a way of making tea'; these allow the inference that performing the action of boiling a kettle of water is a reasonable thing to do, given these circumstances. McGinn

(1979) allows that behaviour may be caused by unconscious reasons, thus overcoming one of the stumbling-blocks of explanations of behaviour in terms of rationalisation. He makes it clear that rationalisation is idiographic and not deductive-nomological; that is, particular rationalisations cannot be subsumed under general laws. There are no laws relating reasons and actions. However, this does not mean that, differently described, they may not be covered by general laws.

For a persuasive attempt to demonstrate that hermeneutics (the interpretation of action in terms of intentions and reasons) is a different language from that of natural science, see Gauld and Shotter (1977), and for the view that the everyday prediction of individual behavioural episodes is distinct from scientific psychology which deals with general competences, see Russell (1984).

EMPATHIC UNDERSTANDING

Artistic empathy is distinct from scientific explanation (Grünbaum, 1952; Holt, 1967; Kendler, 1970). *Verstehen* in art involves subjective, empathic feeling, direct non-intellective knowing, non-explanatory understanding; scientific explanation on the other hand involves the grasp of structure and is concerned with how things work and their necessary and/or sufficient conditions. They have different aims and criteria.

> An artist's quest for 'truth' differs from a scientist's in being a striving not for strict verisimilitude but for allusive illumination. The criterion of this kind of understanding is the effect on some audience; the ultimate criterion of scientific understanding may be verified precision, or . . . an elegant and comprehensive account of facts already available, like the Darwinian theory of evolution.
>
> (Holt, 1967: 50–1)

Intuition and empathy are desirable in deciding what to study and what strategies to use in formulating hypotheses and making discoveries. But they are not sufficient. 'The methodology of verification, the hypothesis testing phase of scientific work, involves well-developed rules and consensually established procedures, and . . . intuition and empathy have no place in it' (Holt, 1967).

In some ways, however, the dichotomy between science and art is less than the nomothetic–idiographic controversy would have us believe. Scientists need to be artistic in theory construction and communication and the best of them combine traits from both art and science. As Holt observes: 'The more secure the scientists are in their methodological position, the more respect they usually have for intuition.' Art can inform and science be beautiful.

Bibliography

Abel, T. (1948) 'The operation called *Verstehen*', *American Journal of Sociology* 54: 211–18.

Allport, D.A. (1975) 'Critical notice: the state of cognitive psychology', *Quarterly Journal of Experimental Psychology* 27: 141–52.

Allport, D.A. (1980) 'Patterns and actions: cognitive mechanisms are content-specific', in G. Claxton (ed.) *Cognitive Psychology: New Directions*, London: Routledge and Kegan Paul.

Allport, F.H. (1955) *Theories of Perception and the Concept of Structure*, New York: Wiley.

Allport, G.W. (1961) *Pattern and Growth in Personality*, New York: Holt, Rinehart and Winston.

Allport, G.W. (1962) 'The general and the unique in psychological science', *Journal of Personality* 30: 405–22.

Allport, G.W., Vernon, P.E. and Lindzey, G. (1960) *A Study of Values*, 3rd edn, Boston: Houghton Mifflin.

Anand, B.K., Chhina, B.S. and Singh, B. (1961) 'Some aspects of electroencephalographic studies in yogis', *Electroencephalography and Clinical Neurophysiology* 13: 452–6.

Annett, J. (1969) *Feedback and Human Behaviour*, Harmondsworth: Penguin.

Antaki, C. (ed.) (1988) *Analysing Everyday Explanation*, London: Sage.

Antrobus, J., Antrobus, J.S. and Fisher, C. (1965) 'Discrimination of dreaming and non-dreaming sleep', *Archives of General Psychiatry* 12: 395–401.

Apter, M.J. (1973) 'The computer modelling of behaviour', in M.J. Apter and G. Westby (eds) *The Computer in Psychology*, London: Wiley.

Apter, M.J. (1989) *Reversal Theory: Motivation, Emotion and Personality*, London: Routledge.

Argyris, C. (1968) 'Some unintended consequences of rigorous research', *Psychological Bulletin* 70: 185–97.

Armstrong, D.M. (1968) *A Materialist Theory of Mind*, London: Routledge and Kegan Paul.

Armstrong, J.R. (1982) 'Barriers to scientific contributions: the author's formula', *Behavioral and Brain Sciences* 5: 197–9.

Aserinsky, E. and Kleitman, N. (1953) 'Regularly occurring periods of eye motility, and concomitant phenomena, during sleep', *Science* 118: 273–4.

Ashby, W.R. (1940) 'Adaptiveness and equilibrium', *Journal of Mental Science* 86: 478–83.

Ashby, W.R. (1948) 'Design for a brain', *Electronic Engineering* 20: 379–83.

Ayer, A.J. (1946) 'Freedom and necessity', in *Philosophical Essays*, 1954, London: Macmillan.

Ayer, A.J. (1959) 'Privacy', *Proceedings of the British Academy* 45: 43–65.
Baars, B.J. (1988) *A Cognitive Theory of Consciousness*, Cambridge: Cambridge University Press.
Bacon, F. (1620) *Novum Organum*, T. Fowler (ed.) 1979, Darby, PA: Arden Library.
Baddeley, A.D. (1976) *The Psychology of Memory*, New York: Harper and Row.
Baddeley, A.D. (1982) 'Implications of neuropsychological evidence for theories of normal memory', *Philosophical Transactions of the Royal Society of London B* 298: 59–72.
Baddeley, A.D. and Lieberman, K. (1980) 'Spatial working memory', in R. Nickerson (ed.) *Attention and Performance* VIII, Hillsdale, NJ: Erlbaum.
Bakan, D. (1967) *On Method*, San Francisco: Jossey-Bass.
Baldwin, A.L. (1942) 'Personal structure analysis: a statistical method for investigation of the single personality', *Journal of Abnormal and Social Psychology* 37: 163–83.
Baloff, N. and Becker, S.E. (1967) 'On the futility of aggregating individual learning curves', *Psychological Reports* 20: 183–91.
Bannister, D. (1968) 'The myth of physiological psychology', *Bulletin of the British Psychological Society* 21: 229–31.
Barber, T.X. and Silver, M.J. (1968) 'Fact, fiction, and the experimenter bias effect', *Psychological Bulletin Monographs Supplement* 70: 1–29.
Barlow, D.H. and Hersen, M. (1984) *Single-Case Experimental Designs*, 2nd edn, Oxford: Pergamon.
Bartlett, F.C. (1932) *Remembering*, Cambridge: Cambridge University Press.
Bass, M.J. and Hull, C.L. (1934) 'The irradiation of a tactile conditioned reflex in man', *Journal of Comparative Psychology* 17: 47–65.
Beach, F.A. (1950) 'The snark was a boojum', *American Psychologist* 5: 115–24.
Beach, F.A. (1955) 'The descent of instinct', *Psychological Review* 62: 401–10.
Bechtel, W. (1986a) 'The nature of scientific integration', in W. Bechtel (ed.) *Integrating Scientific Disciplines*, Dordrecht: Martinus Nijhoff.
Bechtel, W. (1986b) 'Teleological functional analysis and the hierarchical organization of nature', in N. Rescher (ed.) *Teleology and Natural Science*, Landham, MD: University Press of America.
Bechtel, W. (1988a) *Philosophy of Mind: an Overview for Cognitive Science*, Hillsdale, NJ: Erlbaum.
Bechtel, W. (1988b) *Philosophy of Science: an Overview for Cognitive Science*, Hillsdale, NJ: Erlbaum.
Becker, D.E. and Shapiro, D. (1981) 'Physiological responses to clicks during zen, yoga and TM meditation', *Psychophysiology* 18: 694–9.
Bekerian, D.A. and Bowers, J.M. (1983) 'Eyewitness testimony: Were we misled?', *Journal of Experimental Psychology: Learning, Memory and Cognition* 9: 139–45.
Bem, D. (1972) 'Self-perception theory', in L. Berkowitz (ed.) *Advances in Experimental Psychology*, vol. 6, New York: Academic Press.
Bem, D.J. and McConnell, H.J. (1970) 'Testing the self-perception explanation of dissonance phenomena: on the salience of premanipulation attitudes', *Journal of Personality and Social Psychology* 14: 23–31.
Bennett, J. (1983) 'Cognitive ethology: theory or poetry?', *Behavioral and Brain Sciences* 6: 356–8.
Berger, R.J. and Oswald, I. (1962) 'Eye movements during active and passive dreams', *Science* 137: 601.
Bergmann, G. (1957) *Philosophy of Science*, Madison: University of Wisconsin Press.
Berkeley, G. (1710) *A Treatise concerning the Principles of Human Knowledge*, 1963, LaSalle, IL: Open Court.
Bindra, D. (1976) *A Theory of Intelligent Behavior*, New York: Wiley.

Binet, A. (1903) *L'Etude experimentale de l'intelligence*, Paris: Schleicher Frères.
Binet, A. and Passy, J. (1895) 'Etudes de psychologie sur des auteurs dramatiques', *L'Année Psychologique* 1: 60–118.
Birrell, P.C. (1983) 'Behavioral, subjective, and electroencephalographic indices of sleep onset latency and sleep duration', *Journal of Behavioral Assessment* 5: 179–90.
Blanshard, B. and Skinner, B.F. (1967) 'The problem of consciousness – a debate', *Philosophy and Phenomenological Research* 27: 317–37.
Blattberg, R.C. and Hoch, S.J. (1990) 'Database models and managerial intuition: 50% model + 50% manager', *Management Science* 36: 887–99.
Block, N. and Fodor, J.A. (1972) 'What psychological states are not', *Philosophical Review* 81: 158–81.
Boden, M.A. (1972) *Purposive Explanation in Psychology*, Cambridge, MA: Harvard University Press.
Boden, M.A. (1978) 'Human values in a mechanistic universe', in G.A. Vesey (ed.) *Human Values*, Hassocks, Sussex: Harvester Press.
Boden, M.A. (1979) 'The computational metaphor in psychology', in N. Bolton (ed.) *Philosophical Problems in Psychology*, London: Methuen.
Boden, M.A. (1987) *Artificial Intelligence and Natural Man*, 2nd edn, London: MIT Press.
Boden, M.A. (1988) *Computer Models of Mind*, Cambridge: Cambridge University Press.
Bolles, R.C. (1962) 'The difference between statistical hypotheses and scientific hypotheses', *Psychological Reports* 11: 639–45.
Bolton, N. (1978) 'Reflecting on the pre-reflective: phenomenology', in A. Burton and J. Radford (eds) *Thinking in Perspective*, London: Methuen.
Bolton, N. (1979) 'Phenomenology and psychology: being objective about the mind', in N. Bolton (ed.) *Philosophical Problems in Psychology*, London: Methuen.
Boring, E.G. (1927) 'The problem of originality in science', *American Journal of Psychology* 39: 70–90.
Boring, E.G. (1942) 'Human nature *vs.* sensation: William James and the psychology of the present', *American Journal of Psychology* 55: 310–27.
Boring, E.G. (1954) 'Psychological factors in scientific progress', *American Scientist* 42: 639–45.
Braithwaite, R.B. (1947) 'Teleological explanation', *Proceedings of the Aristotelian Society* 1946–47: i–xx.
Braithwaite, R.B. (1953) *Scientific Explanation*, Cambridge: Cambridge University Press.
Braithwaite, R.B. (1962) 'Models in the empirical sciences', in E. Nagel, P. Suppes and A. Tarski (eds) *Logic, Methodology and Philosophy of Science*, Stanford, CA: Stanford University Press.
Bransford, J.D. and Franks, J.J. (1971) 'The abstraction of linguistic ideas', *Cognitive Psychology* 2: 331–50.
Brentano, F. (1874) *Psychologie vom empirischen Standpunkt*, Leipzig: Duncker and Humboldt.
Bricker, P.D. and Chapanis, A. (1953) 'Do incorrectly perceived tachistoscopic stimuli convey some information?', *Psychological Review* 60: 181–8.
Bridgman, P.W. (1927) *The Logic of Modern Physics*, New York: Macmillan.
Broadbent, D.E. (1957) 'A mechanical model for human attention and immediate memory', *Psychological Review* 64: 205–15.
Broadbent, D.E. (1961) *Behaviour*, London: Eyre and Spottiswoode.
Broadbent, D.E. (1977) 'Levels, hierarchies and the locus of control', *Quarterly Journal of Experimental Psychology* 29: 181–201.

Brody, N. and Oppenheim, P. (1966) 'Tensions in psychology between the methods of behaviorism and phenomenology', *Psychological Review* 73: 295–305.
Bromberger, S. (1966) 'Why-Questions', in R.G. Colodny (ed.) *Mind and Cosmos*, Pittsburgh, PA: University of Pittsburgh Press.
Bromberger, S. (1968) 'An approach to explanation', in R.J. Butler (ed.) *Analytic Philosophy: Second Series*, Oxford: Blackwell.
Broverman, D.M. (1960) 'Cognitive style and intra-individual variation in abilities', *Journal of Personality* 28: 240–56.
Brown, D.P. (1977) 'A model for the levels of concentrative meditation', *International Journal of Clinical and Experimental Hypnosis* 25: 236–73.
Brown, G.W. and Harris, T. (1978) *Social Origins of Depression*, London: Tavistock.
Bruner, J.S. (1983) *In Search of Mind*, New York: Harper and Row.
Bruner, J.S. and Postman, L. (1949) 'On the perception of incongruity: a paradigm', *Journal of Personality* 18: 206–23.
Brunswik, E. (1939) 'The conceptual focus of some psychological systems', *Journal for the Unification of Science* 8: 36–49.
Brunswik, E. (1947) *Systematic and Unrepresentative Design of Psychological Experiments with Results in Physical and Social Perception*, Berkeley: University of California Press.
Brush, S.G. (1974) 'Should the history of science be rated X?', *Science* 183: 1164–72.
Burns, B.D. (1968) *The Uncertain Nervous System*, London: Edward Arnold.
Burt, C. (1962) 'The concept of consciousness', *British Journal of Psychology* 53: 229–43.
Bush, R.R. and Mosteller, F. (1955) *Stochastic Models for Learning*, New York: Wiley.
Caine, T.M., Wijesinghe, O.B.A. and Winter, D.A. (1981) *Personal Styles in Neurosis: Implications for Small Group Psychotherapy and Behaviour Therapy*, London: Routledge and Kegan Paul.
Capra, F. (1975) *The Tao of Physics*, London: Wildwood House.
Caramazza, A. (1986) 'On drawing inferences about the structure of normal cognitive systems from the analysis of patterns of impaired performance: the case for single-patient studies', *Brain and Cognition* 5: 41–66.
Carlson, V.R. (1960) 'Overestimation in size-constancy judgements', *American Journal of Psychology* 73: 199–213.
Carr, E.H. (1961) *What is History?*, London: Macmillan.
Castaneda, C. (1968) *The Teachings of Don Juan: a Yacqui Way of Knowing*, Berkeley: University of California Press.
Causey, R.L. (1977) *Unity of Science*, Dordrecht: D. Reidel.
Chapanis, A. (1961) 'Men, machines, and models', *American Psychologist* 16: 113–31.
Chapanis, A. (1967) 'The relevance of laboratory studies to practical situations', *Ergonomics* 10: 557–77.
Charniak, E. and McDermott, D.V. (1985) *Introduction to Artificial Intelligence*, Reading, MA: Addison-Wesley.
Chisholm, R.M. (1967) 'Intentionality', in P. Edwards (ed.) *The Encyclopaedia of Philosophy* IV: 201–4.
Chomsky, N. (1959) 'Review of *Verbal Behavior* by B.F. Skinner', *Language* 35: 26–58.
Chomsky, N. (1980) *Rules and Representations*, Oxford: Blackwell.
Churchland, P.M. (1981) 'Eliminative materialism and the propositional attitudes', *Journal of Philosophy* 78: 67–90.
Churchland, P.M. (1985) 'Reduction, qualia, and the direct introspection of brain states', *Journal of Philosophy* 82: 8–28.
Churchland, P.M. (1986) 'Some reductive strategies in cognitive biology', *Mind* 95: 279–309.

Churchland, P.M. and Churchland, P.S. (1981) 'Functionalism, qualia, and intentionality', *Philosophical Topics* 12: 121–45.
Churchland, P.S. (1986) *Neurophilosophy*, Cambridge, MA: Bradford/MIT Press.
Clark, A. (1980) *Psychological Models and Neural Mechanisms*, Oxford: Clarendon.
Clark, J.H. (1972) 'A map of inner space', in R. Ruddock (ed.) *Six Approaches to the Person*, London: Routledge and Kegan Paul.
Clark, J.H. (1983) *A Map of Mental States*, London: Routledge and Kegan Paul.
Clark, P. (1987) 'Determinism and probability in physics', *Proceedings of the Aristotelian Society*, Supplementary Volume 61: 185–210.
Claxton, G. (1980) 'Cognitive psychology: a suitable case for what sort of treatment?', in G. Claxton (ed.) *Cognitive Psychology: New Directions*, London: Routledge and Kegan Paul.
Claxton, G. (ed.) (1986) *Beyond Therapy*, London: Wisdom.
Coan, R.W. (1979) *Psychologists: Personal and Theoretical Pathways*, New York: Irvington.
Cochrane, R. and Duffy, J. (1974) 'Psychology and scientific method', *Bulletin of the British Psychological Society* 27: 117–21.
Cohen, J. (1962) 'The statistical power of abnormal-social psychological research', *Journal of Abnormal and Social Psychology* 65: 145–53.
Cohen, N.J. and Squire, L.R. (1980) 'Preserved learning and retention of pattern-analyzing skill in amnesia: dissociation of knowing how and knowing that', *Science* 210: 207–10.
Colby, K.M. (1963) 'Computer simulation of a neurotic process', in S.S. Tomkins and S. Messick (eds) *Computer Simulation of Personality*, New York: Wiley.
Colby, K.M., Weber, S. and Halif, F.D. (1971) 'Artificial paranoia', *Artificial Intelligence* 2: 1–26.
Coltheart, M. (1980) 'Deep dyslexia: A review of the syndrome', in M. Coltheart, K.E. Patterson and J.C. Marshall (eds) *Deep Dyslexia*, London: Routledge and Kegan Paul.
Coltheart, M. (1981) 'Disorders of reading and their implications for models of normal reading', *Visible Language* 15: 245–86.
Coltheart, M., Patterson, K.E. and Marshall, J.C. (1986) *Deep Dyslexia*, 2nd edn, London: Routledge and Kegan Paul.
Comte, A. (1842) *Cours de Philosophie Positive*, Paris: Bachelier.
Conklin, E.G. (1943) *Man: Real and Ideal*, New York: Scribner.
Conrad, H.S. (1932) 'The validity of personality ratings of pre-school children', *Journal of Educational Psychology* 23: 671–80.
Coombs, C.H., Dawes, R.M. and Tversky, A. (1970) *Mathematical Psychology: An Elementary Introduction*, Englewood Cliffs, NJ: Prentice-Hall.
Cornman, J.W. (1962) 'The identity of mind and body', *Journal of Philosophy* 59: 486–92.
Costall, A. and Still, A. (eds) (1987) *Cognitive Psychology in Question*, Brighton: Wheatsheaf.
Crick, F.H.C. (1984) 'Function of the thalamic reticular cortex: the searchlight hypothesis', *Proceedings of the National Academy of the United States of America, Biological Sciences* 81: 4586–90.
Cronbach, L.J. (1957) 'The two disciplines of scientific psychology', *American Psychologist* 12: 671–84.
Crook, J.H. (1987a) 'The nature of conscious awareness', in C. Blakemore and S. Greenfield (eds) *Mindwaves*, Oxford: Blackwell.
Crook, J.H. (1987b) 'The experiential context of intellect', in R.W. Byrne and A. Whiten (eds) *Social Expertise and the Evolution of Intellect*, Oxford: Oxford University Press.
Crook, J.H. and Fontana, D. (eds) (1990) *Space in Mind*, London: Element.

Csikszentmihalyi, M. (1975) *Beyond Boredom and Anxiety: the Experience of Play in Work and Games*, San Francisco: Jossey-Bass.
Cummins, R. (1983) *The Nature of Psychological Explanation*, Cambridge, MA: MIT Press.
Darden, L. and Maull, N. (1977) 'Interfield theories', *Philosophy of Science* 43: 44–64.
Davidson, D. (1963) 'Actions, reasons and causes', *Journal of Philosophy* 60: 685–700.
Davidson, D. (1970) 'Mental events', in L. Foster and J.W. Swanson (eds) *Experience and Theory*, Amherst: University of Massachusetts Press.
Day, W.D. (1969) 'Radical behaviorism in reconciliation with phenomenology', *Journal for the Experimental Analysis of Behavior* 12: 315–28.
Day, W.F. (1976) 'The case for behaviorism', in M.H. Marx and F.E. Goodson (eds) *Theories in Contemporary Psychology*, London: Macmillan.
De Bono, E. (1967) *The Use of Lateral Thinking*, London: Cape.
De Groot, A.D. (1965) *Thought and Choice in Chess*, The Hague: Mouton. (First published in Dutch in 1946.)
Deikman, A. (1966) 'De-automatization and the mystic experience', *Psychiatry* 29: 324–38.
Delgado, J.M.R. (1965) 'Sequential behavior induced repeatedly by stimulation of the red nucleus in free monkeys', *Science* 148: 1361–3.
Dement, W.C. (1955) 'Dream recall and eye movements during sleep in schizophrenics and normals', *Journal of Nervous and Mental Disorders* 122: 263–9.
Dement, W.C. (1972) *Some must Watch while Some must Sleep*, San Francisco: W.H. Freeman.
Dement, W.C. and Kleitman, N. (1957) 'The relation of eye movements during sleep to dream activity: an objective method for the study of dreaming', *Journal of Experimental Psychology* 53: 339–46.
Dennett, D.C. (1971) 'Intentional systems', *Journal of Philosophy* 68: 87–106.
Dennett, D.C. (1978) *Brainstorms: Philosophical Essays on Mind and Psychology*, Montgomery, VT: Bradford Books.
Dennett, D.C. (1979) 'Artificial intelligence as philosophy and psychology', in M.H. Ringle (ed.) *Philosophical Perspectives in Artificial Intelligence*, New York: Humanities Press.
Dennett, D.C. (1983) 'Intentional systems in cognitive ethology: the "Panglossian paradigm" defended', *Behavioral and Brain Sciences* 6: 343–90.
Dennett, D.C. (1984) *Elbow Room*, Oxford: Clarendon.
Dennett, D.C. (1987) 'Consciousness', in R.L. Gregory (ed.) *The Oxford Companion to the Mind*, Oxford: Oxford University Press.
Dennett, D.C. (1988) *The Intentional Stance*, Cambridge, MA: Bradford/ MIT Press.
Descartes, R. (1641) *Discourse on Method*, transl. J. Veitch, 1953, London: Dent.
Deutsch, J.A. (1960) *The Structural Basis of Behaviour*, Cambridge: Cambridge University Press.
Dewey, J. (1896) 'The reflex arc concept in psychology', *Psychological Review* 3: 357–70.
Dilthey, W. (1937) *Historik*, Munich: Oldenbourg.
Dimond, S.J. (1972) *The Double Brain*, Edinburgh: Churchill Livingstone.
Dixon, N.F. (1971) *Subliminal Perception: the Nature of a Controversy*, London: McGraw-Hill.
Dixon, N.F. (1981) *Preconscious Processing*, New York: Wiley.
Doerr, H.O. and Hokanson, J.E. (1965) 'A relation between heart-rate and performance in children', *Journal of Personality and Social Psychology* 2: 70–7.
Dreyfus, H.L. (1979) *What Computers Can't Do*, 2nd edn, New York: Harper and Row.
Dreyfus, H.L. and Dreyfus, S.E. (1988) 'Making a mind versus modeling the brain: artificial intelligence back at a branchpoint', *Daedalus*, March: 15–43.

Droysen, J.G. (1858) *Grundriss der Historik*, 1925, Halle-Salle: Niemeyer, translated as *Outlines of the Principles of History*, 1893, Boston: Ginn.
Dubuisson, D. and Melzack, R. (1976) 'Classification of clinical pain descriptions by multiple group discriminant analysis', *Experimental Neurology* 51: 480–87.
Dulany, D.E. Jr (1962) 'The place of hypotheses and intention: an analysis of verbal control in verbal conditioning', in C.W. Eriksen (ed.) *Behavior and Awareness*, Durham, NC: Duke University Press.
Duncker, K. (1945) 'On problem solving', *Psychological Monographs* 58, whole no. 270: 1–113.
Dunnette, M.D. (1966) 'Fads, fashions, and folderol in psychology', *American Psychologist* 21: 343–52.
Duval, S. and Wicklund, R.A. (1972) *A Theory of Object Self-awareness*, New York: Academic Press.
Eccles, J.C., Ito, M. and Szentagothai, J. (1967) *The Cerebellum as a Neuronal Machine*, New York: Springer-Verlag.
Eccles, J.C. and Robinson, D.N. (1984) *The Wonder of Being Human*, New York: Free Press.
Einhorn, H.J. (1972) 'Expert measurement and mechanical combination', *Organizational Behavior and Human Performance* 7: 86–106.
Elashoff, J.D. and Snow, R.E. (1971) *Pygmalion Reconsidered*, Worthington, OH: Jones.
Erickson, M.H. (1965) 'A special inquiry with Aldous Huxley into the nature and character of various states of consciousness', *American Journal of Clinical Hypnosis* 8: 17–33.
Ericsson, K.A. and Simon, H.A. (1980) 'Verbal reports as data', *Psychological Review* 87: 215–51.
Ericsson, K.A. and Simon, H.A. (1984) *Protocol Analysis*, Cambridge, MA: MIT Press.
Estes, W.K. (1950) 'Toward a statistical theory of learning', *Psychological Review* 57: 94–107.
Estes, W.K. (1959) 'The statistical approach to learning theory', in S. Koch (ed.) *Psychology: a Study of a Science*, vol. 2, New York: McGraw-Hill.
Evans, J.StB.T. (1980) 'Thinking: experiential and information processing', in G. Claxton (ed.) *Cognitive Psychology: New Directions*, London: Routledge and Kegan Paul.
Evans, J.StB.T. and Wason, P.C. (1976) 'Rationalization in a reasoning task', *British Journal of Psychology* 67: 479–86.
Eysenck, H.J. (1966) 'Personality and experimental psychology', *Bulletin of the British Psychological Society* 19: 1–28.
Eysenck, H.J. and Slater, E. (1958) 'Effects of practice and rest on fluctuations in the Müller-Lyer illusion', *British Journal of Psychology* 49: 246–56.
Eysenck, M.W. (1977) *Human Memory: Research, Theory and Individual Differences*, Oxford: Pergamon.
Farah, M.J. (1988) 'Electrophysiological evidence for a shared representational medium for visual images and visual percepts', *Psychological Review* 117: 248–57.
Feigl, H. (1958) 'The 'mental' and the 'physical'', in H. Feigl, G. Maxwell and M. Scriven (eds) *Concepts, Theories and the Mind–Body Problem*, Minneapolis: University of Minnesota Press.
Feigl, H. (1960) 'Mind–body, *not* a pseudo-problem', in S. Hook (ed.) *Dimensions of Mind*, New York: New York University Press.
Fenwick, P., Canavan, T., Anderson, E. and Brown, R. 'Neurophysiological and psychophysiological investigation of a Zen master', unpublished paper.
Feyerabend, P.K. (1962) 'Explanation, reduction, and empiricism', in H. Feigl and G. Maxwell (eds) *Minnesota Studies in the Philosophy of Science* 3: 29–97, Minneapolis: University of Minnesota Press.

Feyerabend, P.K. (1963) 'Materialism and the mind–body problem', *Review of Metaphysics* 17: 49–66.
Feyerabend, P.K. (1975) *Against Method: an Outline of an Anarchistic Theory of Knowledge*, London: NLB.
Field, G.C. (1921) 'Faculty psychology and instinct psychology', *Mind* 30: 257–70.
Fischer, R. (1971) 'A cartography of the ecstatic and meditative states', *Science* 174: 897–904.
Fishbein, M. and Ajzen, I. (1975) *Belief, Attitude, Intention and Behavior*, Reading, MA: Addison-Wesley.
Flourens, P. (1842) *Recherches Expérimentales sur les Propriétés et les Fonctions du Système Nerveux dans les Animaux Vertébrés*, 2nd edn, Paris: Baillière.
Fodor, J.A. (1965) 'Could meaning be an r_m?', *Journal of Verbal Learning and Verbal Behavior* 4: 73–81.
Fodor, J.A. (1968) *Psychological Explanation: an Introduction to the Philosophy of Psychology*, New York: Random House.
Fodor, J.A. (1974) 'Special sciences (Or: Disunity of science as a working hypothesis)', *Synthese* 28: 77–115.
Fodor, J.A. (1975) *The Language of Thought*, New York: Crowell.
Fodor, J.A. (1980) 'Methodological solipsism considered as a research strategy in cognitive psychology', *Behavioral and Brain Sciences* 3: 63–110.
Fodor, J.A. (1981) 'The mind–body problem', *Scientific American* 244 (4): 124–32.
Fodor, J.A. (1983) *The Modularity of Mind*, Cambridge, MA: MIT Press.
Fodor, J.A. (1987) *Psychosemantics*, Cambridge, MA: Bradford/MIT Press.
Fodor, J.A. and Pylyshyn, Z.W. (1988) 'Connectionism and cognitive architecture: a critical analysis', *Cognition* 28: 3–71.
Foss, B.M. (1974) 'On taking sides', *Bulletin of the British Psychological Society* 27: 347–51.
Fougasse and McCullough, D. (1935) *You have been Warned*, London: Methuen.
Foulkes, W.D. (1962) 'Dream reports from different stages of sleep', *Journal of Abnormal and Social Psychology* 65: 14–25.
Foulkes, W.D. and Vogel, G. (1965) 'Mental activity at sleep onset', *Journal of Abnormal Psychology* 70: 231–43.
Frankel, C. (1973) 'The nature and sources of irrationalism', *Science* 180: 927–31.
Fransella, F. (1975) *Need to Change?*, London: Methuen.
Frijda, N.H. (1967) 'Problems of computer simulation', *Behavioral Science* 12: 59–67.
Funkenstein, D.H. (1955) 'The physiology of fear and anger', *Scientific American* 192 (5): 74–80.
Furneaux, W.D. (1961) 'Neuroticism, extraversion, drive and suggestibility', *International Journal of Clinical and Experimental Hypnosis* 9: 195–214.
Gagné, R.H. and Smith, E.C. (1962) 'A study of the effects of verbalization on problem solving', *Journal of Experimental Psychology* 63: 12–18.
Galdston, I. (1956) 'Freud and romantic medicine', *Bulletin of the History of Medicine* 30: 489–507.
Gallwey, W.T. (1975) *The Inner Game of Tennis*, London: Jonathan Cape.
Garner, W.R., Hake, H.W. and Eriksen, C.W. (1956) 'Operationism and the concept of perception', *Psychological Review* 63: 149–59.
Gauld, A. and Shotter, J. (1977) *Human Action and its Psychological Investigation*, London: Routledge and Kegan Paul.
Gazzaniga, M.S. (1970) *The Bisected Brain*, New York: Appleton-Century-Crofts.
Gazzaniga, M.S. and LeDoux, J.E. (1978) *The Integrated Mind*, New York: Plenum Press.
Gelernter, H. (1959) 'Realization of a geometry-theorem proving machine', in E.A.

Feigenbaum and J. Feldman (eds) *Computers and Thought*, 1963, New York: McGraw-Hill.
Gelernter, H., Hansen, J.R. and Loveland, D.W. (1960) 'Empirical explorations of the geometry-theorem proving machine', in E.A. Feigenbaum and J. Feldman (eds) *Computers and Thought*, New York: McGraw-Hill, 1963.
Geller, L. (1982) 'The failure of self-actualization theory: a critique of Carl Rogers and Abraham Maslow', *Journal of Humanistic Psychology* 22 (2): 56–73.
George, F.H. (1953) 'Formalization of language systems for behavior theory', *Psychological Review* 60: 232–40.
Ghiselli, E.E. (1963) 'Moderating effects and differential reliability and validity', *Journal of Applied Psychology* 47: 81–6.
Gholson, B. and Barker, P. (1985) 'Kuhn, Lakatos, and Laudan: applications in the history of physics and psychology', *American Psychologist* 40: 755–69.
Gibson, J.J. (1979) *The Ecological Approach to Visual Perception*, Boston: Houghton Mifflin.
Goethals, G.R. and Reckman, R.F. (1973) 'The perception of consistency in attitudes', *Journal of Experimental Social Psychology* 9: 491–501.
Goffman, E. (1959) *The Presentation of Self in Everyday Life*, New York: Anchor Books.
Goldberg, L.R. (1965) 'Diagnosticians vs. diagnostic signs: the diagnosis of psychosis vs. neurosis from the MMPI', *Psychological Monographs* 79 (9, whole no. 602).
Goldmann, L. (1959) *Recherches dialectiques*, Paris: Gallimard.
Goodson, F.E. and Morgan, G.A. (1976) 'Evaluation of theory', in M.H. Marx and F.E. Goodson (eds) *Theories in Contemporary Psychology*, New York: Macmillan.
Gordon, P., Valentine, E. and Wilding, J. (1984) 'One man's memory: a study of a mnemonist', *British Journal of Psychology* 75: 1–14.
Gordon, R. (1950) 'An experiment correlating the nature of imagery with performance on a test of reversal perspective', *British Journal of Psychology* 41: 63–7.
Gorman, M.E., Gorman, M.E., Latta, R.M. and Cunningham, G. (1984) 'How disconfirmatory, confirmatory and combined strategies affect group problem-solving', *British Journal of Psychology* 75: 65–79.
Gray, J.A. (1971) 'The mind–brain identity theory as a scientific hypothesis', *Philosophical Quarterly* 21: 247–54.
Gray, J.A. (1975) *Elements of a Two-Process Theory of Learning*, London: Academic Press.
Gregory, R.L. (1961) 'The brain as an engineering problem', in W.H. Thorpe and O.L. Zangwill (eds) *Current Problems in Animal Behaviour*, Cambridge: Cambridge University Press.
Gregory, R.L. (1970) 'On how little information controls so much behaviour', *Ergonomics* 13: 25–35.
Grünbaum, A. (1952) 'Causality and the science of behavior', *American Scientist* 40: 665–76, 689.
Gunter, R. (1951) 'Binocular fusion of colours', *British Journal of Psychology* 42: 363–72.
Gustav, A. (1962) 'Students' attitudes towards compulsory participation in experiments', *Journal of Psychology* 53: 119–25.
Haber, R.N. (1965) 'Effect of prior knowledge of the stimulus on word recognition processes', *Journal of Experimental Psychology* 69: 282–6.
Haber, R.N. and Haber, R.B. (1964) 'Eidetic imagery: I Frequency', *Perceptual and Motor Skills* 19: 131–8.
Haldane, J.B.S. (1927) *Possible Worlds*, 1940, London: Heinemann.
Haldane, J.B.S. (1954) 'I repent an error', *Literary Guide*, 7 April: 29.
Haldane, J.B.S. (1963) 'Life and mind as physical realities', *Penguin Science Survey B*: 224–38.

Hanson, N.R. (1958) *Patterns of Discovery*, Cambridge: Cambridge University Press.
Hardin, C.L. (1988) *Color for Philosophers*, Indianapolis, IN: Hacket Publishing.
Harré, R. and Secord, P.F. (1972) *The Explanation of Social Behaviour*, Oxford: Blackwell.
Hatfield, G. (1988) 'Neuro-philosophy meets psychology: reduction, autonomy, and physiological constraints', *Cognitive Neuropsychology* 5: 723–46.
Hayes, J.R. (1973) 'On the function of imagery in elementary mathematics', in W.G. Chase (ed.) *Visual Information Processing*, London: Academic Press.
Heather, N. (1976) *Radical Perspectives in Psychology*, London: Methuen.
Hebb, D.O. (1949) *The Organization of Behavior*, New York: Wiley.
Hebb, D.O. (1968) 'Concerning imagery', *Psychological Review* 75: 466–77.
Heisenberg, W. (1927) 'Uber den anschlauchichen Inhalt der quantentheoretischen Kinetik und Mechanik', *Zeitschrift für Physik* 43: 172–98.
Hempel, C.G. (1959) 'The logic of functional analysis', in L. Gross (ed.) *Symposium on Sociological Theory*, New York: Harper and Row.
Hempel, C.G. and Oppenheim, P. (1948) 'Studies in the philosophy of explanation', *Philosophy of Science* 15: 135–75.
Herbart, J.F. (1824) *Psychologie als Wissenschaft*, Leipzig.
Hinton, G.E. and Anderson, J.A. (eds) (1981) *Parallel Models of Associative Memory*, Hillsdale, NJ: Erlbaum.
Hobbes, T. (1651) *Leviathan*, 1969, Menston, Yorkshire: The Scolar Press.
Holmes, D.S. (1967) 'Amount of experience in experiments as a determinant of performance in later experiments', *Journal of Personality and Social Psychology* 7: 403–7.
Holst, E. von (1954) 'Relations between the central nervous system and the peripheral organs', *British Journal of Animal Behaviour* 2: 89–94.
Holt, R.R. (1964) 'Imagery: the return of the ostracized', *American Psychologist* 19: 254–64.
Holt, R.R. (1967) 'Individuality and generalization in the psychology of personality', in R.L. Lazarus and J.R. Opton (eds) *Personality*, Harmondsworth: Penguin.
Hooker, C.A. (1981) 'Towards a general theory of reduction. Part I: Historical and scientific setting', *Dialogue* 20: 38–59.
Hovland, C.I. (1939) 'Experimental studies in rote learning theory. V. Comparison of distribution of practice in serial and paired-associate learning', *Journal of Experimental Psychology* 25: 622–33.
Howard, G.S., Youngs, W.H. and Siatczynski, A.M. (1989) 'A research strategy for studying telic behavior', *Journal of Mind and Behavior* 10: 393–412.
Howes, D.H. and Solomon, R.L. (1951) 'Visual duration threshold as a function of word-probability', *Journal of Experimental Psychology* 41: 401–10.
Hudson, L. (1972) *The Cult of the Fact*, London: Johnathan Cape.
Hull, C.L. (1935) 'The mechanism of the assembly of behavior segments in novel situations suitable for problem solving', *Psychological Review* 42: 219–45.
Hull, C.L. (1943) *Principles of Behavior*, New York: Appleton-Century-Crofts.
Hume, D. (1739) *Treatise of Human Nature*, L.A. Selby-Bigge (ed.), Oxford: Clarendon.
Humphrey, G. (1951) *Thinking*, London: Methuen.
Humphrey, N. (1983) *Consciousness Regained: Chapters in the Development of Mind*, Oxford: Oxford University Press.
Hunt, E.B. (1980) 'Intelligence as an information-processing concept', *British Journal of Psychology* 71: 449–74.
Husserl, E. (1901) *Logische Untersuchungen*, Niemeyer: Halle, transl. J.N. Findlay, 1970, New York: Humanities Press.
Husserl, E. (1913) *Ideen zu einer Reinen Phänomenonologie und Phänomenologische Philosophie*, transl. W.R. Boyce Gibson, 1931, London: George Allen and Unwin.
Huxley, A. (1954) *The Doors of Perception*, New York: Harper.

Huxley, T.H. (1874) 'On the hypothesis that animals are automata', *Fortnightly Review* 16: 555–80.

Hyman, R. (1964) *The Nature of Psychological Inquiry*, Englewood Cliffs, NJ: Prentice-Hall.

Idhe, A.J. (1948) 'The inevitability of scientific discovery', *Scientific Monographs* 67: 427–9.

Jackendoff, R. (1987) *Consciousness and the Computational Mind*, Cambridge, MA: Bradford/MIT.

Jackson, C.W. and Pollard, J.C. (1966) 'Some nondeprivation variables which influence the "effects" of experimental sensory deprivation', *Journal of Abnormal Psychology* 71: 383–8.

Jackson, F. (1982) 'Epiphenomenal qualia', *Philosophical Quarterly*, 32: 127–36.

Jackson, J.H. (1878) *Selected Writings of John Hughlings Jackson*, 2 vols, ed. J. Taylor, 1931, London: Hodder and Stoughton.

James, W. (1880) 'Great men, great thoughts and the environment', *Atlantic Monthly* 46: 441–59.

James, W. (1890) *Principles of Psychology*, New York: Holt.

James, W. (1907) *Pragmatism*, New York: Longmans.

James, W. (1912) *Memories and Studies*, New York: Longmans.

Janis, I.L. and King, B.T. (1954) 'The influence of role-playing on opinion change', *Journal of Abnormal and Social Psychology*, 49: 211–18.

Janke, W. (1964) *Experimentelle Untersuchungen zur Abhängigkeit der Wirkung psychotroper Substanzen von Persönlichkeitsmerkmalen*, Frankfurt: Akademische Verlagsgesellschaft.

Jaspers, K. (1962) *General Psychopathology*, Manchester: Manchester University Press.

Jaynes, J. (1976) *The Origin of Consciousness in the Breakdown of the Bicameral Mind*, Boston, MA: Houghton Mifflin.

Jennett, B., Snoek, J., Bond, M.R. and Brooks, N. (1981) 'Disability after severe head injury: observations on the use of the Glasgow Outcome Scale', *Journal of Neurology, Neurosurgery and Psychiatry* 44: 285–93.

Jensen, A.R. (1962) 'Extraversion, neuroticism and serial learning', *Acta Psychologica* 20: 69–77.

Jessor, R. (1958) 'The problem of reductionism in psychology', *Psychological Review* 65: 170–8.

Johnson, L.C. (1977) 'Psychophysiological research: its aims and methods', in Z.J. Lipowski, D.R. Lipsitt and P.C. Whybrow (eds) *Psychosomatic Medicine*, New York: Oxford University Press.

Johnson-Laird, P.N. (1983a) *Mental Models*, Cambridge: Cambridge University Press.

Johnson-Laird, P.N. (1983b) 'A computational analysis of consciousness', *Cognition and Brain Theory* 6: 499–508.

Johnson-Laird, P.N. (1988) *The Computer and the Mind*, London: Fontana.

Jones, B. (1974) 'The role of central monitoring of efference in motor short-term memory', *Journal of Experimental Psychology* 102: 37–43.

Jones, E. (1955) *Sigmund Freud: Life and Work*, London: Hogarth.

Jones, G.S. (1968) *Treatment or Torture*, London: Tavistock.

Jones, M.B. and Fennell, R.S. (1965) 'Runway performance by two strains of rats', *Quarterly Journal of the Florida Academy of Science* 28: 289–96.

Joynson, R.B. (1958) 'An experimental synthesis of the Association and Gestalt accounts of the perception of size', *Quarterly Journal of Experimental Psychology* 10: 65–76, 124–54.

Joynson, R.B. (1970) 'The breakdown of modern psychology', *Bulletin of the British Psychological Society* 23: 261–9.

Joynson, R.B. (1980) 'Models of man: 1879–1979', in A.J. Chapman and D.M. Jones (eds) *Models of Man*, Leicester: British Psychological Society.

Kamin, L.J. (1968) ' "Attention-like" processes in classical conditioning', in M.R. Jones (ed.) *Miami Symposium on the Prediction of Behavior: Aversive Stimulation*, Miami, FL: University of Miami Press.

Kant, I. (1781) *Kritik der reinen Vernunft*, transl. J.M.D. Meikeljohn, 1974, London: Dent.

Kasamatsu, A. and Hirai, T. (1966) 'An electroencephalographic study on the zen meditation (zazen)', *Folia Psychiatrica et Neurologica Japonica* 20: 315–16.

Kellogg, R.T. (1982) 'When can we introspect accurately about mental processes?', *Memory and Cognition* 10: 141–4.

Kelly, G.A. (1955) *The Psychology of Personal Constructs*, New York: Morton.

Kelvin, R.P. (1956) 'Thinking: psychologists and physiology', *Acta Psychologica* 12: 136–51.

Kemeny, J.G. and Oppenheim, P. (1956) 'On reduction', *Philosophical Studies* 7: 6–19.

Kendler, H.H. (1970) 'The unity of psychology', *Canadian Psychologist* 11: 30–47.

Kendler, H.H. and Kendler, T.S. (1962) 'Vertical and horizontal processes in problem solving', *Psychological Review* 69: 1–16.

Kendler, H.H. and Spence, J.T. (1971) *Essays in Neobehaviorism: a Memorial Volume to Kenneth W. Spence*, Englewood Cliffs, NJ: Prentice-Hall.

Kilpatrick, F.P. and Cantril, H. (1960) 'Self-anchoring scale: a measure of the individual's unique reality world', *Journal of Individual Psychology* 16: 158–70.

Kimble, G.A. (1964) 'Categories of learning and the problem of definition', in A.W. Melton (ed.) *Categories of Human Learning*, New York: Academic Press.

Kimble, G.A and Perlmuter, L.C. (1970) 'The problem of volition', *Psychological Review* 77: 361–84.

Kleinmuntz, B. (1990) 'Why we still use our heads instead of formulas: toward an integrative approach', *Psychological Bulletin* 107: 296–310.

Kluckholn, C.M. and Murray, H.A. (1953) 'Personality formation: its determinants', in C.M. Kluckholn and H.A Murray (eds) *Personality in Nature, Society and Culture*, 2nd edn, New York: Knopf.

Koch, S. (1959) 'Epilogue', in S. Koch (ed.) *Psychology: a Study of a Science*, vol. 3, New York: McGraw-Hill.

Kogan, N. and Wallach, M.A. (1964) *Risk Taking: a Study in Cognition and Personality*, London: Holt, Rinehart and Winston.

Köhler, W. (1918) 'Nachweis einfacher Strukturfunktionen beim Schimpanses und beim Haushuhn: Uber eine neue Methode zur Untersuching des bunten Farbensystems', *Abhandlungen Preussische Akadamie der Wissenschaften* 2: 1–101.

Kripke, S. (1972) 'Naming and necessity', in D. Davidson and G. Harmon (eds) *Semantics of Natural Languages*, Dordrecht: Reidel.

Krishnamurti, J. (1956) *Commentaries on Living*, D. Rajagopal (ed.), London: Gollancz.

Kroll, N.E.A. and Kellicutt, M.H. (1972) 'Short-term recall as a function of covert rehearsal and of intervening task', *Journal of Verbal Learning and Verbal Behavior* 11: 196–204.

Kuhn, T.S. (1962) *The Structure of Scientific Revolutions*, Chicago: Chicago University Press.

Kuhn, T.S. (1963) 'The essential tension: tradition and innovation in scientific research', in C.W. Taylor and F. Barron (eds) *Scientific Creativity*, New York: Wiley.

Kuhn, T.S. (1970) 'Postscript – 1969', in *The Structure of Scientific Revolutions*, 2nd edn, Chicago: Chicago University Press.

Kvale, S. and Grenness, C.E. (1967) 'Skinner and Sartre: towards a radical phenomenology of behaviour?' *Review of Existentialist Psychology and Psychiatry* 7: 128–48.

Lachman, R. (1960) 'The model in theory construction', *Psychological Review* 67: 113–29.
Lachman, R., Lachman, J.L. and Butterfield, E.C. (1979) *Cognitive Psychology and Information Processing*, Hillsdale, NJ: Erlbaum.
Laird, J.D. (1974) 'Self-attribution of emotion: the effect of expressive behavior on the quality of emotional experience', *Journal of Personality and Social Psychology* 29: 475–86.
Lakatos, I. (1970) 'Falsification and the methodology of scientific research programmes', in I. Lakatos and A. Musgrave (eds) *Criticism and the Growth of Knowledge*, Cambridge: Cambridge University Press.
Landauer, A.A. and Rodger, R.S. (1964) 'The effect of "apparent" instructions on brightness judgements', *Journal of Experimental Psychology* 68: 80–4.
Laplace, P.S. (1820) *Théorie analytique des probabilités*, 1967, Brussels: Culture et Civilization.
Lashley, K.S. (1929) *Brain Mechanisms and Intelligence*, Chicago: Chicago University Press.
Lashley, K.S. (1930) 'Basic neural mechanisms in behavior', *Psychological Review* 37: 1–24.
Lashley, K.S. (1942) 'An examination of the "continuity theory" as applied to discrimination learning', *Journal of General Psychology* 26: 241–65.
Lashley, K.S. (1951) 'The problem of serial order in behavior', in L.A. Jefress (ed.) *The Hixon Symposium*, New York: Wiley.
Lashley, K.S. (1956) 'Cerebral organization and behavior', in H. Solomon, S. Cobb and W. Penfield (eds) *The Brain and Human Behavior*, Baltimore: Williams and Wilkins.
Lashley, K.S., Chow, K.L. and Semmes, J. (1951) 'An examination of the electrical field theory of cerebral integration', *Psychological Review* 58: 123–36.
Lassen, N.A., Ingvar, D.H. and Skinhøj, E. (1978) 'Brain function and blood flow', *Scientific American* 239 (4): 50–9.
Latané, B. and Darley, J.M. (1970) *The Unresponsive Bystander: Why doesn't he help?*, New York: Appleton-Century-Crofts.
Laudan, L. (1977) *Progress and its Problems*, Berkeley: University of California Press.
Lawrence, D.H. (1950) 'Acquired distinctiveness of cues: II Selective association in a constant stimulus situation', *Journal of Experimental Psychology* 40: 175–88.
Leavitt, F. and Garron, D.C. (1980) 'Validity of a back pain classification scale for detecting psychological disturbance as measured by the MMPI', *Journal of Clinical Psychology* 36: 186–9.
LeDoux, J.E., Wilson, D.H. and Gazzaniga, M.S. (1979) 'Beyond commisurotomy: clues to consciousness', in M.S. Gazzaniga (ed.) *Handbook of Behavioral Neurobiology*, New York: Plenum Press.
Lehman, H.C. and Witty, P.A. (1931) 'Certain attitudes of present-day physicists and psychologists', *American Journal of Psychology* 43: 664–78.
Leibniz, G.W. von (1714) *Monadologie*, transl. R. Latta, 1898, Oxford: Oxford University Press.
Lenat, D.B. (1982) 'The nature of heuristics', *Artificial Intelligence* 19: 189–249.
Lenat, D.B. (1983) 'EURISKO: a program that learns new heuristics and domain concepts', *Artifical Intelligence* 21: 61–98.
Lenneberg, E.H. (1967) *The Biological Foundations of Language*, New York: Wiley.
Lettvin, J.Y., Maturana, H.R., Pitts, W. and McCulloch, W.R. (1959) 'What the frog's eye tells the frog's brain', *Proceedings of the Institute of Radio Engineers* 47: 1940–59.
Lewin, K. (1951) *Field Theory in Social Science*, New York: Harper.
Lewis, D. (1969) 'Review of art, mind, and religion', *Journal of Philosophy* 66: 23–5.
Lewis, D. (1983) 'Postscript to "Mad pain and Martian pain" ', in *Philosophical Papers*, vol. 1, New York: Oxford University Press.

Liberman, A.M., Harris, K.S., Hoffman, H.S. and Griffith, B.C. (1957) 'The discrimination of speech sounds within and across phoneme boundaries', *Journal of Experimental Psychology* 54: 358–68.
Libet, B. (1985) 'Unconscious cerebral initiative and the role of conscious will in voluntary action', *Behavioral and Brain Sciences* 8: 529–66.
Libet, B., Wright, E.W. Jr, Feinstein, B. and Pearl, D.K. (1979) 'Subjective referral of the timing for a conscious sensory experience: a functional role for the somatosensory specific projection system in man', *Brain* 102: 191–222.
Lieberman, D. (1979) 'Behaviorism and the mind: a (limited) call for a return to introspection', *American Psychologist* 34: 319–33.
Locke, D. (1974) 'Action, movement and neurophysiology', *Inquiry* 17: 23–42.
Lorenz, K. (1950) 'The comparative method in studying innate behaviour patterns', *Symposium of the Society for Experimental Biology* 4: 221–68.
Lorenz, K. (1966) *The Evolution and Modification of Behaviour*, London: Methuen.
Lycan, W. (1981) 'Form, function and feel', *Journal of Philosophy* 78: 24–50.
McClearn, G.E. (1962) 'Genetic differences in the effect of alcohol upon behaviour of mice', Proceedings of the Third International Conference on Alcohol and Road Traffic, London.
McClintock, M.K. (1971) 'Menstrual synchrony and suppression', *Nature* 229: 244–5.
MacCorquodale, K. and Meehl, P.H. (1948) 'On a distinction between hypothetical constructs and intervening variables', *Psychological Review* 55: 95–107.
McDougall, W. (1912) *Psychology: the Study of Behavior*, London: Williams and Norgate.
McDougall, W. (1925) *An Introduction to Social Psychology*, 20th edn, London: Methuen.
McDougall, W. (1932) *The Energies of Men: a Study of the Fundamentals of Dynamic Psychology*, London: Methuen.
McDougall, W. (1936) *An Introduction to Social Psychology*, 23rd edn, London: Methuen.
McFarland, D. (1981) *The Oxford Companion to Animal Behaviour*, Oxford: Oxford University Press.
McFarland, D. (1985) *Animal Behaviour*, London: Pitman.
McFie, J. (1972) 'Factors of the brain', *Bulletin of the British Psychological Society* 25: 11–14.
McGeoch, J.A. (1933) 'The formal criteria of a systematic psychology', *Psychological Review* 40: 1–12.
McGinn, C. (1979) 'Action and its explanation', in N. Bolton (ed.) *Philosophical Problems in Psychology*, London: Methuen.
McGinn, C. (1982) *The Character of Mind*, Oxford: Oxford University Press.
Mach, E. (1897) *Beiträge zur Analyse der Empfindungen*, transl. C.M. Williams, Chigaco: Chigaco University Press.
MacKay, D.M. (1981) 'Neural basis of cognitive experience', in G. Szekely, E. Labos and S. Damjanovich (eds) *Neural Communication and Control, Advances in Physiological Sciences*, vol. 30, Oxford: Pergamon.
MacKay, D.M. (1987) 'Determinism and free will', in R.L. Gregory (ed.) *The Oxford Companion to the Mind*, Oxford: Oxford University Press.
McKellar, P. (1962) 'The method of introspection', in J.M. Scher (ed.) *Theories of the Mind*, New York: Free Press of Glencoe.
MacLeod, C.M., Hunt, E.B. and Matthews, N.N. (1978) 'Individual differences in the verification of sentence–picture relationships', *Journal of Verbal Learning and Verbal Behaviour* 17: 493–507.
McNaughton, B.L. and Morris, R.G.M. (1987) 'Hippocampal synaptic enhancement

and information storage within a distributed memory system', *Trends in Neurosciences* 10: 408–15.
Mahoney, M.J. (1976a) 'The truth seekers', *Psychology Today*, April: 60–5.
Mahoney, M.J. (1976b) *Scientists as Subject: the Psychological Imperative*, Cambridge, MA: Ballinger.
Mahoney, M.J. and DeMonbreun, B.G. (1978) 'Psychology of the scientist: an analysis of problem solving bias', *Cognitive Therapy and Research* 1: 229–55.
Maier, N.R.F. (1931) 'The solution of a problem and its appearance in consciousness', *Journal of Comparative Psychology* 12: 181–94.
Malcolm, N. (1959) *Dreaming*, New York: Humanities Press.
Malebranche, N. (1675) *Oeuvres complètes*, 1979, Paris: Vrin.
Mandler, G. (1975) *Mind and Emotion*, New York: Wiley.
Mandler, G. (1984) *Mind and Body: Emotion and Stress*, New York: Norton.
Mandler, G. (1985) *Cognitive Psychology*, Hillsdale, NJ: Erlbaum.
Mandler, G. and Kessen, W. (1974) 'The appearance of free will', in S.C. Brown (ed.) *Philosophy of Psychology*, London: Macmillan.
Mannheim, K. (1952) *Essays in the Sociology of Knowledge*, P. Kecskemeti (ed.), London: Routledge and Kegan Paul.
Marcel, A.J. (1983a) 'Conscious and unconscious perception: experiments on visual masking and word recognition', *Cognitive Psychology* 15: 197–237.
Marcel, A.J. (1983b) 'Conscious and unconscious perception: an approach to the relations between phenomenal experience and perceptual processes', *Cognitive Psychology* 15: 238–300.
Marr, D. (1969) 'A theory of the cerebellar cortex', *Journal of Physiology* 202: 432–70.
Marr, D. (1982) *Vision*, San Francisco: W.H. Freeman.
Marx, M.H. (1963) 'The general nature of theory construction', in M.H. Marx (ed.) *Theories in Contemporary Psychology*, New York: Macmillan.
Marx, M.H. (1976) 'Formal theory', in M.H. Marx and F.E. Goodson (eds) *Theories in Contemporary Psychology*, New York: Macmillan.
Maslow, A.H. (1954) *Motivation and Personality*, 2nd edn 1970, New York: Harper and Row.
Maslow, A.H. (1966) *The Psychology of Science*, New York: Harper and Row.
Maslow, A.H. (1969) 'Toward a humanistic biology', *American Psychologist* 24: 724–35.
Masterman, M. (1970) 'The nature of a paradigm', in I. Lakatos and A. Musgrave (eds) *Criticism and the Growth of Knowledge*, Cambridge: Cambridge University Press.
May, M.A. (1948) 'Experimentally acquired drives', *Journal of Experimental Psychology* 38: 66–77.
Maze, J.R. (1954) 'Do intervening variables intervene?', *Psychological Review* 61: 226–34.
Medawar, P.B. (1969) *Induction and Intuition in Scientific Thought*, London: Methuen.
Mednick, S. (1970) 'Breakdown in individuals at high risk for schizophrenia: possible predispositional and perinatal factors', *Mental Hygiene* 54: 50–63.
Meehl, P. (1954) *Clinical vs. Statistical Prediction*, Minneapolis: University of Minnesota Press.
Meehl, P. (1957) 'When shall we use our heads instead of the formula?', *Counseling Psychology* 4: 268–73.
Mehler, J., Morton, J. and Jucszyk, P.W. (1984) 'On reducing language to biology', *Cognitive Neuropsychology* 1: 83–116.
Melden, A. (1961) *Free Action*, London: Routledge and Kegan Paul.
Merleau-Ponty, M. (1942) *The Structure of Behaviour*, 1963, Boston, MA: Beacon.
Merleau-Ponty, M. (1945) *Phenomenology of Perception*, 1962, New York: Humanities Press.
Mill, J.S. (1882) *August Comte and Positivism*, 3rd edn, London: Trubner.

Millenson, J. (1967) 'An isomorphism between S–R notation and information processing flow diagrams', *Psychological Record* 17: 305–19.
Miller, G.A (1956) 'The magical number seven, plus or minus two: some limits on our capacity for processing information', *Psychological Review* 63: 81–97.
Miller, G.A. (1964) *Psychology: the Science of Mental Life*, London: Hutchinson.
Miller, G.A. (1980) 'Computation, consciousness and cognition', *Behavioral and Brain Sciences* 3: 146.
Miller, G.A., Galanter, E. and Pribram, K. (1960) *Plans and the Structure of Behaviour*, New York: Holt, Rinehart and Winston. (Reprinted by Adams, Bannister, Cox, 1986).
Miller, N.E. (1956) 'Effects of drugs on motivation: the value of using a variety of measures', *Annals of the New York Academy of Science* 65: 318–33.
Milner, P.M. (1957) 'The cell assembly: Mark II', *Psychological Review* 64: 242–57.
Mischel, T. (1973) 'Toward a cognitive social learning reconceptualization of personality', *Psychological Review* 80: 252–83.
Mitroff, I.I. (1974) *The Subjective Side of Science*, Amsterdam: Elsevier.
Morgan, C.L. (1894) *Introduction to Comparative Psychology*, London: Scott.
Mowrer, O.H. (1954) 'The psychologist looks at language', *American Psychologist* 9: 660–94.
Munkelt, P. (1965) 'Persönlichkeitsmerkmale als Bedingungsfaktoren der Psychotropen Arzneimittelwirkung', *Psychologische Beiträge* 8: 98–183.
Mynatt, C.R., Doherty, M.E. and Tweney, R.D. (1977) 'Confirmation bias in a simulated research environment: an experimental study of scientific inference', *Quarterly Journal of Experimental Psychology* 29: 85–95.
Mynatt, C.R., Doherty, M.E. and Tweney, R.D. (1978) 'Consequences of confirmation and disconfirmation in a simulated research environment', *Quarterly Journal of Experimental Psychology* 30: 395–406.
Nagel, E. (1953) 'Teleological explanation and teleological systems', in S. Ratner (ed.) *Vision and Action*, New Brunswick, NJ: Rutgers University Press.
Nagel, E. (1961) *The Structure of Science*, London: Routledge and Kegan Paul.
Nagel, E. (1967) 'What is true and what is false in science: Medawar and the anatomy of research', *Encounter* 29: 68–70.
Nagel, T. (1974) 'What is it like to be a bat?', *Philosophical Review* 83: 354–450.
Nagel, T. (1986) *The View from Nowhere*, Oxford: Oxford University Press.
Natsoulas, T. (1967) 'What are perceptual reports about?', *Psychological Bulletin* 67: 249–72.
Natsoulas, T. (1970) 'Concerning introspective "knowledge" ', *Psychological Bulletin* 73: 89–111.
Natsoulas, T. and Levy, E. (1965) 'A further study of the verbal transformation effect', unpublished manuscript, University of California, Davis (cited in Natsoulas, 1967).
Neisser, U. (1963) 'The imitation of man by machine', *Science* 139: 193–7.
Neisser, U. (1970) 'Visual imagery as process and as experience', in J. Antrobus (ed.) *Cognition and Affect*, Boston: Little, Brown.
Neisser, U. (1976) *Cognition and Reality*, San Francisco: W.H. Freeman.
Neumann, J. von (1958) *The Computer and the Brain*, New Haven, CT: Yale University Press.
Neurath, O. (1938) 'Unified science as encyclopaedic integration', in O. Neurath, R. Carnap and C.W. Morris (eds) *Encyclopaedia and Unified Science*, *International Encyclopaedia of Unified Science*, vol. 1, no. 1, Chicago: Chicago University Press.
Newcombe, F. (1985) 'Neuropsychology of consciousness: a review of human clinical evidence', in D. Oakley (ed.) *Brain and Mind*, London: Methuen.
Newcombe, F. and Marshall, J.C. (1988) 'Idealisation meets psychometrics: the case for the right groups and the right individuals', *Cognitive Neuropsychology* 5: 549–64.
Newell, A. (1973) 'You can't play 20 questions with nature and win', in W.G. Chase (ed.) *Visual Information Processing*, London: Academic Press.

Newell, A., Shaw, J.C. and Simon, H.A. (1957) 'Empirical explorations with the logic theory machine', *Proceedings of the Western Joint Computer Conference* 15: 218–39.
Newell, A. and Simon, H.A. (1961) 'Computer simulation of human thinking', *Science* 134: 201–17.
Newell, A. and Simon, H.A. (1972) *Human Problem Solving*, Englewood Cliffs, NJ: Prentice-Hall.
Nisbett, R.E. and Ross, L. (1980) *Human Inference: Strategies and Shortcomings of Social Judgment*, Englewood Cliffs, NJ: Prentice-Hall.
Nisbett, R.E. and Wilson, T. DeC. (1977) 'Telling more than we can know: verbal reports on mental processes', *Psychological Review* 84: 231–59.
Norman, D. and Shallice, T. (1986) 'Attention to action: willed and automatic control of behavior', in R.J. Davidson, G.E. Schwartz and D. Shapiro (eds) *Consciousness and Self-regulation: Advances in Research and Theory*, New York: Plenum.
Nunnally, J.C. (1955) 'An investigation of some propositions of self-conception: the case of Miss Sun', *Journal of Abnormal and Social Psychology* 50: 87–92.
Nunnally, J. (1960) 'The place of statistics in psychology', *Educational and Psychological Measurement* 20: 641–50.
O'Connor, D.J. (1971) *Free Will*, New York: Doubleday.
Ogburn, W.F. and Thomas, D. (1922) 'Are inventions inevitable?', *Political Science Quarterly* 37: 83–93.
O'Keefe, J. (1985) 'Is consciousness the gateway to the hippocampal cognitive map? A speculative essay on the neural basis of mind', in D. Oakley (ed.) *Brain and Mind*, London: Methuen.
O'Keefe, J. and Nadel, L. (1978) *The Hippocampus as a Cognitive Map*, Oxford: Clarendon.
Oliver, W.D. and Landfield, A.W. (1963) 'Reflexivity: an unfaced issue of psychology', *Journal of Individual Psychology* 20: 187–201.
Olson, D. (1986) 'The cognitive consequences of literacy', *Canadian Psychologist* 27: 109–21.
Oppenheim, P. and Putnam, H. (1958) 'Unity of science as a working hypothesis', in H. Feigl (ed.) *Minnesota Studies in the Philosophy of Science* 2: 3–36.
Orne, M.T. (1959) 'The nature of hypnosis: artefact and essence', *Journal of Abnormal and Social Psychology* 58: 277–99.
Orne, M.T. (1962) 'On the social psychology of the psychological experiment: with particular reference to demand characteristics and their implications', *American Psychologist* 17: 776–83.
Orne, M.T. and Scheibe, K.E. (1964) 'The contribution of non-deprivation factors in the production of sensory deprivation effects: the psychology of the "panic button" ', *Journal of Abnormal and Social Psychology* 68: 3–12.
Osgood, C.E. (1953) *Method and Theory in Experimental Psychology*, New York: Oxford University Press.
Osgood, C.E. (1956) 'Behavior theory and the social sciences', *Behavioral Science* 1: 167–85.
Osgood, C.E. (1963) 'On understanding and creating sentences', *American Psychologist* 18: 735–51.
Outhwaite, W. (1975) *Understanding Social Life*, London: George Allen and Unwin.
Overall, J.E. (1969) 'Classical statistical hypothesis testing within the context of Bayesian theory', *Psychological Bulletin* 71: 285–92.
Palermo, D.S. (1971) 'Is a scientific revolution taking place in psychology?', *Science Studies* 1: 133–55.
Paranjpe, A. (1984) *Theoretical Psychology: the Meeting of East and West*, New York: Plenum.

Paxton, R. (1976) 'Some criteria for choosing between explanations in psychology', *Bulletin of the British Psychological Society* 29: 396–9.
Pearson, K. (1892) *The Grammar of Science*, London: Scott.
Pellionisz, A. and Llinas, R. (1979) 'Brain modeling by tensor network theory and computer simulation. The cerebellum: distributed processor for predictive coordination', *Neuroscience* 4: 323–48.
Penfield, W. (1955) 'The permanent record of the stream of consciousness', *Acta Psychologica* 11: 47–69.
Penfield, W. (1958) *The Excitable Cortex in Conscious Man*, Liverpool: Liverpool University Press.
Penfield, W. (1969) 'Consciousness, memory, and man's conditioned reflexes', in K.H. Pribram (ed.) *On the Biology of Learning*, New York: Harcourt, Brace and World.
Perkins, M. (1953) 'Intersubjectivity and Gestalt psychology', *Philosophy and Phenomenological Research* 13: 437–51.
Perrett, D.I., Smith, P.A.J., Potter, D.D., Mistlin, A.J., Head, A.S., Milner, A.D. and Jeeves, M.A. (1985) 'Visual cells in the temporal cortex sensitive to face view and gaze direction', *Philosophical Transactions of the Royal Society of London B* 223: 293–317.
Perry, R.B. (1918) 'Docility and purposiveness', *Psychological Review* 25: 1–21.
Peters, D.P. and Ceci, S.J. (1982) 'Peer-review practices of psychological journals: the fate of published articles submitted again', *Behavioral and Brain Sciences* 5: 187–255.
Peters, R.S. (ed.) (1953) *Brett's History of Psychology*, London: George Allen and Unwin.
Peters, R.S. (1958) *The Concept of Motivation*, London: Routledge and Kegan Paul.
Pettigrew, J.D. and Konishi, M. (1976) 'Neurons selective for orientation and binocular disparity in the visual wulst of the barn owl (*tyto alba*)', *Science* 193: 675–8.
Pettit, P. (1979) 'Rationalisation and the art of explaining action', in N. Bolton (ed.) *Philosophical Problems in Psychology*, London: Methuen.
Pfungst, P. (1911) *Clever Hans (the Horse of Mr van Osten): A Contribution to Experimental, Animal and Human Psychology*, transl. C.L. Rahn, New York: Holt.
Pilkington, G.W. and Glasgow, W.D. (1967) 'Towards a rehabilitation of introspection as a method in psychology', *Journal of Existentialism* 7: 329–50.
Pinneo, L.R. (1966) 'Electrical control of behavior by programmed stimulation of the brain', *Nature* 211: 705–8.
Place, U.T. (1956) 'Is consciousness a brain process?', *British Journal of Psychology* 47: 44–51.
Place, U.T. (1988) 'Thirty years on – is consciousness still a brain process', *Australasian Journal of Philosophy* 66: 208–19.
Platt, J.R. (1964) 'Strong inference', *Science* 146: 347–53.
Polanyi, M. (1966) *The Tacit Dimension*, London: Routledge and Kegan Paul.
Popper, K.R. (1950) 'Indeterminism in quantum physics and in classical physics', *British Journal for the Philosophy of Science* 1: 117–33, 173–95.
Popper, K.R. (1959) *The Logic of Scientific Discovery*, London: Hutchinson.
Popper, K.R. (1963) *Conjectures and Refutations*, London: Routledge and Kegan Paul.
Popper, K.R. and Eccles, J.C. (1977) *The Self and its Brain*, Berlin: Springer-Verlag.
Postman, L.J. (1947) 'The history and present status of the law of effect', *Psychological Bulletin* 44: 489–563.
Prince, M. (1905) *The Dissociation of Personality: a Biographical Study in Abnormal Psychology*, New York: Longmans.
Putnam, H. (1960) 'Minds and machines', in S. Hook (ed.) *Dimensions of Mind*, New York: New York University Press.
Putnam, H. (1967) 'Psychological predicates', in W.H. Capitan and D.D. Merrill (eds) *Art, Mind, and Religion*, Pittsburgh, PA: University of Pittsburgh Press.

Putnam, H. (1973) 'Reductionism and the nature of psychology', *Cognition* 2: 131–46.
Putnam, H. (1975) 'The meaning of meaning', in H. Putnam (ed.) *Mind, Language and Reality: Philosophical Papers of Hilary Putnam*, vol. 2, Cambridge: Cambridge University Press.
Putnam, H. (1978) *Meaning and the Moral Sciences*, London: Routledge and Kegan Paul.
Putnam, H. (1983) *Realism and Reason*, Cambridge: Cambridge University Press.
Pylyshyn, Z.W. (1980) 'Computation and cognition: issues in the foundations of cognitive science', *Behavioral and Brain Sciences* 3: 111–34.
Pylyshyn, Z.W. (1984) *Computation and Cognition*, Cambridge, MA: MIT Press.
Radford, J. and Burton, A. (1974) *Thinking: Its Nature and Development*, London: Wiley.
Reason, J.T. (1984) 'Absentmindedness and cognitive control', in J.E. Harris and P.E. Morris (eds) *Everyday Memory, Action and Absentmindedness*, New York: Academic Press.
Reason, P. and Rowan, J. (eds) (1981) *Human Inquiry: a Sourcebook of New Paradigm Research*, Chichester: Wiley.
Reese, H.W. and Overton, W.F. (1970) 'Models of development and theories of development', in L.R. Goulet and P.B. Baltes (eds) *Life-span Developmental Psychology*, New York: Academic Press.
Reeves, J.W. (1958) *Body and Mind in Western Thought*, London: Penguin.
Reeves, J.W. (1965) *Thinking about Thinking*, London: Secker and Warburg.
Reichenbach, H. (1938) *Experience and Prediction*, Chicago: Chicago University Press.
Reid, L.S. (1953) 'The development of noncontinuity behavior through continuity learning', *Journal of Experimental Behavior* 46: 107–12.
Reitman, W.R. (1965) *Cognition and Thought: an Information Processing Approach*, New York: Wiley.
Riecken, H.W. (1962) 'A program for research on experiments in social psychology', in N.F. Washburne (ed.) *Decisions, Values and Groups*, vol. 2, New York: Pergamon.
Rochester, N., Holland, J.H., Haibt, L.H. and Duda, W.L. (1956) 'Test of a cell assembly theory of the action of the brain, using a large digital computer', *IRE Transactions in Information Theory* IT–2 (3): 80–93.
Roe, A. (1953) *The Making of a Scientist*, New York: Dodd Mead.
Rogers, C.R. (1956) 'Some issues concerning the control of human behavior', *Science* 124: 1057–66.
Rogers, C.R. (1965) *Client-Centered Therapy*, New York: Houghton Mifflin.
Rolls, E.T. (1987) 'Information representation, processing, and storage in the brain: analysis at the single neuron level', in J-P. Changeux and M. Konishi (eds) *The Neural and Molecular Bases of Learning*, New York: Wiley.
Rorty, R. (1970) 'In defense of eliminative materialism', *Review of Metaphysics* 24: 112–21.
Rosenblueth, A., Wiener, N. and Bigelow, J. (1943) 'Behavior, purpose and teleology', *Philosophy of Science* 10: 18–24.
Rosenthal, R. (1963) 'Experimenter attributes as determinants of subjects' responses', *Journal of Projective Techniques* 27: 324–31.
Rosenthal, R. (1965) 'The volunteer subject', *Human Relations* 18: 389–406.
Rosenthal, R. (1966) *Experimenter Effects in Behavioral Research*, New York: Appleton-Century-Crofts.
Rosenthal, R. (1967) 'Covert communication in the psychological experiment', *Psychological Bulletin* 67: 356–67.
Rosenthal, R. and Fode, K.L. (1963) 'The effect of experimenter bias on the performance of the albino rat', *Behavioral Science* 8: 183–9.
Rosenthal, R., Fode, K.L., Friedman, C.J. and Vikan-Kline, L. (1960) 'Subjects'

perception of their experimenter under conditions of experimenter bias', *Perceptual and Motor Skills* 11: 325–31.

Rosenthal, R. and Jacobson, L. (1966) 'Teachers' expectancies: determinants of pupils' IQ gains', *Psychological Reports* 19: 115–18.

Rosenthal, R., Kohn, P., Greenfield, P.M. and Carota, N. (1965) 'Experimenters' hypothesis confirmation and mood as determinants of experimental results', *Perceptual and Motor Skills* 20: 1237–52.

Rosenthal, R., Kohn, P., Greenfield, P.M. and Carota, N. (1966) 'Data desirability, experimenter expectancy, and the results of psychological research', *Journal of Personality and Social Psychology* 3: 20–7.

Rosenthal, R., Persinger, G.W., Vikan-Kline, L. and Fode, K.L. (1963) 'The role of the research assistant in the mediation of experimenter bias', *Journal of Personality* 31: 313–35.

Rosenthal, R. and Rosnow, R.L. (eds) (1969) *Artifact in Behavioral Research*, New York: Academic Press.

Rosenthal, R. and Rubin, D.B. (1978) 'Interpersonal expectancy effects: the first 345 studies', *Behavioral and Brain Sciences* 3: 377–415.

Rozin, P. (1976) 'The evolution of intelligence and access to the cognitive unconscious', in J.M. Sprague and A.N. Epstein (eds) *Progress in Psychobiology and Physiological Psychology*, vol. 6, New York: Academic Press.

Rumelhart, D.E. and McClelland, J.L. (1986) 'On learning the past tenses of English verbs', in D.E. Rumelhart, J.L. McClelland and the PDP Research Group (eds) *Parallel Distributed Processing*, Cambridge, MA: MIT Press.

Rumelhart, D.E., McClelland, J.L. and the PDP Research Group (eds) (1986) *Parallel Distributed Processing*, Cambridge, MA: MIT Press.

Russell, B. (1913) 'On the notion of cause', *Proceedings of the Aristotelian Society*, 1912–13: 1–26.

Russell, B. (1927) *The Analysis of Matter*, London: George Allen and Unwin.

Russell, E.S. (1945) *The Directiveness of Organic Activities*, Cambridge: Cambridge University Press.

Russell, J. (1984) *Explaining Mental Life*, London: Macmillan.

Rychlak, J.F. (1981) *A Philosophy of Science for Personality Theory*, 2nd edn, Malabar, FL: Robert E. Krieger.

Rycroft, C. (1966) 'Causes and meaning', in C. Rycroft (ed.) *Psychoanalysis Observed*, London: Constable.

Ryle, G. (1949) *The Concept of Mind*, London: Hutchinson.

Salmon, W.C. (1978) 'Why ask "Why?" ', *Proceedings and Addresses of the American Philosophical Association* 51: 683–705.

Salmon, W.C. (1984) *Scientific Explanation and the Causal Structure of the World*, Princeton, NJ: Princeton University Press.

Samuel, A.L. (1959) 'Some studies in machine learning using the game of checkers', in E.A. Feigenbaum and J. Feldman (eds) *Computers and Thought*, 1963, New York: McGraw-Hill.

Savage, I.R. (1957) 'Non-parametric statistics', *Journal of the American Statistical Association* 52: 331–44.

Sawyer, J. (1966) 'Measurement and prediction, clinical and statistical', *Psychological Bulletin* 66: 178–200.

Schaffner, K.F. (1967) 'Approaches to reduction', *Philosophy of Science* 34: 137–47.

Schelting, A. von (1934) *Max Weber's Wissenschafteslehre*, Tübingen: Mohr.

Schlick, M. (1925) *Philosophy of Nature*, transl. A. von Zepperlin, 1943, London: Greenwood Press.

Schoenfeld, W.N. and Cumming, W.W. (1963) 'Behavior and perception', in S. Koch (ed.) *Psychology: a Study of a Science*, vol. 5, New York: McGraw-Hill.
Schrödinger, E. (1958) *Mind and Matter*, Cambridge: Cambridge University Press.
Schultz, D.P. (1969) 'The human subject in psychological research', *Psychological Bulletin* 72: 214–28.
Schutz, A. (1932) *Der sinnhafte Aufbau der Sozialen Welt Eine Einfürhrung in die verstehende Soziologie*, translated as *The Phenomenology of the Social World*, 1972, London: Heinemann.
Scriven, M. (1960) 'The compleat robot: a prolegomena to androidology', in S. Hook (ed.) *Dimensions of Mind*, New York: New York University Press.
Scriven, M. (1962) 'Explanations, predictions, and laws', in H. Feigl and G. Maxwell (eds) *Minnesota Studies in the Philosophy of Science*, Minneapolis: University of Minnesota Press.
Searle, J.R. (1980) 'Minds, brains, and programs', *Behavioral and Brain Sciences* 3: 417–57.
Searle, J.R. (1983) *Intentionality: an Essay in the Philosophy of Mind*, Cambridge: Cambridge University Press.
Sejnowski, T.J. and Rosenberg, C.R. (1986) 'NETtalk: a parallel network that learns to read aloud', Johns Hopkins University Electrical Engineering and Computer Science Technical Report JHU/EECS-86/01.
Seligman, M.E.P. (1970) 'On the generality of the laws of learning', *Psychological Review* 77: 406–18.
Shaffer, J.A. (1965) 'Recent work on the mind–body problem', *American Philosophical Quarterly* 2: 81–104.
Shallice, T. (1972) 'Dual functions of consciousness', *Psychological Review* 79: 383–93.
Shallice, T. (1978) 'The dominant action system: an information processing approach to consciousness', in K.S. Pope and J.L. Singer (eds) *The Stream of Consciousness*, New York: Plenum Press.
Shallice, T. (1988) *From Neuropsychology to Mental Structure*, Cambridge: Cambridge University Press.
Shapiro, D. (1976) 'The effects of therapeutic conditions: positive results revisited', *British Journal of Medical Psychology* 49: 315–23.
Shapiro, M.B. (1961) 'The single case in fundamental clinical psychological research', *British Journal of Medical Psychology* 34: 255–62.
Sheehan, P.W. (1967) 'A shortened form of Betts' questionnaire upon mental imagery', *Journal of Clinical Psychology* 23: 386–9.
Sheehan, P.W. and Neisser, U. (1969) 'Some variables affecting the vividness of imagery in recall', *British Journal of Psychology* 60: 71–80.
Shiffrin, R.M. and Schneider, W. (1977) 'Controlled and automatic human information processing: II Perceptual learning, automatic attending, and a general theory', *Psychological Review* 84: 127–90.
Shoemaker, S. (1975) 'Functionalism and qualia', *Philosophical Studies* 27: 291–315.
Shweder, R.A. (1977) 'Likeness and likelihood in everyday thought: magical thinking and everyday judgements about personality', *Current Anthropology* 18: 637–658.
Sidman, M. (1960) *Tactics of Scientific Research*, New York: Basic Books.
Silva, P. de (1984) 'Buddhism and behaviour modification', *Behaviour Research and Therapy* 22: 661–78.
Silva, P. de (1990) 'Self-management strategies in early Buddhism', in J.H. Crook and D. Fontana (eds) *Space in Mind*, London: Element.
Simon, H.A. (1952) 'A formal theory of interaction in social groups', *American Sociological Review* 17: 202–11.

Simon, H.A. and Kotovsky, K. (1963) 'Human acquisition of concepts for sequential patterns', *Psychological Review* 70: 534–46.
Simon, H.A. and Newell, A. (1956) 'Models: their uses and limitations', in L.D. White (ed.) *The State of the Social Sciences*, Chicago: Chicago University Press.
Skinner, B.F. (1938) *The Behavior of Organisms: an Experimental Analysis*, New York: Appleton-Century-Crofts.
Skinner, B.F. (1948) *Walden Two*, New York: Macmillan.
Skinner, B.F. (1950) 'Are theories of learning necessary?', *Psychological Review* 57: 193–216.
Skinner, B.F. (1953) *Science and Human Behavior*, New York: Macmillan.
Skinner, B.F. (1964) 'Behaviorism at fifty', in T.W. Wann (ed.) *Behaviorism and Phenomenology*, Chicago: Chicago University Press.
Skinner, B.F. (1971) *Beyond Freedom and Dignity*, New York: Knopf.
Slovic, P. and Lichtenstein, S. (1971) 'Comparison of Bayesian and regression approaches to the study of information processing in judgement', *Organizational Behavior and Human Performance* 6: 649–744.
Smart, J.J.C. (1959) 'Sensations and brain processes', *Philosophical Review* 68: 141–56.
Smart, R. (1966) 'Subject selection bias in psychological research', *Canadian Psychologist* 7: 115–21.
Smith, E.R. and Miller, F.D. (1978) 'Limits on perception of cognitive processes: a reply to Nisbett and Wilson', *Psychological Review* 85: 355–62.
Smith, M.B. (1969) *Social Psychology and Human Values*, Chicago: Aldine.
Spence, K.W. (1937) 'The differential response in animals to stimuli varying within a single dimension', *Psychological Review* 47: 271–88.
Spence, K.W. (1950) 'Cognitive vs. S–R theories of learning', *Psychological Review* 57: 159–72.
Spence, K.W. (1951) 'Theoretical interpretations of learning', in S.S. Stevens (ed.) *Handbook of Experimental Psychology*, New York: Wiley.
Sperry, R.W. (1966) 'Brain bisection and mechanisms of consciousness', in J.C. Eccles (ed.) *Brain and Conscious Experience*, New York: Springer-Verlag.
Sperry, R.W. (1968) 'Hemisphere deconnection and unity in conscious awareness', *American Psychologist* 23: 723–33.
Sperry, R.W. (1974) 'Lateral specialization in the surgically separated hemispheres', in F.O. Schmitt and F. Worden (eds) *Neurosciences: Third Study Program*, Cambridge, MA: MIT Press.
Sperry, R.W. (1980) 'Mind–brain interaction: Mentalism, yes: dualism, no', *Neuroscience* 5: 195–206.
Sperry, R.W., Gazzaniga, M.S. and Bogen, J.E. (1969) 'Interhemispheric relationships: the neocortical commissures; syndromes of hemisphere deconnection', in P.J. Vinken and G.W. Bruyn (eds) *Handbook of Clinical Neurology*, Amsterdam: North Holland.
Spiegelberg, H. (1971) *The Phenomenological Movement: a Historical Introduction*, 2nd edn, The Hague: Nijhoff.
Spinoza, B. de (1677) *Ethics*, transl. A. Boyle, 1959, London: Dent.
Squire, L.R. and Cohen, N.J. (1984) 'Human memory and amnesia', in G. Lynch, J.L. McGaugh and N.M. Weinberger (eds) *Neurobiology of Learning and Memory*, New York: Guilford.
Standing, L. and McKelvie, S. (1986) 'Psychology journals: a case for treatment', *Bulletin of the British Psychological Society* 39: 445–50.
Steiner, I.D. (1970) 'Perceived freedom', in L. Berkowitz (ed.) *Advances in Experimental Social Psychology*, vol. 5, New York: Academic Press.
Stephenson, W. (1953) *The Study of Behavior*, Chicago: University of Chicago Press.

Stevens, S.S. (1939) 'Psychology and the science of science', *Psychological Bulletin* 36: 221–63.

Stich, S.P. (1983) *From Folk Psychology to Cognitive Science: the Case Against Belief*, New York: MIT Press.

Still, A. (1979) 'Perception and representation', in N. Bolton (ed.) *Philosophical Problems in Psychology*, London: Methuen.

Stolorow, R.D. and Atwood, G.E. (1979) *Faces in a Cloud: Subjectivity in Personality Theory*, New York: Aronson.

Storms, M.D. and Nisbett, R.E. (1970) 'Insomnia and the attribution process', *Journal of Personality and Social Psychology* 2: 319–28.

Stoyva, J. and Kamiya, J. (1968) 'Electrophysiological studies of dreaming as the prototype of a new strategy in the study of consciousness', *Psychological Review* 75: 192–205.

Stretch, R. (1966) 'Operant conditioning in the study of animal behaviour', in B.M. Foss (ed.) *New Horizons in Psychology*, Harmondsworth: Penguin.

Stromeyer, C.F. and Psotka, J. (1970) 'The detailed texture of eidetic images', *Nature* 225: 346–49.

Suppes, P. (1967) 'What is a scientific theory?', in S. Morgenbesser (ed.) *Philosophy of Science Today*, New York: Basic Books.

Suppes, P. (1969) 'Stimulus theories of finite automata', *Journal of Mathematical Psychology* 6: 327–55.

Sussman, G.J. (1975) *A Computer Model of Skill Acquisition*, New York: American Elsevier.

Sutherland, N.S. (1959) 'Motives as explanations', *Mind* 68: 145–59.

Sutherland, N.S. (1970) 'Is the brain a physical system?' in R. Borger and F. Cioffi (eds) *Explanation in the Behavioural Sciences*, Cambridge: Cambridge University Press.

Sutherland, N.S. (1974) 'Computer simulation of brain function', in S.C. Brown (ed.) *Philosophy of Psychology*, London: Macmillan.

Sutherland, N.S. and Mackintosh, N. (1971) *Mechanisms of Animal Discrimination Learning*, London: Academic Press.

Tart, C.W. (ed.) (1969) *Altered States of Consciousness*, New York: Wiley.

Taylor, C. (1964) *The Explanation of Behaviour*, London: Routledge and Kegan Paul.

Taylor, C. (1970) 'The explanation of purposive behaviour', in R. Borger and F. Cioffi (eds) *Explanation in the Behavioural Sciences*, Cambridge: Cambridge University Press.

Taylor, C.W. and Barron, F. (1963) *Scientific Creativity: its Nature and Development*, New York: Wiley.

Thayer, R.E. (1970) 'Activation states as assessed by verbal report and four psychophysiological variables', *Psychophysiology* 7: 86–94.

Thigpen, C.H. and Cleckley, H.M. (1957) *The Three Faces of Eve*, London: Secker and Warburg.

Thinès, G. (1977) *Phenomenology and the Science of Behaviour*, London: George Allen and Unwin.

Thinès, G., Costall, A. and Butterworth, G. (1991) *Michotte's Experimental Phenomenology of Perception*, Hillsdale, NJ: Erlbaum.

Thorndike, E.L. (1911) *Animal Intelligence: Experimental Studies*, New York: Macmillan.

Thorndike, E.L. (1935) *The Psychology of Wants, Interests and Attitudes*, New York: Appleton-Century-Crofts.

Thorndike, R.L. (1968) 'Review of *Pygmalion in the Classroom*', *American Educational Research Journal* 5: 708–11.

Titchener, E.B. (1899) *An Outline of Psychology*, New York: Macmillan.

Tolman, E.C. (1925) 'Behaviorism and purpose', *Journal of Philosophy* 22: 36–41.

Tolman, E.C. (1932) *Purposive Behavior in Animals and Men*, New York: Appleton-Century-Crofts.

Toulmin, S. (1970) 'Reasons and causes', in R. Borger and F. Cioffi (eds) *Explanation in the Behavioural Sciences*, Cambridge: Cambridge University Press.

Tukey, D.D. (1968) 'A philosophical and empirical analysis of subjects' modes of inquiry in Wason's 2–4–6 task', *Quarterly Journal of Experimental Psychology* 38A: 5–33.

Turing, A.M. (1950) 'Computing machinery and intelligence', *Mind* 59: 433–60.

Tversky, A. and Kahneman, D. (1971) 'Belief in the law of small numbers', *Psychological Bulletin* 76: 105–110.

Tversky, A. and Kahneman, D. (1974) 'Judgment under uncertainty: heuristics and biases', *Science* 125: 1124–31.

Underwood, B.J. (1963) 'Stimulus selection in verbal learning', in C.N. Cofer and B.S. Musgrave (eds) *Verbal Learning and Behavior*, New York: McGraw-Hill.

Valentine, E.R. (1978) 'Perchings and flights: introspection', in J. Radford and A. Burton (eds) *Thinking in Perspective*, London: Methuen.

Valentine, E.R. (1985) 'Misticismo, fenomenologia e psicologia strutturalista: un confronto di metodi', *Teorie e Modelli* 2: 61–72.

Valentine, E.R. (1988) 'Teleological explanations and their relation to causal explanations in psychology', *Philosophical Psychology* 1: 61–8.

Valentine, E.R. (1989a) 'A cognitive psychological analysis of meditation techniques and mystical experiences', *Ethical Record* 94: 9–10, 14–20.

Valentine, E.R. (1989b) 'Neural nets: from Hartley and Hebb to Hinton', *Journal of Mathematical Psychology* 33: 348–57.

Valentine, E.R. (1989c) 'Perception and action in East and West', in J.P. Forgas and M.J. Innes (eds) *Social Psychology: An International Perspective*, Amsterdam: Elsevier (North Holland).

Valentine, E.R. (1991) 'The use of religious literature in understanding and teaching psychology', in J. Radford and D. Smith (eds) *Uses of Literature in Understanding and Teaching Psychology*, Leicester: British Psychological Society.

Valentine, J.D. (1982) 'Towards a physics of consciousness', *Psychoenergetics* 4: 257–74.

Valins, S. (1966) 'Cognitive effects of false heart-rate feedback', *Journal of Personality and Social Psychology* 4: 400–8.

Van Fraassen, B.C. (1977) 'The pragmatics of explanation', *American Philosophical Quarterly* 14: 143–50.

Van Fraassen, B.C. (1980) *The Scientific Image*, Oxford: Clarendon.

Vaughan, C.J. (1964) 'The development and use of an operant technique to provide evidence for visual imagery in the rhesus monkey under "sensory deprivation" ', doctoral dissertation, University of Pittsburgh.

Velmans, M. (1989) 'The function of consciousness in human information processing', paper presented to the British Psychological Society, History and Philosophy of Psychology Section Conference, Lincoln, April.

Walker, S.F. (1990) 'A brief history of connectionism and its psychological implications', *AI and Society* 4: 17–38.

Wallach, H., O'Connell, D.N. and Neisser, U. (1953) 'The memory effect of visual perception of three-dimensional form', *Journal of Experimental Psychology* 45: 360–8.

Walter, W.G. (1953) *The Living Brain*, London: Duckworth.

Waltz, D.L. (1982) 'Artificial intelligence', *Scientific American* 247 (4): 101–22.

Wann, T.W. (ed.) (1964) *Behaviorism and Phenomenology: Contrasting Bases for Modern Psychology*, Chicago: Chicago University Press.

Warren, N. (1971) 'Is a scientific revolution taking place in psychology?' *Science Studies* 1: 407–13.
Warshaw, D.R. and Davis, F.D. (1984) 'Self-understanding and the accuracy of behavioural expectations', *Personality and Social Psychology Bulletin* 10: 111–18.
Wason, P.C. (1960) 'On the failure to eliminate hypotheses in a conceptual task', *Quarterly Journal of Experimental Psychology* 12: 129–40.
Wason, P.C. and Evans, J.StB.T. (1975) 'Dual processes in reasoning', *Cognition* 3: 141–54.
Watson, J.B. (1907) 'Kinaesthetic and organic sensations: their role in the reactions of the white rat to the maze', *Psychological Review* 8, Monograph Supplement, whole no. 33: 1–100.
Watson, J.B. (1913) 'Psychology as the behaviorist views it', *Psychological Review* 20: 158–77.
Watson, J.B. (1914) *Behavior: an Introduction to Comparative Psychology*, New York: Holt.
Watson, R.I. and Campbell, D.T. (eds)(1963) *History, Psychology and Science: Selected Papers by Edwin G. Boring*, New York: Wiley.
Webb, E.J., Campbell, D.T., Schwartz, R.D. and Sechrest, L. (1966) *Unobtrusive Measures: Nonreactive Research in the Social Sciences*, Chicago: Rand McNally.
Weimer, W.B. and Palermo, D.S. (1973) 'Paradigms and normal science in psychology', *Science Studies* 3: 211–44.
Weisen, A. (1965) 'Differential reinforcing effects of onset and offset of stimulation on the operant behavior of normals, neurotics and psychopaths', unpublished Ph.D. thesis, University of Florida (cited in Eysenck, 1966).
Weiskrantz, L. (1968) 'Treatments, inferences and brain function', in L. Weiskrantz (ed.) *Analysis of Behavioral Change*, New York: Harper and Row.
Weiskrantz, L. (1980) 'Varieties of residual experience', *Quarterly Journal of Experimental Psychology* 32: 365–86.
Weiskrantz, L. (1986) *Blindsight: a Case Study and its Implications*, Oxford: Oxford University Press.
Weiskrantz, L., Warrington, E.K., Sanders, M.D. and Marshall, J. (1974) 'Visual capacity in the hemianopic field following restricted occipital ablation', *Brain* 97: 709–28.
Wertheimer, M. (1972) *Fundamental Issues in Psychology*, New York: Holt, Rinehart and Winston.
West, M. (ed.)(1987) *The Psychology of Meditation*, Oxford: Clarendon.
Westcott, M.R. (1982a) 'Quantitative and qualitative aspects of experienced freedom', *Journal of Mind and Behavior* 3: 99–126.
Westcott, M.R. (1982b) 'On being free and feeling free', paper presented to the 20th International Congress of Applied Psychology, Edinburgh.
Westcott, M.R. (1988) *The Psychology of Human Freedom*, New York: Springer-Verlag.
Westland, G. (1978) *Current Crises of Psychology*, London: Heinemann.
White, P. (1980) 'Limitations on verbal reports of internal events: a refutation of Nisbett and Wilson and of Bem', *Psychological Review* 87: 105–12.
White, P. (1988) 'Knowing more about what we can tell: "Introspective access" and causal report accuracy 10 years later', *British Journal of Psychology* 79: 13–45.
Whitehurst, G.J. (1982) 'The quandary of manuscript reviewers', *Behavioral and Brain Sciences* 5: 241–2.
Whyte, L.L. (1960) *The Unconscious before Freud*, New York: Basic Books.
Whytt, R. (1751) *An Essay on the Vital and Other Voluntary Motions in Animals*, Edinburgh: Hamilton, Balfour and Neill.
Wiener, N. (1948) *Cybernetics or Communication and Control in the Animal and the Machine*, London: Wiley.

Wiggins, J.S., Renner, K.E., Clore, G.L. and Rose, R.T. (1971) *The Psychology of Personality*, Reading, MA: Addison-Wesley.
Wilding, J.M. (1978) 'Bits and spaces: computer simulation', in A. Burton and J. Radford (eds) *Thinking in Perspective*, London: Methuen.
Wilding, J.M. (1989) 'Developmental dyslexics do not fit in boxes: evidence from the case studies', *European Journal of Cognitive Psychology* 1: 105–27.
Wilks, Y. (1982) 'Machines and consciousness', paper CSCM-8, Cognitive Studies Centre, University of Essex.
Wimsatt, W.C. (1972) 'Teleology and the logical structure of function statements', *Studies in the History and Philosophy of Science* 3: 1–80.
Wimsatt, W.C. (1976) 'Reductionism, levels of organization, and the mind–body problem', in G.G. Globus, G. Maxwell and I. Savodnik (eds) *Consciousness and the Brain*, New York: Plenum.
Winch, P. (1958) *The Idea of a Social Science and its Relation to Philosophy*, London: Routledge and Kegan Paul.
Winston, P.H. (1984) *Artificial Intelligence*, 2nd edn, Reading, MA: Addison-Wesley.
Wittgenstein, L. (1953) *Philosophical Investigations*, Oxford: Blackwell.
Wolins, L. (1962) 'Responsibility for raw data', *American Psychologist* 17: 657–8.
Wolman, B.J. and Ullman, M. (eds) (1986) *Handbook of States of Consciousness*, New York: Van Nostrand.
Wolpert, E.A. (1960) 'Studies in psychophysiology of dreams. II An electromyographic study of dreaming', *Archives of General Psychiatry* 2: 231–41.
Woodworth, R.S. (1906) 'Imageless thought', *Journal of Philosophy, Psychology and Scientific Method* 3: 701–8.
Woodworth, R.S. (1918) *Dynamic Psychology*, New York: Columbia University Press.
Woodworth, R.S. and Schlosberg, H. (1954) *Experimental Psychology*, 3rd edn, London: Methuen.
Wooldridge, D.E. (1963) *The Machinery of the Brain*, New York: McGraw-Hill.
Wright, L. (1976) *Teleological Explanations: an Etiological Analysis of Goals and Functions*, Berkeley: University of California Press.
Wundt, W. (1862) *Beiträge zur Theorie der Sinneswahrnemung*, Leipzig.
Wyckoff, L.B. Jr (1952) 'The role of observing responses in discrimination learning', *Psychological Review* 59: 431–42.
Young, J.Z. (1951) *Doubt and Certainty in Science: a Biologist's Reflections on the Brain*, Oxford: Clarendon.
Zajonc, R.B. (1980) 'Feeling and thinking: preferences need no inferences', *American Psychologist* 35: 151–75.
Zukav, G. (1979) *The Dancing Wu Li Masters*, New York: William Morrow.

Name index

Subject index